# Subject to Change

Polly Young-Eisendrath offers a response that opens new vistas in our understanding of ourselves within the complexity of a postmodern world.

*Subject to Change* is a collection of essays spanning a twenty-year period of theorizing and practice of a highly regarded senior Jungian analyst. The diverse ideas and perspectives discussed in the essays deal with the big issues surrounding how Jungian analysts and psychoanalysts understand their profession and what it teaches us about our subjective lives. The book is divided into four clear and informative sections:

- Subjectivity and uncertainty.
- Gender and desire.
- Transference and transformation.
- Transcendence and subjectivity.

The classic essays presented in this book will have significant appeal to all those concerned with Jungian analysis, psychotherapy, psychoanalysis, gender development, and the interface between psychotherapy and spirituality.

**Polly Young-Eisendrath** is Clinical Associate Professor of Psychiatry at the University of Vermont Medical College and a psychologist and Jungian analyst practicing in central Vermont, USA.

# Subject to Change

## Jung, gender and subjectivity in psychoanalysis

Polly Young-Eisendrath

Brunner-Routledge
Taylor & Francis Group

HOVE AND NEW YORK

First published 2004
by Brunner-Routledge
27 Church Road, Hove, East Sussex BN3 2FA

Simultaneously published in the USA and Canada
by Brunner-Routledge
29 West 35th Street, New York NY 10001

*Brunner-Routledge is an imprint of the Taylor & Francis Group*

Typeset in Times by Mayhew Typesetting, Rhayader, Powys
Printed and bound in Great Britain by TJ International Ltd, Padstow,
Cornwall
Cover design by Hybert Design

This publication has been produced with paper manufactured to strict
environmental standards and with pulp derived from sustainable
forests.

*British Library Cataloguing in Publication Data*
A catalogue record for this book is available from the British Library

*Library of Congress Cataloging-in-Publication Data*
Young-Eisendrath, Polly, 1947–
   Subject to change : Jung, gender, and subjectivity in psychoanalysis /
Polly Young-Eisendrath.
        p. cm.
Includes bibliographical references and index.
   ISBN 1-58391-946-5 (hardback : alk. paper)
1. Psychoanalysis. 2. Jungian psychology. 3. Jung, C. G. (Carl
Gustav), 1875–1961. 4. Subjectivity. 5. Sex role. 6. Psychoanalysis
and religion. I. Title.

   RC506.Y686 2004
   616.89'17–dc22

                                                    2003019590

ISBN 1-58391-946-5 (hbk)

# Contents

# Acknowledgments

The following chapters are reprinted from other sources by permission of the author and publisher. Chapter 3 is taken from Young-Eisendrath, P. (1995) "Struggling with Jung: the value of uncertainty", *Psychological Perspectives*, 31(Spring–Summer): 46–54. Chapter 4 is taken from Young-Eisendrath, P. (1997) "Why it is difficult to be a Jungian analyst in today's world", in M.A. Mattoon (ed.) *Open Questions in Analytical Psychology*, Einsiedeln, Switzerland: Daimon-Verlag. Chapter 6 is taken from Young-Eisendrath, P. (1997) "The self in analysis", *Journal of Analytical Psychology*, 42: 157–166. Chapter 7 is taken from Young-Eisendrath, P. (1997) "Jungian constructivism and the value of uncertainty", *Journal of Analytical Psychology*, 42: 637–652. Chapter 10 is taken from Young-Eisendrath, P. (1987) "The female person and how we talk about her", in M. Gergen (ed.) *Feminist Thought and the Structure of Knowledge*, New York: New York University Press. Chapter 12 is taken from Young-Eisendrath, P. (1997) "Gender and contrasexuality: Jung's contribution and beyond", in P. Young-Eisendrath and T. Dawson (eds) *The Cambridge Companion to Jung*, Cambridge, UK: Cambridge University Press. Chapter 14 is taken from Young-Eisendrath, P. (2002) "The transformation of human suffering: a perspective from psychotherapy and Buddhism", in P. Young-Eisendrath and S. Muramoto (eds) *Awakening and Insight: Zen Buddhism and Psychotherapy*, London: Routledge. Chapter 15 is taken from Young-Eisendrath, P. (2001) "When the fruit ripens: alleviating suffering and increasing compassion as goals of clinical psychoanalysis", *Psychoanalytic Quarterly*, LXX: 265–285. Chapter 16 is taken from Young-Eisendrath, P. (2000) "Psychotherapy as ordinary transcendence: the unspeakable and the unspoken", in P. Young-Eisendrath and M. Miller (eds) *The Psychology of Mature Spirituality: Integrity, Wisdom, Transcendence*, London: Routledge. Chapter 18 is taken from Young-Eisendrath, P. (1993) "Locating the transcendent: inference, rupture, irony", in M.A. Mattoon (ed.) *The Transcendent Function: Individual and Collective Aspects*, Einsiedeln, Switzerland: Daimon-Verlag. Chapter 19 is taken from Young-Eisendrath, P. (2000) "Self and transcendence: a postmodern approach to analytical psychology in practice", *Psychoanalytical Dialogues*, 10(3): 427–441.

I would like to express my gratitude to Courtney Brown and Katherine Masís for their careful help in editing and searching for scholarly references. Courtney helped especially in the early organization of the book, and Katherine was indispensable in gathering last-minute information. Sharon Broll also helped with trimming my prose, as she always does. My husband, Ed Epstein, was his usual supportive self throughout this long project, always encouraging me to bring out a volume of my collected essays that would express my unique perspective on psychotherapy. I deeply appreciate the conscientious help and encouragement from these friends.

# Chapter 1

# Introduction

## Changing the subject – the self as a verb

---

If the doors of perception were cleansed every thing would appear to man as it is, infinite.

*The Marriage of Heaven and Hell* (Blake in Kazin, 1946/1968: 258)

*Subject to Change*, the title I chose for this book, is a play on words that suggests the diverse ideas and perspectives expressed in these essays. They reflect a twenty-year span of my own development as a person, woman, Jungian psychoanalyst, feminist, Buddhist, and developmental psychologist – to name only a few of the categories that are relevant to my own subjective life. As you will see, my ideas have changed in various ways and have come under the influence of different authorities over time. And yet, certain themes have continued to focus my interest over the years: the constraints and forms of human transformation; the dialectic of tensions within and between people; the question of what is universal and what is particular in human life.

My own approach to understanding psychoanalytic work has always been open to not-knowing: it has been "subject to change." I regard not-knowing as an active stance from which to engage with our moment-to-moment experience. I see it as a commitment to reveal ourselves openly and transparently, without too much rigidity or guardedness, so that life can teach us. We discover ourselves and the world by putting forth our thoughts, feelings and actions with a curiosity about how they are supported or resisted by others and the environment around us. The commitment is not only to be transparent, but to remain interested in the responses we get. Naturally, we do this only imperfectly and inconsistently. Not-knowing is a style, not an art or a science.

All of us, as adults, have beliefs and desires and theories about ourselves and others. Uncertainty about what we know keeps us honest and flexible. We can never possess a complete and precise understanding of subjective experience, neither our own nor another's, precisely because it is the lens through which we examine our subjectivity, as well as the subject matter itself. This circularity doesn't mean that psychoanalysis is doomed to subjectivism. To function as a systematic science of subjective life, psychoanalysis must stand for certain methods that govern our inquiry and allow us to craft an objective stance whereby we can make predictions, test our theories, and review our clinical practices. Objectivity is based on consensual agreements about the boundaries and domain of any science – its hypotheses, and the ways in which they are tested. There is *no* objective fact to be discovered outside of such an interpersonal context, as philosophers of science have clarified over the past two decades. As psychoanalysts we need to study ourselves, our therapeutic results, and our theories of personality so that we can continuously refine our views in a disciplined manner, consistent with our goals. But this refinement must be accompanied by ongoing debate, a knowledge of the limitations of our field (including the circularity of its subject matter), and a willingness to change as our understanding changes.

On a more personal level, when we (as practitioners or persons) believe that we already know exactly how things are with ourselves and others, we risk being defined by the emotional habits that drive us. If we are forever open to inquiry into what we might *not* know about ourselves and our lives, then we are more likely to become responsive to the complexity of our being.

Another meaning of the word "subject," to which the title alludes, is the doer of an action or the receiver of an action. In psychoanalysis, we often refer to the subject as the thinking and acting agent, as distinguished from the object of desire or the passive victim of circumstances. This agent is free to change, to experience something which I call "subjective freedom," permitting us to know ourselves well enough that our habits of mind don't weigh us down or trip us up in our movements through life. To know ourselves means becoming familiar with our unconscious and preconscious patterns and complexes until we become unashamedly accountable for the diversity of states within us, even for the reactions that seize us unawares.

Under these circumstances, even our impulses cannot make us wholly subject to *their* emotional power. We become what Jung has called a "psychological individual," acknowledging the range and difficulty of our own personality, with a self-accepting willingness not to enact every feeling or impulse, but rather to return again and again to interpersonal inquiry about, and open-minded reflection on, ourselves and our motives. This subjective freedom is psychological, but depends on the political and social freedoms that allow for a self-determining life.

Subjective freedom leads to the possibility of spiritual freedom: the opportunity to engage in mature spiritual practices and inquiries. In my view, spirituality involves our attempts to answer the bigger questions about our existence: what's the meaning of life, why are we here, why do we die, how do we know what we know? Self-knowledge, self-acceptance and personal responsibility permit us to take ourselves into evermore expansive spiritual landscapes without fraying the edges of the relational fabric on which we depend. There is no religion or spiritual practice that does not rest on an ethic of personal responsibility in which an individual is accountable for her or his actions and expressions. This accountability, and its development into integrity, is the foundation of all mature spiritual or religious practices. Psychoanalysis encourages us to remain engaged in inquiry about ourselves and our motives in order to sharpen our sense of personal responsibility throughout life. It is not possible to know ourselves once and for all, but it is possible to cultivate an openness to inquiry that connects us again and again to both the particular and the universal meanings of a truly human life.

## Change and constraint

The word "change" also has multiple meanings. In psychotherapy and life, change seems to be a fairly predictable process of transformation. Subjective life progresses through paradigms of structuring and restructuring of self/other and self/world. I have been very much influenced by structural developmental psychology that begins with the work of Jean Piaget and continues into a vast array of research and theory that includes important studies of moral and ego development.

Subjective life is always and everywhere constrained in both its patterns of change and its possibilities for openness. That sounds like the opposite of "uncertainty," and in a way it is. As embodied human beings, we are all limited in certain aspects of our knowledge, our bodies (structures and functions) and our life span, our language and culture, and our awareness of ourselves. We are all shaped by our long dependency in childhood and its ambivalent emotional influences on our adult identities and relationships. We are all aware of our mortality from a young age and haunted by it throughout our adult years.

These universal constraints can be studied as *archetypes*, or primary imprints, on the human subject. To study these patterns scientifically we must, of course, include all types and variations of human subjects: people from all walks of life, different societies, different genders and races and ages, and so on. Only by including all can we trace the universal map of the real constraints on our subjectivity. Otherwise, we are dealing with "observer phenomena" – the labels and categories that are imposed from the observer's viewpoint and culture, rather than expressed by the subject. To study the change process we must depend on each other, and our theories, in a process of inquiry. This is the essence of our clinical practice and the direction of our scientific development.

Beyond these universal constraints, though, the particularity of the human subject – the uniqueness of an individual person – makes for a kind of randomness in our experience. The human imagination develops in new and unpredictable ways over a lifetime and throughout centuries. In most of our daily life, though, these aspects of particularity are variations within a powerfully constrained world of human being and relating as persons to persons, other beings, and the world.

I regard change in the human subject as a "dialectic of development" in which opposites, tensions, splits and divisions, both within and outside the personality, are potentially available to new syntheses. When change is possible, we discover a third ground or a new perspective that integrates the original two opposites that were in tension. This occurs in all human relationships at all levels of family and society, as well as within individual reflection. But then new tensions and conflicts will always replace old ones, as we move on in our experience over the life span, just as new problems always replace old ones in human societies. Our insights and solutions are always partial and limited, no matter the accuracy of our machines and sciences, because of the limitations of the human subject. Psychoanalysis was designed specifically to study these limitations in a protected inter-personal environment. Discovering a third perspective in a conflict within or between people does not mean occupying an idealized middle ground. It means remaining open to inquiry and new discovery, as the title of the book suggests.

## Jung, gender and subjectivity in psychoanalysis

The subtitle, on the other hand, narrows the field of my particular inquiry. It names those topics that have stayed with me over the years of my development as a psychologist and psychoanalyst. First, there is Jung and his psychology as they have developed within my own reflection and prac-tice over the past twenty years. My roots are Jungian: I trained to become a Jungian analyst and began my serious study of psychoanalysis from that perspective. I call the discipline that I practice "psychoanalysis," not to obscure the influence of Jungian theory and methods, nor to confuse Jung's contributions with Freud's or others, but rather to be accurate about the context of the work I do and think about. "Psychoanalysis" is the term that has survived in the public domain relating specifically to the study of unconscious life, both within the psychotherapeutic enterprise and in human development. Jung called his approach "analytical psychology" at a time when differing biases were seen as a reason to divorce one "school" from another. Now that the whole field of psychoanalysis has been attacked and devalued by various outside economic and cultural forces, it behooves us to function as a cooperative group, and to heal the step-family mentality that has hurt us badly. As psychoanalysts we need each other in many more ways than we need to be each other's enemies. For these reasons and more,

I envision Jung's psychology and Jungian analysis to fall within the scope of the larger psychoanalytic circle (which is small enough).

The second topic in the subtitle, gender, has been a central focus of mine in studying and researching developmental psychology and in doing couples psychotherapy and individual therapy and analysis. Primarily, I have approached gender from a constructivist perspective: that gender categories are empty of any specific content, but are assigned based on body type at birth (or even earlier now) in order to move people into certain roles, identities, status, and jobs. Sex, by contrast, is a limit on our body type. Although people now manipulate that limit, they cannot wholly transcend it. Our sex presents us with inevitable constraints on our wishes and desires within a human society. Whereas gender is relatively flexible across contexts, and changes over the life span, sex is more inflexible and constant. The division of the human community into two gender groups, based on body architecture, leads to many tensions, divisions, and splits in the ways that people relate to themselves and each other – in couples, families and groups. This situation has deeply interested me throughout my career.

The final term of the subtitle, subjectivity, could have been exchanged for "personality" or "intersubjectivity," but these latter two didn't sound as good to my ears, and didn't really cover the range that "subjectivity" does. Suffice it to say that my interests in subjectivity encompass both the ways in which the human personality forms and functions as an apparent unity – what we call "self" – and how this illusion of singularity and unity always rests on, and is rooted in, self–other functioning. What has interested me throughout my years of study and practice in psychology and life is that the self and the other – not the individual mind, brain, or body – are the fundamental subjective unit, both in our earliest becoming (we come into being inside of someone else) and in every moment in which we conceive of a self. The "other" in this case may be a person, another being, or the environment; it is whatever is providing the contrast to "self" in a moment of perception. Along these lines, I want to introduce my own version of the human self as an action that makes us feel and perceive ourselves as individual subjects. If I could change our language, I would cast the self as a verb rather than a noun. I hope that this account of self will set the tone for the remainder of the book.

## Some personal background

I need first to begin with my own background. I started my training to be a Jungian analyst in 1979. Eight (or so) years before that, I had become a student of Zen Buddhism. In my twenties, as I was at that time, I blithely assumed that *everything* that interested me should fit nicely into a seamless fabric of meaning. Over the years, I have been forced to sew many seams into that fabric. Indeed, my fabric of meaning is a veritable patchwork quilt of highly contrasting pieces combined into a pattern that emphasizes and blends differences. Back in 1979, my seamless fabric was rudely ripped apart when many of my analytic colleagues, especially my Jungian colleagues, were suspicious of Zen as an alien philosophy that produced a disengaged stance. My Zen colleagues were also suspicious of psychotherapists who were "restoring the ego to equilibrium" – as they were described – rather than making it more transparent and fluid. This was before Buddhism became a popular middle-class American religion and the Dalai Lama was a worldwide celebrity. In the 1980s, I stayed in the closet as a Buddhist, as many other psychoanalysts did, as became clear in the late 1990s when the closet doors opened.

In the 1980s and early 1990s, I found that Western postmodern philosophy helped to close the gap in my conceptual understanding between psychology and meditation. I became the Jungian poster child for "constructivism" and "phenomenological hermeneutics" in relation to such concepts as self, instinct, archetype, complex, and therapeutic action. I read and studied contemporary philosophical arguments and engaged in many debates about what might be useful, valid, and reasonable to say about the self, clinically and developmentally. I want to summarize now what I have gleaned in fitting together a couple of pieces in my quilt that connect my experiences in psychoanalysis, psychology, psychotherapy, meditation, and philosophy.

## Self and no-self as verbs

I regard the human self as an "action" or a "function" of a "person." The self does not "do" any actions or think any thoughts; it is the person who does these things. In the 1980s I began to hold a strong distinction between self and person, having read what was then called "philosophy of the person," especially the contributions of Rom Harré (1984: 76) who wrote: "I propose . . . a distinction between the individuality of a human being as it is publicly identified and collectively defined and the individuality of the unitary subject of experience."

"Persons," claimed Harré, "are identified by public criteria" that emphasize the "intentionality of their actions and speeches" and are interpreted "within a social framework of interpersonal commitments rather than as the outward expression of some inner state." Selves, on the other hand, are "psychological individuals, manifested in the unified organization of perceptions, feelings and beliefs of each human being . . . organized in that fashion." He added that there may also be human beings who are "organized in some non-unitary way" (pp. 76–77). Although this early distinction now seems awkward and more than a little abstract, it initiated a process of clarification in my own thinking that has been refined through my meditative and clinical practices in the last two decades, as well as the theories connected to each.

In formal discussions of psychoanalysis, I frequently find that the distinction between self and person is unfortunately erased, leading to unnecessary confusions and awkward descriptions. This is true even though Roy Schafer (1978: 86, for instance) offered many cogent critiques of our self-language more than twenty years ago. For example, he wrote: "The self is . . . something one learns to conceptualize in one's capacity as agent; it is not a door of actions. In this light, we can see that Heinz Kohut [1971] and other analytic theoreticians of the self have been wrong in speaking of the experiential self as playing its own regulatory role in human action."

When we make the mistake of saying that the "self," rather than the person, is intending, feeling or doing, we lose our ability to be precise and convincing in our descriptions of how we work with subjective life. Instead of regarding the self as an action *of* a person, the self is then named as the actor, opening the door to all sorts of confusions in our conversations with one another.

These problems are nowhere thornier or more troublesome than in our attempts to develop a dialogue between practitioners of psychoanalysis and practitioners of Buddhism, an important conversation of the twenty-first century between two different (and sometimes similar) systematic approaches to subjectivity. We find ourselves at a special loss to describe the actions of a person who has reached states of non-separateness or "no-self." If we speak of the self as actor, then *who* is the actor when there is no self? The relational psychoanalyst Stephen Mitchell (2003: 96), for example, in a written dialogue with a psychologist who is also a Buddhist teacher, comments on the "centeredness" of such no-self states by asking "Who then is the one who is centered? Is this not a version of the self?" Another example of this confusion is in an essay by Zen teacher and psychoanalyst Barry Magid, who wants to describe what is constant and familiar in his own Zen teacher, although she exemplifies the unfixed no-self in her actions and expressions. Reaching for a way to characterize this seeming paradox of her being, Magid (2003: 295) quotes another Zen teacher, Robert Aitken Roshi, who describes the liberated person in the following way: "The self is still present – but it is not self-preoccupied. It washes the dishes and puts them away."

If we preserved a clear distinction between self and person, we might say, "this person acts in a non-self-preoccupied way. She just washes the dishes and puts them away." On the surface this may seem trivial, but preserving this distinction clears up a lot of unnecessary troubles in conversations about self and no-self in both psychoanalysis and Buddhism.

A major barrier in translating the language of Buddhism into Western meanings surrounds the discussion of self. Let me use just one more short passage from Buddhist scholar Robert Thurman (1994: 32–33) to further develop my point:

> All the world is in some sense created by the mind, from the infinitely positive to the infinitely negative. If you step out in front of a freight train, its painful crushing of you is all in the mind as well. A liberated person, viscerally aware of the precise sense of "just being in the mind," would have no problem standing in front of such a train if there were any benefit for beings from doing so.

Such a "liberated person" would be one who has mastered the fluid movements back and forth between the actions of self and the actions of no-self, but this person would still objectively experience the pain and death of the physical body. And yet, the perceived experience of being crushed by a freight train would be vastly different for such a person than for the rest of us. The liberated person would feel pain, but not suffering – physical sensation, but not misery and anguish. The rest of us would be just crushed in every awful imaginable way.

All discussions of self in psychoanalysis and Buddhism are vastly improved by retaining the distinction between a person, as an embodied agent who exists in a public context, and a self that is the action of a person and lacks such embodied public existence. This is not just a trick of language. We changed a great deal in our thinking about gender when we disciplined ourselves to use the pronouns "she or he" to refer to "a person." Similarly, I believe that we can open whole new horizons of meaning if we discipline ourselves to speak of self as an action of a person, rather than the actor.

It seems to me that the Buddhist language of no-self has emphasized the importance of being precise about the self. Experiences of no-self problematize the experience of self. Along these lines, I also believe that it might be useful to distinguish no-self states, as those states when the separateness of individual being is entirely absent, from non-self states when a sense of being a separate individual is still present, but not as the focus of our actions, sensations, thoughts or feelings. Both no-self and non-self states can be pathological, healthy or liberating. In other words, the term "no-self" should not be reserved only for liberated states because no-self states can be used by people to serve pathological aims, as Brian Victoria's (1997) book *Zen at War* clearly illustrated.

And so, I regard the self as the action of a person who is perceiving oneself as being and behaving as a separate individual subject. The self is an action of a person, rather than the sum total of a person or a deep internal state of a person. It is possible for a person to be functionally centered in her or his awareness without a self – as, for example, in certain advanced meditative states or other no-self experiences such as childbirth. It is also possible for a person to be dysfunctional or non-functional in either a no-self or a non-self state – for example, in certain momentary states that are delusional or drug-induced, or in profoundly pathological psychotic or depersonalized states. Questions about "who" is acting in such circumstances are answered by the category "person" – the public criteria of a mind-and-body being who is intending and acting in these ways. In the future, when we understand the actions that we call "self" more clearly, as we are bound to do between the discoveries of neuroscience and the discoveries of psychoanalysis and Buddhism, we may find a verb for this kind of self-ing. In the meantime, I am forced to use the noun to refer to the action.

Thanks to my current meditation teacher Shinzen Young, and his Zen teacher Sasaki Roshi (of Mt. Baldy Zen Center in California), I would describe the action of the self as micro-movements of change in our perceptions that escape our attention most of the time. These are similar to the micro movements of the human eye that permit us to have a clear image of "some thing" existing "outside" ourselves. A recent article about the scientific study of these micro-movements of the eye by Haseltine (2003: 88) in *Discover Magazine* says that direct experiential evidence is "hard to come by because the sensors that must detect such movements – your eyes – are the same sensors that are constantly being repositioned by the micro-movements. It's like trying to catch your eyes moving in the mirror. Under very special circumstances, however, micro-movements can be coaxed out into the open". This description is a perfect analog of the difficulty of directly detecting the micro-movements of self. And yet, the self micro-movements can also be coaxed out into the open in the special conditions of certain forms of meditation that have been designed and refined for just this purpose. When this happens, we can perceive ourselves creating self states, and we can also see how to act and perceive without creating this separateness. No-self states are ways of behaving and perceiving in which there is *non-interference* from a boundaried separate subject – or self – with our perceptions of seeing, hearing, smelling, tasting, touching, sensing, feeling (emotion), and thinking. As the opening quote from William Blake states, we experience our perceptions as infinite when the self does not interfere. In fact, it is possible for people to be consciously aware of their embodied thoughts and feelings while being in a state of no-self. Under these conditions a person functions as a person in all respects by public criteria, while functioning without the interference of the sense of being separate.

In another essay on the dialogue between Buddhism and psychoanalysis, psychologist and Buddhist teacher Jack Engler (2003) describes the action of self:

> the division of experience into "inside" and "outside," "self" and "object," "self" and "other," "self and body" arises within the

perceptual process itself, from the patterning of the first input to the final stage in which we become conscious of our perceptions and weave them into a framework of meaning.

He goes on to describe how people perceive no-self, first through meditation training, and eventually in walking-around experience:

> we can observe the moment-to-moment way in which we bring these [self] elements of our ordinary experiences into being . . . It's possible to directly see the constructed, momentary, and interdependent nature of self and 'reality' by actually experiencing the steps of their construction (p. 92).

Only within the province of the sciences of subjectivity, such as Buddhism and psychoanalysis, can we investigate, describe, clarify and theorize how people create and sustain selves and no-selves. Over the past twenty-five years, I have been pursuing an investigation of these issues in my own meditation training, my studies in psychology and psychoanalysis and philosophy, and my clinical practice of psychotherapy and analysis. Neuroscience and biology address these matters from the observer standpoint, not from subjective involvement. Natural science findings cannot directly influence our subjective lives nor include accounts of human desires, beliefs, intentions and actions in the subject matter of their investigations. The unique circumstances of the subjective sciences allow for the possibility of systematic observations of self, non-self and no-self in the actions of persons, while we learn through experience to change our minds in the process.

In Western societies, we have tended to perceive the self as a thing, like a body. For Westerners especially, I like to compare the micro-movements of self to the micro-movements of the bodily organ that we call "the pancreas." The pancreas changes all of its cells almost every twenty-four hours, but it appears to us as a thing. Upon close examination, we discover that its apparent thing-ness is a transformative action that we can observe through special instruments designed for magnification. Of course, Western physics has provided evidence that all "things" are actual energy forms or actions. But these statements from physics, no matter how convincing and appealing they are, seem to remain outside of the web of the beliefs and desires that influence our subjective being. Having direct experience of the pancreas-like nature of the self, on the other hand, strongly affects the way we see and feel ourselves as persons.

## What are the actions of self, no-self and non-self?

What is the action we call self? It is the micro-movements in our perceptions that separate us from the environment and convince us that we are a continuous unified individual subject, a "something in here" with a "something else out there," as we have seen. When we act, think, and feel ourselves as continuous, embodied, separate subjects (without specific consciousness of doing so), we are using the self automatically and unself-consciously. We regularly use the self non-defensively in such a manner. This is analogous to driving your car without thinking specifically about driving or focusing your eyes through micro-movements without knowing you are doing it.

Sometimes we unintentionally or accidentally lose this sense of self, even our identification with a particular ("my") body. We may lose our sense of time, our sense of being contained in our bodies, our ability to use our own agency or initiative to direct ourselves, and/or our feelings of being separate from other people. A loss of self-as-separate-being is a normal occurrence when we are asleep; in our dreams, we may change bodies, find our bodies disappearing or move out of our bodies. We may also have a sense of being someone else in a dream – a person of the opposite sex or an animal, for example. In waking life, when we are in shock, in intense physical pain, in states of merger or ecstasy, and in various states of psychic distress, we may find that we pop into no-self states in which we no longer embody the being of a separate individual subject.

The intentional cultivation of no-self states in some forms of Buddhist meditation practices is designed to help us witness exactly how we create a separate self, how this creation is related to our suffering, and how it can be made more transparent on a walking-around basis so that we don't have to habitually do it. People can be aware, alert, responsible and attuned without creating a separate self if they have carefully cultivated the kind of awareness that is necessary, as I have said.

Outside of such practices and careful development, our experiences of no-self states may seem frightening and may even engender psychopathology. Some people learn to escape their ordinary subjective being and their accountability for themselves by diving into no-self states, such as psychotic fantasies, hallucinations, and de-personalizations or de-realizations (when people get out of their bodies or become identified with other bodies as in reliving trauma and other kinds of dissociation).

Non-self states – when we act without the ordinary sense of a self being unitary or focused – may be felt as being "beside ourselves" or "not myself today." Chronic symptomatically rigid forms of reactivity in personality disorders, neuroses, and psychoses, as well as benign or troubling identifications, are often experienced as non-self states. Without any particular insight, people often remark "I was beside myself when I did that." In psychoanalysis, we refer to non-self states by names such as symptoms, primary process, prototaxic, parataxic, unconscious complexes, repetition compulsions, paranoid-schizoid, autistic-contiguous, compromise formations, resistances, and defenses. With these kinds of names, we are pointing to states of being in which the ordinary micro-movements of creating a unitary or separate subject have broken down. Painful and chronic breakdowns of self typically bring people into psychotherapy, although ordinary disruptions are a part of everyday life.

In all people, everywhere, the action of self is expected to produce a fairly reliable experience of feeling and being an individual subject. In all cultures and societies, adults are expected to be accountable for their actions and bodies over time. As a Jungian, I would call the self an archetype or universal imprint: a predisposition in the human personality to act and feel as an individual subject and then to develop that experience over a lifetime.

## Reading this book

What you have just read is my most up-to-date formal account of self and no-self psychology that integrates my thinking about psychoanalysis and Buddhism as practices of subjective science. I have offered this account here because I believe that it will give you an umbrella of understanding for encountering the chapters throughout this book. I have struggled hard to find definitions and descriptions that I hope are useful for treating and developing our subjectivity and intersubjectivity, self and no-self, in clinical and meditational practices. I believe that we should always question and refine our language of subjective life because our linguistic categories teach us if we use them in a disciplined and open-minded manner.

In the following, I make some suggestions for reading this book in order to meet my ideas in an optimal way. My overarching invitation to you is that you form a relationship with me: argue with me, mark down your thoughts (even in the margins), agree or disagree with me, but find yourself here while questioning my ideas. I hope that you also find that your ideas and feelings are subject to change.

The rest of the book is divided into four parts. These organize the chapters according to certain topics that are relevant to the abiding interests that I mentioned at the beginning: the constraints and forms of transformation, the dialectic of tensions within and between people, and the question of what is universal and what is particular in human life.

Part 1 entitled "Subjectivity and uncertainty," continues to develop some of the material that I have introduced in this chapter. Chapter 2 sets the stage for the way I understand the larger field of psychoanalysis, and how I believe the field should develop if it is to survive. The chapter title, "The science of intentions and the intentions of science," argues that psychoanalysis is a special kind of science that needs to discover systematic and scientific foundations on the grounds of its own being: the study of subjective life. I describe psychoanalysis as a "science of intentions" and show how it can help us to clarify the "intentions of science" as we face a massive contemporary illusion: that we should investigate our subjective distress through biological determinism. As I mentioned in this Introduction, our goals and methods in psychoanalysis, as a systematic study of subjective life, explicitly contrast with the assumptions and forms of investigation in biology and neuroscience. We cannot ground psychoanalysis (or Buddhism, for that matter) in studies of organic processes because our questions cannot be answered by such studies.

Chapter 2 introduces the framework that I flesh out in the other chapters of Part 1. As a Jungian psychoanalyst who has collided with aspects of Jung's life and theories, and a constructivist theorist who values uncertainty and dialogue, I am constantly examining the nature of my assumptions, and the methods and context of my clinical and theoretical inquiries. Chapters 3 and 4 concern my autobiographical experience as a Jungian psychoanalyst; I give a complete account of my struggles to be fully who I am – a Jungian, Buddhist, feminist psychoanalyst, who is also a developmental psychologist. These various identifications have constantly clashed with one another over the years and have often left me feeling marginalized in my various arenas of discourse and engagement. I talk about how and why this is so and then go on to show the reader the fruits of my struggles in Chapters 5–7 that exemplify my particular approach to psychoanalytic work: "Subject to change: feminism, psychoanalysis and subjectivity," "The self in analysis: a postmodern account" and "Jungian constructivism and the value of uncertainty." I believe that Part 1 reveals quite clearly my own theoretical and clinical journey with its patchwork quilt of influences.

Part 2 entitled "Gender and desire" reviews my work in analyzing gender and gendered relationships from a Jungian, developmental, feminist, constructivist perspective. This section evolves from the problem of "Woman as the object of desire" to a comprehensive treatment of the Jungian psychology of gender, revising the concept of "contrasexual complex" in terms that are non-essentialist and developmental. In Chapter 8 called "Myth and body: Pandora's legacy in a postmodern world," I talk especially about the unique struggles and images involved with the female body in how it is experienced and seen. Then in Chapter 9, "Feminism and narrating female persons," I investigate the philosophy of the female person from the perspective of feminist and psychoanalytic theories. This discussion moves into more philosophical terrain in Chapter 10, "The female person and how we talk about her", where I question our categories of meaning and suggest new ones. Finally, in Chapter 11, "Revisiting identity" – a paper that was written originally to commemorate the psychology of Erik Erikson – and in Chapter 12, "Gender and contrasexuality: Jung's contribution and beyond," I show how we can work within various aspects of developmental and psychoanalytic theory to liberate our concepts into new ways of understanding the whole field of gender, especially from an intersubjective perspective on projection and projective identification.

Parts 1 and 2 prepare the reader, through a complete introduction to my own orientations and ideas, to encounter the more contemporary final two Parts 3 and 4: "Transference and transformation" and "Transcendence and subjectivity." These last two parts contain only my more recent works that deal with the cutting edge of my own thinking about the therapeutic action of psychoanalysis in the transformation of human suffering, and the ways in which love and compassion participate in this transformation.

Chapter 13, "What's love got to do with it? Transference and transformation in psychoanalysis and psychotherapy" and Chapter 14, "The transformation of human suffering: a perspective from psychotherapy and Buddhism", look at the complexity of the therapeutic relationship, its frame and transferences – from a perspective that is informed by my many years of practicing Zen and Vipassana alongside psychoanalysis. These chapters continue to develop, in more practical and clinical ways, some of the themes I have introduced in this introductory chapter while they also add a critically minded account of how I regard relationship, transference and love as catalysts of therapeutic transformation and life span development. Then in Chapter 15, "When the fruit ripens: alleviating suffering and increasing compassion as goals of clinical psychoanalysis," I turn my attention exclusively to understanding the goals and process of transformation in psychoanalysis, from a postmodern, intersubjective, Young-Eisendrath point of view.

In Part 4, almost every chapter involves an account of "transcendence" by which I mean, as I make clear in Chapter 16, "Psychotherapy as ordinary transcendence," not the traditional religious sense of moving beyond or outside of our quotidian realities, but rather embracing the apparent limitations of ordinary experiences as the means of transcending ourselves – our suffering, our identities, our addictions. I have come to a conclusion that it's best to stick with the ordinary in our quest to discover the extraordinary. How to do this authentically and personally is a work-in-progress for all of us, but I do my best to say what I have discovered. Taking my cues from Jung's theory of the "transcendent function," which is roughly equivalent to Odgen's theory of "dialogical space" and Winnicott's account of "potential space," I develop a way of looking at our search for mental "space" within ourselves and our relationships, including psychotherapy. What do we mean by "reflective space" or "spacious mind"? How do we find such spaces in ourselves and with others? Each of the final five chapters in this part addresses in its own way, often including some myths and stories, the problem of finding the divine in the ordinary and being ever surprised by what life teaches us. Is it possible to be no longer distressed or offended by our encounters with misery, ignorance and limitation in ourselves and others because everything teaches us? This is a question I raise in one way and then another in these final five chapters, concluding with a plea for us, as a society, to transcend the biological realism of our contemporary thinking about being human – a theme that intertwines with Chapter 2 in Part 1.

Seven of the chapters in this book have not been previously published and the other twelve, while they have been published elsewhere, have been edited and changed to fit the needs of this particular work. All the same, in a volume of essays that have been written over time for different occasions and publications, some repetition of themes and ideas is to be expected. I have worked hard to revise these chapters so that the book can be read as a single work. I have tried to eliminate the worst repetitions while repeating themes and ideas that I felt needed to be restated in a new context. I have also allowed a certain amount of overlap because I assume that readers may want to dip into this collection and read according to interest, and thus may need basic references in a particular chapter.

Along these lines, reading the first chapter in each section is a good introduction to the main concerns of the section. Then a reader may skip around by individual interest. If you want to know my perspective in depth, you should feel comfortable reading the book from start to finish, even though there are some repetitions and overlaps. Such a reading will surely reveal how I have changed my mind over time and subject matter.

I am, of course, deeply and forever grateful to all of my teachers, including those teachers in my high school years who recognized me as having something unique or significant to add to the world. Among my college teachers three stand out in my memory: Leslie Rollins, John Chandler and Harrison Butterworth. They all encouraged me with the grace, charm and wit of their own being to become fully myself. In graduate school, Jane Loevinger and Richard deCharms were intellectual giants, in my view, and transformed my thinking and skills as a writer, scientist, and clinician. In my postgraduate years, the writers and teachers to whom I am most grateful are June Singer, Charles Taylor, Arnold Modell, Roy Schafer, Philip Kapleau and Shinzen Young.

Having acknowledged these major influences on my development, I hasten to add that my own clients and patients in psychotherapy and psychoanalysis have always been the true grit of my formation and development as a psychotherapist and psychologist, often as a human being. It is hard to find adjectives that are adequate to express my admiration and love for the people who have sought help from me. Those who have stayed for the full course of their treatment have allowed me into an adventure of inquiry and change that would be unimaginable in any other life setting. I am forever grateful to all of them. I hope that these essays do justice to the worlds they have opened in our shared transformative space.

# Part 1

## Subjectivity and uncertainty

# Chapter 2

# The science of intentions and the intentions of science

One of my most passionate wishes for the twenty-first century is for the further development of a human science of subjectivity, rooted in the ideas and practices of psychoanalysis and analytic therapies, that can stand toe to toe with biological explanations of human behaviors. The abandonment of such a science of subjectivity by many departments of psychiatry in the past decade or more is due more to political and economic conditions than to scientific or clinical findings. I am deeply concerned about the loss in our ability to study and hypothesize issues of human desire, intention, will, action and freedom in a scientific way. We need a systematic study of human subjective responses in order for psychology to enter into dialogue with biology, biochemistry and neuroscience in attempting to understand consciousness and unconsciousness in human actions.

In the absence of such a dialogue at the beginning of the twenty-first century, both popular and academic media have lapsed into an ideology of scientific materialism – a knee-jerk biological determinism – that does not serve us well in our attempts to ameliorate human suffering. This ideology endorses a false assumption that many human characteristics are fixed at birth, and it portends an era of detailed information about group and individual "genetic predispositions" for many human traits from the undesirable to the sublime. This kind of thinking endows the "master molecule" of the gene with almost autonomous power that replaces human intentions and desires. Everything from happiness to criminality, from aesthetics to addictions, from romance to religiosity has been dubbed "genetic" in such accounts. To understand ourselves as organisms propagating our genes eliminates the complexity of our own motives and dulls our ability to encounter people as moral agents.

Before I go into more detail about some clinical and scientific problems that stem from this kind of thinking, I'd like to define a few terms. By the term "intention" I mean purpose, desire, or aim: what one consciously or unconsciously *wants or wants to do*. By the word "suffering" I mean specifically the anguish and discontent that are directly related to our emotional habits, impulses and unrealistic ideals. Here I distinguish suffering as a subjective state, different from objective pain and necessary adversity. Suffering, as I use it, is the unnecessary difficulty that we add to our experiences through evaluating, fantasizing, aggrandizing and diminishing both objective and subjective events.

In this chapter, I will speak about "psychoanalysis" as a science of subjectivity and intention, by which I mean a study of subjective states that depends on the practice of psychodynamic psychotherapies, and on related scientific studies of personality, therapeutic change, and development. I consider the general field of psychoanalysis and analytical therapies to be composed of the following: a means to ameliorate human suffering through therapeutic treatment, a way of thinking about subjective life, and a set of testable hypotheses (contrary to Grunbaum, 1984) about such phenomena as defense mechanisms, attachment behaviors, motivations, core conflicts, therapeutic change, personality development, emotional memory, and more. And finally, when I speak of "science" I mean systematized knowledge – the product of agreed-upon objective methods of investigation - that becomes the basis for truth claims in whatever field of study.

Through our clinical work and scientific studies in the psychoanalytic therapies, we discover the complex, conflicted and often unknown intentions that are at the very core of human suffering. I agree with psychoanalyst and theoretician Carlo Strenger (1991: 62–63) when he says the following about psychoanalysis:

> The assumption is that every aspect of human behavior is intelligible; i.e. behavior is seen as intentional action all the way down. Furthermore, it is assumed that by correctly understanding the meaning of actions, we help the patient to take full responsibility for who he is, and give him the freedom to change if he truly wants to.

This responsibility is now considered almost a luxury for the wealthy few, rather than a necessity for helping people who are suffering in all kinds of life circumstances. In order to fully develop and make use of this science of subjectivity, we need to expand and articulate further our models of the human psyche through study and research that does not import wholecloth the epistemological categories of the natural sciences. The sciences of numbers, objects, and processes – mathematics, physics, biochemistry, biology, genetics – necessarily distort our understanding of human desire, choice, agency and responsibility because the natural sciences are grounded in assumptions that mostly eliminate all categories of subjectivity.

In order to investigate human subjectivity in any comprehensive or adequate way, it must be understood on its own terms, accounting for meaning and purpose, and distinguished from biological processes and fixed characteristics. Using the methods of the human sciences, I believe that we can develop a systematic understanding of subjective states that could eventually clarify the nature of human suffering and address its complexities in terms of relationships and society. Under these circumstances, a dialogue with biology, biochemistry and neuroscience could *then* become extremely fertile, especially in regard to such important topics as the nature of human consciousness and emotion. Without an adequate account of human subjectivity, on the other hand, we are likely to evolve more and more reductive scientific ideologies that interfere with our abilities to remain open-minded in scientific and clinical practices. I hope that my comments here will increase our interest in the future of such dialogue by recognizing the importance of the human sciences such as psychology, linguistics, economics, anthropology, sociology, history, and psychoanalysis as complementary to the natural sciences of life processes. Before I talk about the human sciences, a few personal remarks.

## Professional and personal contexts

Many patients now seeking analysis and psychotherapy with me come with vague theories of genetic or biological determinism, such as "I am depressed because I inherited depression from my mother's family" or "I have an addiction because my genetic history is loaded for substance dependency" or "I have attention deficit disorder because of my genetic background" and so on. These people feel hopeless because after they have taken the appropriate medications, and comforted themselves with the company of their ancestors, they are still stuck with their suffering. This certainly can be helped by effective psychotherapy, but for those who never consider psychotherapy – and of course, most people don't – these vaguely organic explanations only block any desire to understand the personal motives and meanings that shape much of their suffering.

In another professional context, I encounter even greater trouble engendered by our *zeitgeist* of biological determinism. Over the past twelve years I have held clinical appointments in departments of psychiatry and have witnessed the "eradication" of dynamic psychiatry. In this brief period of time, most psychiatric residents in the USA have lost their connection to any psychological understanding of human suffering. The majority of psychiatric residents I now encounter, in lectures and workshops all over the country, know how to provide only the shortest term care, mostly through medication and some short-term therapies. They often lack even basic counseling skills, have no knowledge of personality dynamics, and have the most minimal understanding of human development, without even mentioning the unconscious dynamics of psychopathology and any methods of intensive psychotherapy. These residents want to help their patients. As human beings themselves, they often feel that something very fundamental is being overlooked.

As we have all been encouraged to explain more and more of our personal difficulties in terms of organic and biological processes, and less and less in terms of our own desires and actions, we providers of mental health services now risk obscuring the complexity of subjective life. If we respond to our patients' and our own questions about why we suffer, without any insight into human motivations, conflicts, and desires, we may short-circuit the formation of certain questions of meaning and purpose. And if we explain human moods, emotional difficulties, and other shortcomings mostly, or most adequately, in terms of biochemical or other organic processes, we betray the thimbleful of social awareness of the role of unconscious human intentions that has only recently become a part of Western culture.

When I was in graduate school in developmental psychology in the late 1970s, just at the time that I began my training to be a psychoanalyst, I studied the complexity of human desires in a seminar on motivation. In this and other seminars, I learned that human agency and language demand a non-reductive method of study. At that time, we believed that the freedom to think abstractly – even to theorize about one's thoughts and moods – sets humans sufficiently apart from other organisms and animals to create a "psychology of the person" which is rooted in intention, rather than reactivity or organic process. I was taught that it is dangerous to believe that humans are biologically or psychologically determined animals because an adequate theory of human action must account for intentions that go beyond determining forces. For example, when humans are condemned to horrific torture, some will continue to find a meaningful way to engage with their lives, as is illustrated in Viktor Frankl's (1984) *Man's Search for Meaning*. Even when diagnosed with a terminal illness, we are still free to see it as a personal adventure as writer Anatole Broyard (1992) shows us in *Intoxicated by My Illness*. These freedoms are not the product of organic processes or biochemical reactions, but they are critically important in living a fulfilling life.

In the late 1970s, psychodynamic types thought that cognitive-behaviorism was the reductionism to oppose. We did not see what was coming around the biochemical corner. A mere twenty years later, most American journalists would concur with English journalist Brian Appleyard (1998: 15) who, in a study of the ethical issues inherent in applying genetic methods to humans, states as a fact that "Almost every aspect of human life has a large and frequently decisive genetic component". Even though he is a critic, he like most other popularizers of science is a true believer in genetic ideology. Organic explanations of human life have very quickly come to overshadow the nascent understanding of ourselves as complex intentional actors, the sort who can both create theories of DNA and debate their validity.

Twenty years ago, in graduate school, I learned that there is no way to explain human experience without including the ideas of agency, action and intentionality. Even the human infant depends on intentional action rather than an adaptation to an environment. The infant cannot, of course, think for itself and yet it cannot live without thinking; so someone else must think for it. The infant cannot foresee its own needs and provide for them; so someone else must use foresight. Human beings develop inherently personal relationships that include intention, meaning, and reflection from the very beginning. Although our temperament and biology may affect how sensitive we are to certain interactions with others, our relationships and their meanings also affect how relevant these biological factors may be.

There is a hidden distortion in applying organic theories to explain human actions in any kind of comprehensive way. Philosopher John MacMurray ([1961] 1979: 46) says it like this: "To affirm the organic conception of the personal field is implicitly to deny the possibility of action . . . If organic theory overlooks human freedom, organic practice must suppress it." As we shall see, biological determinism makes human behavior unintelligible as intentional action, and transforms the goal of psychodynamic therapies – greater subjective freedom through increased awareness – into gibberish.

From my many years practicing dynamic therapies, I am certain that much of human suffering comes from grandiose and unrealistic expectations and ideals, blind repetitions of past emotional patterns, impulses based on unconscious conflicts, and obsessions with conscious and unconscious desires and fears. This suffering is composed largely of emotional and perceptual habits that were initially shaped in our earliest relational and family life in which we were powerless to protect ourselves by any means other than molding our subjective awareness into something that was liveable. Unless we become conscious of our emotional habits, and their attendant trigger points and images, we are doomed to treat various aspects of the present or future as if they were the past. "Neurosis," Jung once wrote (*Letters* I, 1973: 333), "is a protracted crisis degenerated into a habit, the daily catastrophe ready for use".

For all of these reasons, I passionately believe that psychoanalysis should develop its identity and methods as a human science within psychology, remaining true to the multi-leveled intentional and relational character of human subjectivity.

## The human sciences

When I first encountered the philosophy of science, also in the late 1970s through the well-known work of T.S. Kuhn from the Massachusetts Institute of Technology and Princeton University, I was enlightened by the notion of scientific "paradigms" or exemplary models that are used as if they were reality. Kuhn showed that the natural sciences, such as physics and chemistry, have grown through revolutionary shifts in these paradigms, rather than through linear accumulation of new knowledge or information. From time to time, some scientists discover and investigate anomalies in the exemplary model, and these anomalies eventually lead to a whole new worldview that topples the old paradigm and allows scientists to see data in a new way. Kuhn's theory appealed to psychological clinicians because we believed that we were helping our patients shift their paradigms of reality by examining the anomalies in their worldviews. But Kuhn strongly objected to applying his structural theory of the natural sciences to any understanding of the human sciences of psychology, anthropology, socio-logy, linguistics, economics or history.

The original line drawn in the nineteenth century between the natural sciences and the human sciences was as follows: the natural sciences explain events mathematically and organically in terms of the laws of nature, while the human sciences explain events in terms of human intentions. This distinction came from the German philosopher Wilhelm Dilthey who died in 1911. He claimed that the goal of the natural sciences is the discovery of causal principles and generalized physical laws, whereas the goal of the human sciences is to understand the purpose and meaning of human action. Dilthey argued that because of this difference, the natural sciences are inadequate for the study of human intentionality and experience at their most complex levels.

Throughout most of the twentieth century, philosophers of science debated the question of whether there are true differences between the natural and human sciences and if there are, what are they. Is it the subject matter, the attitude of the scientist, or the method of study that makes the two endeavors seem so different? There now appears to be some consensus among philosophers of science that all sciences are interpretive at base. This means that all of the assumptions and methods of science occur in par-ticular contexts of meaning and are not necessarily generalizable from one to another. We can no longer claim that the simple facts of reality are discovered, even by natural scientists, because no fact exists outside of some context of shared assumptions. Rather than discovering objective facts that are beyond interpretation, scientists are now understood to pursue their particular subject matter within a community of thinkers who share a worldview or way of seeing something. So what are the distinctions between the natural and human sciences that can still be defended as valid?

In 1989, I heard Kuhn (published in 1991) lecture on his own long-term conclusions about this issue, and I find myself very much in agreement with him. He claimed that the main difference between these two kinds of science is practical, in terms of what practitioners normally *do*, not how or what they study. What natural scientists do, given their hermeneutic base:

> is not ordinarily hermeneutic. Rather, they put to use the paradigm
> received from their teachers in an . . . enterprise that attempts to solve

puzzles like those of improving and extending the match between theory and experiment at the advancing forefront of the field.

(Kuhn, 1991)

On the other hand, human scientists rarely work with such received knowledge. Their sciences "appear to be hermeneutic, interpretive, through and through. Very little of what goes on in them at all resembles the normal puzzle-solving research of the natural sciences. Their aim is . . . to understand behavior, not to discover the laws, if any, that govern it" (Kuhn, 1991: 22–23). Asking himself the question of whether the human sciences could eventually find paradigms that would support normal puzzle-solving research, Kuhn said he was "totally uncertain," stating that some aspects of economics and psychology already seem to use models that could be generalized in developing a puzzled-solving science. On the other hand, when the unit of study is a social or psychological system (or psychotherapeutic relationship, I would add), Kuhn wondered if there would be any real gain in abstracting principles that might lead to puzzle-solving rather than continuing to engage in a thoroughly hermeneutic enterprise.

In my view, psychoanalysis, as a science of subjective experience, is short-circuited and distorted if we attempt to ground it in the causal laws of the natural sciences whether they derive from relativity theory, chaos theory, or biochemistry. And yet, I believe that psychoanalysis should be systematized and researched as a science of human intentions with its own consensual forms and methods, and its own means of reliability, validity and prediction.

Many psychological investigations that have emerged in dialogue with psychoanalysis are already exemplary models of such a hermeneutic human science of subjectivity with strong records of reliability, validity and prediction. Those which come easily to mind are research programs in the following: (Loevinger's) ego development theory, affect theory and regulation, infant–mother observation, attachment theory, defense mechanisms research, psychodynamic psychotherapy outcome studies, some dream studies, and the core-conflict studies of psychotherapy. All of these have contributed important new understandings and expanded old ones, while they have used complex hermeneutical methods to investigate human emotions and intentions.

Of course, it is also fruitful to draw on certain findings in the natural sciences. Many of these are useful as heuristics and analogies. For example, recent neuroscientific findings on emotional memory from studies by Gerard Edelman and Joseph LeDoux can be interpreted as supporting and expanding some psychoanalytic ideas such as repetition compulsion, impulsive enactments of unconscious memory, and so on. On the other hand, if we try to ground our theories in natural science paradigms –

whether they are described as causes, teleologies, genetic tendencies or organic processes – we will warp our views of intentional life and also tend to do very bad science. In the words of contemporary philosopher Charles Taylor (1985: 1), natural science explanations of our subjective experiences:

> end up in wordy elaborations of the obvious, or they fail altogether to address the interesting questions, or their practitioners end up squandering their talents and ingenuity in the attempt to show that they can after all recapture the insights of ordinary life in their manifestly reductive explanatory languages.

### Biological determinism

Biological determinism, as it has been imported into the language and methods of psychodynamic psychotherapy is one such example of bad science. The typical way that this kind of thinking enters our explanations is through what Harvard geneticist Richard Lewontin (1991) calls the "empty bucket metaphor." This metaphor depicts human beings as empty buckets of different sizes, waiting to be filled with the water of experience. If the environment provides all of the necessary resources, then every bucket is filled to its capacity. Still – the metaphor implies – there will be differences in our abilities, capacities, and limitations because there are differences in how much water each bucket can hold. These differences are natural and inherent in the different sizes of the buckets from the start.

Lewontin claims that a major error is committed through the use of this metaphor because "A change in environment . . . can change abilities by many orders of magnitude . . . [and] the differences between individuals are abolished by cultural and mechanical inventions." For example, "Although there may be biologically based average differences in physique and strength between a random group of men and a random group of women (and these are less than usually supposed), these differences rapidly become irrelevant and disappear from practical view in a world of electrically driven hoists, power steering, and electronic controls" (pp. 29–30). Environmental variation and genetic variation are not independent causal pathways; in fact, the interaction between the two is indissoluble.

In a book written for the general public entitled *Biology as Ideology* (1991), Lewontin defines biological determinism as three main ideas: (1) that humans differ in fundamental abilities because of innate differences; (2) that those innate differences are biologically inherited; and (3) that human nature, therefore, guarantees the formation of a hierarchical society. He then carefully reveals the profound flaws in the largest twin and population studies that make claims for major genetic tendencies in human behavior. These studies discover no causal laws (because their methods are correlational and statistical), but they claim to separate genetic and environmental influences for traits such as happiness and schizophrenia. Lewontin shows how their methods and conclusions are misleading, stating himself that "[T]here is at present simply no convincing measure of the role of genes in influencing human behavioral variation." But we (scientists and public) have developed a problematic confusion "between inherited and unchangeable" (p. 33) in our beliefs about these studies.

Reviewing these beliefs, Lewontin (1991) asks why so many successful, intelligent scientists support the massively expensive project of sequencing the human genome when the results will have little practical consequence for human welfare. Advocates of this project argue that the results will improve our ability to treat and even eliminate various threatening diseases, but the immense and immeasurable variation among normal individuals in the functioning of DNA makes generalization impossible. This fact raises the question of whose genome is going to provide the sequence for the catalog of "the normal person." A medical model that aspires to account for all human variation means a medical dictate of normality which has dangerous implications for society. So far, no actual therapies have been devised for the diseases whose genetic conditions have been identified. This is largely because we cannot deduce a causal story of disease from defective genes, nor generate a therapy. We can do little more than test for the presence of the offensive gene.

So why do so many intelligent scientists argue for the benefits of sequencing the human genome? Lewontin answers that they are "so completely devoted to the ideology of unitary causes that they believe in the efficacy of the research and do not ask themselves more complicated questions" (p. 51). He also adds, "No prominent molecular biologist of my acquaintance is without a financial stake in the biotechnology business" (p. 74).

The complexity of human desire, both conscious and unconscious, has played a determining role in our current version of scientific materialism and the story of the mighty gene. But this is not the first time that a theory of inherited traits has played a powerful role in persuading people that the roots of human misery are "in the blood" rather than in our intentions and actions. English journalist Brian Appleyard (1998) traces the history of this notion from Plato (who advocated an improved species as a necessary aspect of an ideal society), to the Christian Inquisition (whose priests believed that faith and heresy were "in the blood"), and finally to the modern Nazi Final Solution – the extermination of those people considered to be "genetically inferior."

When we shift our focus from the intentional freedom of the person to determining causes of human behavior and actions, we automatically lose track of moral reasoning and responsibility because these are not accounted for in the paradigms of determining causes. In recent history, Marxism and

Nazism were both based on radical scientific reductionism. The Marxist would claim that all truth could be boiled down to a scientific analysis of history, specifically the means of production. The Nazi would claim that the best development of human society would be the scientific use of eugenics – the genetic improvement of a race or breed. Without a science of human intention that fundamentally and convincingly argues the other side of reductionist tendencies in the natural sciences, we are at risk of falling into unchecked desires for omnipotent control of our environment or ourselves through whatever form of scientific determinism we might temporarily embrace.

### The science of intentions

Psychoanalysis has the capacity – as a framework for studying human desires and intentions – to develop a systematic understanding of even the most unsavory human desires, including the desire for power. From a psychoanalytic point of view, we would say that the ideology of biological determinism arises from infantile longings for omnipotence, and the grandiose belief that we can bring our own instinctual life, maybe even death itself, wholly under our own control. In place of acknowledging and accepting at least some human limitations such as illnesses, weaknesses, and fallibility, the biological idealogue claims to have the power to overcome all human limits.

The early founders of psychoanalysis established their science on the basis of an irreducible principle of humanity: that neurotic, psychotic and psychosomatic symptoms – the demons of the past and the bad genes of the present – could be understood as intelligible actions that had psychological motives or purposes. The basic working assumption of any psychoanalyst is that there is meaning to be found on every level of a person's actions, from momentary impulses and slips of the tongue to dreams and inhibitions. As psychoanalyst Carlo Strenger (1991: 78) has described it, the analyst or analytic therapist is always "listening for *subjectively determined, idiosyncratic patterns in the patient's ways of acting, feeling, and thinking*" (italics in original). This kind of listening allows less conscious and unconscious intentions to be formulated from the clues that the patient presents. The goal is to bring out hidden subjective and affective patterns into the light of informed reflection so that we can become accountable and responsible for them.

Those of us who practice psychodynamic therapies share in an ethic about human suffering: that one is the creator of oneself and that whatever one does, one becomes heir to those intentions. To free ourselves from destructive emotional habits or change our irrational fears or reduce our discontent, we must come to know our own desires and motives, especially those that we repeatedly project into others. I borrow some words from contemporary psychoanalyst Roy Schafer (1978: 180) who describes the course of a psychoanalysis in the following way:

> The analysand progressively recognizes, accepts, revises, refines, and lives in terms of the idea of the self as agent. This is to say that, in one way or another and more and more, the analysand sees himself or herself as being the person who essentially has been doing the things from which he or she was apparently suffering upon entering analysis.

It should be sufficiently clear that this ethic stands as a stark contrast to the ideology of biological determinism and the bad gene.

Over the next few decades, I hope that we can work together in the mental health professions to shape a human science of subjective meanings that can come into dialogue with the sciences of biological predispositions and genetic inheritance. I hope that we can, much more than we have in the past decade, steer clear of reductive materialist ideologies that critically undermine human responsibility for suffering. I hope that we can define and develop our young psychoanalytic science of intentions more systematically. Practitioners of psychodynamic therapies, no matter their particular orientations, share fundamental beliefs and methods: we are all committed to understanding human beings as intentional persons, even when they do not understand themselves in this way. We are committed to acknowledging that human experience is filled with discontents, conflicts, and failures because of the ways in which we are all largely unconscious of many of our motives. Claiming this common ground of concern, we need to stop our feuding and gather our strength to develop better scientific practices in the field of psychodynamic therapies. We will certainly need the help of academic scientists in doing this.

In this next decade the best of psychoanalytic science must be formulated in such a way that can be shared with the general public, while research programs are established to investigate both the workings of our therapeutic methods and the assumptions that we make about human personality. Some of these studies are already underway, as I mentioned above. Fully expanded and researched as a science of human intentions, psychoanalysis could assist all people in living more responsibly and cooperatively as a unitary species within families, groups, and societies through recognizing the nature of our limitations and responsibilities. This is my passionate wish.

# Chapter 3

# Struggling with Jung: the value of uncertainty

As I look back over my long relationship with Carl Jung, beginning in 1969 when I read Erich Neumann's *The Great Mother* as a college senior writing an honors thesis on the image of the Virgin in the Middle Ages, I am struck by one theme: transference. Finding Neumann's ideas both wonderful and confusing, I went to my thesis advisor to ask about Jung. He said "Stay away from Jung and all that mysticism." His response was strong enough to interest me, and so I dove headfirst into *Memories, Dreams, Reflections* on the advice of my roommate who seemed to know a lot about mysticism. Opening that book was the start of an idealizing transference to Jung. He would be *my* perfect analyst because his life mirrored mine; I would also be *his* perfect analyst because I understood him from the inside – how he struggled and why he felt so alienated.

Like Jung, I had experienced a lonely, other-worldly childhood with many inexplicable and emotionally charged happenings. I too had a parent (father, not mother as with Jung) who had a "number one" and a "number two" personality. Like Jung, I grew up in the country and spent my early years with animals and very simple folk. I had had a terrible school phobia from age seven to eight and, like Jung, had "snapped out of it" because I overheard my parents' decision to send me to a child psychiatrist.

After reading Jung's autobiography, I yearned to know Jung – not to know more about his ideas, but to know *him*. When I read that Anaïs Nin, after she became acquainted with Jung's work, wanted to go to Zürich to be his lover, I resonated, and became more sympathetic to Nin who had previously seemed impossibly self-centered to me. (Of course, I could not have known then how droves of women, young and old, must have flocked to Zürich with the same fantasy, conscious or not.)

In 1971, ten years after Jung's death, I visited Zürich for the first time. It was July and there were few people at the Jung Institute, the only place in the world that I was interested in pursuing my own psychotherapy. With tremendous excitement and trepidation, I approached the secretary, explaining that I was an American who was interested in Jungian analysis. I was in Zürich for only a few days, I said, but had come expressly to visit the

Jung Institute. She said that another American, an analytic training candidate, was in the library and perhaps I should talk with her.

There I met Linda Leonard and immediately had an idealizing transference to her! Everything she said seemed significant to me, and when I left the hour or so conversation we had, I announced to my husband (to his great dismay) that now I wanted to *become* a Jungian analyst; being in analysis was not enough. I knew nothing more about analytical psychology than that I liked recording my dreams and that I identified with Jung's life! I had no real awareness of my psychological problems or my development. Incidentally I've seen many people seeking Jungian analysis over the years with the same condition: idealized identification with Jung, wanting to become an analyst rather than an analysand. Although I was merely twenty-four years old at the time, I was the sort of person who says what she does and does what she says. The fact that I put my desire into words almost broke up my marriage on the spot. Indeed, my marriage did break up when I returned to Zürich for analysis.

I begin with this idealized identification with Jung not only because it's true or even a good story, but because through reading about Jung's life I received a lot of psychological help. I suspect this is true for many others.

His life story had turned him into what self psychologists call a "self-object" for me when I was twenty-two years old. His autobiography gave coherence and transparency to my young life. Because the autobiography deals mostly with his inner life and his fantasies, I could project my own images of his relationships and life in the world. I did not have to deal with facts, with others' accounts, the reactions of those who loved him or hated him. I felt I understood who and what he was, and that knowing more about *him* was vitally important to my knowing more about me. In short, to become Jung would be to become myself.

For me, Jung (1916/1969: 74) fulfilled the idealizing transference that he described so well in his paper on the transcendent function:

> For the patient . . . the analyst has the character of an indispensable figure absolutely necessary for life. However infantile this dependence may appear to be, it expresses an extremely important demand which, if disappointed, often turns into bitter hatred of the analyst.

## Disillusionment and "analyzing with Jung"

As I have come to know Jung's work and life in greater detail over the years, he has often disappointed me. Because I have been able to analyze the complexity of my relationship to him, I have not developed a bitter hatred. I'm often in conflict with some of his ideas – especially his theories of gender and ethnic differences. In my ongoing analysis, we dissolved the persona-restoring stage a long time ago, have been through the madness of discharging our complexes at each other, and now seem to be entering the stage of secure symbolizing. I'm still working through a rather intensely negative transference, as I will describe later, but I feel quite contained in being able to resolve it. I appreciate the depth and richness of our relationship. As in any good analysis, I feel also that I have helped Jung, by revising and furthering some of his fundamental contributions so that they cannot be easily dismissed by contemporary philosophers, psychoanalysts and feminists. I try to save him from the stumbling blocks of reification and essentialism. He has already saved me from self-hatred, dissociation and alienation.

In working through my idealization of Jung over the years, I have increasingly learned to value uncertainty. By uncertainty, I mean the kind of reflective space in which there is no premature foreclosure on meaning. Just when I think I understand something between Jung and me – as, for example, where we each stand on the theory of contrasexuality – I discover something new in his writings or rediscover something I've forgotten. Then the dialogue moves on. In the remainder of this chapter, I will describe in greater detail why this dialogue depends on both trust and conflict, and how it has saved me from turning my idealization into "bitter hatred of the analyst," as Jung puts it.

## Postmodernism and constructivism

Although Jung lived far into the twentieth century, he saw only the dimmest beginnings of post-structuralism and its development into postmodernism. Jung's interests after about 1944 turned increasingly to ethology, evolutionary biology, and developmental processes of all sorts. I believe he was moving in the direction of contemporary developmental and postmodern psychologies, but he left behind him a trail of different assumptions and interpretations that span the range from realist to idealistic, from essentialist to postmodern, from traditional to radical. It is possible to read Jung from highly divergent perspectives and believe (and find "proof" in the form of quotations) that Jung agrees with you.

I want to take a moment to explain why I think the postmodern critique of truth and culture is important in my relationship with Jung. What I mean by "postmodern" is the critique of truth, history, fact, or reality as being simply found or discovered "out there" or "in here." Postmodern critiques have been successfully aimed at both realism and idealism. The belief that reality lies within the physical and chemical processes of our world has been (in my view) fundamentally defeated by a number of philosophers, particularly Thomas Kuhn and Hilary Putnam.

Similarly, the belief that our mental or perceptual experiences are primarily imposed on us by forms, ideals or categories that structure the mind (such as Kantian categories) has also been fundamentally put to rest, especially by philosophers like Rom Harré and Richard Rorty.

There is a branch of postmodern theory called "deconstruction" that often gets confused with all of postmodernism. Deconstruction originated with the philosopher Jacques Derrida in France. It has been carried into psychoanalysis, especially by some followers of Jacques Lacan. Deconstruction explicitly rejects a psychology of coherence, integration or universal principles of development in favor of a psychology of discontinuity, lack of coherence, and local influences on development. Deconstruction is also a political critique of human ideals and virtues. Often I have heard my Jungian colleagues attack postmodernism, confusing it with desconstruction. Deconstruction is a skeptical philosophy of doubt and criticism. I see little resonance between Jung and deconstruction.

Instead, I have come to believe that Jung is an implicit supporter of a branch of affirmative postmodernism: "constructivism". Constructivism does not reject universals such as archetypes or universal emotions, but it assumes that both the concepts and the experiences to which they refer come directly from human interpretation. On this view, archetypes do not move and shape human consciousness; nor are we caught in morphogenic structures. We humans create our worlds through active encounters between our embodied being and "something out there." Our experience is interdependent, an interaction of our perceptions and attitudes with an environment in flux. Even our very perceptions are interpretations, and so nothing is absolutely fixed and eternal in our phenomenal world. And yet, we are all human beings who are universally constrained and endowed in certain predispositions to perceive ourselves and the world. These can be studied as universal aspects of our subjectivity. In many passages of Jung's later work, I find significant traces of constructivism.

For instance, in 1939 Jung (1939/1992: 58) described how human beliefs about the really real shift around over time, and how these beliefs inescapably constitute "reality":

> On a primitive level people are afraid of witches; on the modern level we are apprehensively aware of microbes. There everybody believes in ghosts, but here everybody believes in vitamins. Once upon a time men were possessed by devils, now they are . . . obsessed by ideas.

But Jung's claims and premises are contradictory. Sometimes he sounds like a constructivist, then he sounds like a Platonic idealist, and then again occasionally like a biological realist. Consequently, I have learned that Jung also is a shifting project of interpretation and complexity that demands an ongoing dialogue.

With this as background then, I want to introduce a framework that has helped me enormously in working through my transferences to Jung. The framework comes from psychoanalyst Arnold Modell.

## Three realities of psychoanalysis

In *Other Times, Other Realities: toward a theory of psychoanalytic treatment*, Modell (1990) describes three competing and equally valid realities within psychoanalysis. Before I go into these in detail, I want to review Modell's central point about these three realities. For analysis to be effective as a transformation of perspective, the analyst and analysand have to become aware of these realities and explore them as different, but overlapping, worlds. When the analytic couple gets stuck in one reality, there tends to be a standstill or a rupture.

This fluidity of perspective that Modell advocates is consonant with Jung's transcendent function – the dialectic of opposites – and with D.W. Winnicott's (e.g., 1971) play space or potential space, and with Tom Ogden's (e.g., 1989) dialectical space. All of these point to a particular kind of uncertainty: an ability to hold multiple meanings in mind without latching onto a single conclusion.

Constructivism adds the caveat that to create an interpretation *is* to constitute a reality. Holding in mind three different realities and moving among them interpretively, both patient and therapist are able to try on meanings and to discover what seems safe, exciting, coherent or persuasive in the moment.

Let me outline Modell's three realities and then return to Jung and me. Modell (1990) proposes two different kinds of transference in the psychoanalytic situation. One kind of transference cannot be fully analyzed and continues to develop even after treatment has ended. He calls it the "dependent-containing transference." It is the core of the therapeutic alliance. It depends on the ritual of analysis (time, place, fee, confidentiality, safe boundaries, etc.), the relative anonymity of the analyst, and the idealizing beliefs about the analyst (e.g., that the analyst is more powerful than one's symptoms). This kind of transference is what Jung referred to in the above passage as "an extremely important demand" that, if disappointed, can turn into "bitter hatred of the analyst."

The second kind of transference is called "iconic-projective" by Modell. This is what we usually call transference proper. It is the projection of images and complexes into the intersubjective field between the therapist and the patient. Of course, it occurs from both sides, but I am talking here only about transference from my side as Jung's "analysand." It would be hard to talk about Jung's countertransference for he has been dead throughout my analysis!

The important contrasts between these two transferences are usefully summarized by Modell (1990: 48–52): the dependent transference is continually present throughout treatment, but the iconic transference is episodic and eventually absent. Within the dependent transference, both analysand and analyst experience symbolic enactments of developmental conflicts (such as attachment–separation, dependence–independence and aggression–love). But in the iconic transference, both experience the recreation of specific images, such as "mother," "father," "child," from the general dynamic themes of the patient's early dependencies and traumas, or other powerful affective experiences. Effective interpretations enhance and strengthen the dependent-containing transference, but they resolve or diminish the iconic-projective one. The dependent-containing transference actually provides the safety, trust, and holding environment that allow the iconic transference to emerge and be understood. Poorly timed or ineffective interpretations of the iconic transference can be felt as a threat to the dependent-containing one.

Finally, the third reality is the ordinary relationship – what Jung calls the kinship libido – between two people struggling together through life difficulties in the face of the demands of treatment. Within the ordinary relationship, it is important to keep in mind that the patient has hired the analyst. When we think of the "asymmetry" of the analytic situation we are often thinking only in terms of the dependent-containing transference, or in terms of the powerful images of the iconic-projective transference. From the perspective of the ordinary relationship, the asymmetry is reversed. The therapist's livelihood depends on the patient.

### Jung and I in three realities

So back to Jung and me: I would like to describe how I see my psychoanalysis in each of these realities. I have already described my dependent-containing transference to Jung as he appeared to me initially in an idealizing identification. That changed as I began training to become an analyst in 1979. Careful and close reading of Jung's collected works often shocked me and ruptured the containing transference. I found some of his ideas, especially about women, to be belittling and insulting. I doubt that I could have sustained our analytical relationship had I not begun reading his letters at about the same time.

In the letters I found a different voice: more flexible, often more imaginative and uncertain, and frequently inspiring. Over the years, the letters have helped to create in me a trusting interplay between different feelings about Jung. Especially in his letters, Jung criticizes any and all dogma, and vows that his approach is not a fixed set of ideas.

In regard to the iconic-projective transference, initially I had fantasized Jung as Great Father. Having myself been fathered by a tortured, maddening, aggressive, but loving man I had known little solid predictable fathering. I longed for the Oedipal romance. I wanted to know that it was possible to feel both proud of and close to Father. Jung at first seemed wiser, more cultured, and more knowledgeable than any man in my life.

Although I can barely recall the time (until I was four years old or so) in which I idealized my own father, I have many clear memories of being disgraced or demeaned by him. Gradually, as I learned more of Jung's history, of his love affairs with various women including his patients, and of his advice to men about women, I could feel the old familiar shame and rage that I felt with my own father. When I first met Jung's concept of contrasexuality I found it freeing and enhancing. But as I read and heard more, the images of anima and animus, and masculine and feminine, seemed like stereotypes into which one's experiences had to be fitted. Even more damaging was my suspicion that Jung misunderstood himself in part because he never seriously respected *any* woman with whom he had had a close relationship. Instead, he insisted that women carry for him various powerfully projected aspects of his own personality. The more I read new accounts of Jung's life, the more I found images that contrasted with my ideal Jung of the autobiography. I probably would have quit our relationship altogether had I not been able to renew again and again my dependent-containing transference by reading his letters.

This process culminated finally in a book that I wrote with James Hall called *Jung's Self Psychology: A Constructivist Perspective* (1991). There I was able to dialogue in depth with the Jung I found in the letters. Through that book especially, I spoke to Jung about our differences. He answered in a way that strengthened our bond. I can't say that the negative father transference has been resolved. New information about Jung's life history is constantly emerging. Some of it has increased my familiar sense of disgrace and shame. But now I trust that I can resolve enough of my negative transference to sustain the dependent-containing one that I need to go on developing in my analysis with Jung.

Our ordinary relationship often enriches me. Many times I remind myself that I chose to pursue all of this; I hired Jung (not Freud or Winnicott or Kohut) to treat me, so to speak. No one forced me into this. No one else is responsible for the pain or transformation, and besides, I feel how much Jung needs *me* for his livelihood! I sustain and expand his ideas and take them into new worlds.

This is a way of claiming my roots: I am a Jungian; this is where I fell in love. Although it's been a complicated relationship, it's produced fertile material in the transcendent function, the play space in which I can entertain his ideas and mine from many different perspectives.

Considering my relationship to Jung to be a psychoanalysis brings me hope that it will never deaden or rigidify. Even if I fully resolve my negative transference, it will be replaced by some other projection, equally rich in its analytical possibilities. In expanding my understanding of the transcendent function, I made it a priority to keep open a dialectical space. In this space I review Jungian concepts, analyze the iconic transference, develop the containing transference, and take responsibility for having hired Jung.

*Being a Jungian*

Sometimes, though, I encounter a kind of narrow-mindedness among my Jungian colleagues, both analysts and other followers of Jung. Either it is an idealizing transference that has never permitted an experience of deep conflict with Jung or it is a "Great Father–Mother" or "Genius" projection that remains stuck in the form of seeing Jung as all-good or all-knowing. Sometimes the image seems even to be of God: to doubt Jung is blasphemous. In such cases there is little recognition of the ordinary human relationship in which Jung is a human being like oneself, and in which one has helped Jung by hiring him to be the analyst/theorist.

I used to paraphrase Jung (who said he was glad to be Jung and not a Jungian) and say that I was glad that I was a Jungian and not Jung. I was glad not to be forced into the hothouse of the dichotomies and splits of early psychoanalysis. Sometimes now, I'm not so sure. Although I still wouldn't want to be Jung, I often feel better when I think of myself as a psychoanalyst rather than a "Jungian" per se. My psychoanalytic colleagues have long since given up the idolizing of Freud. They expect that I also have a conflict-ridden evolving relationship with Jung, as they have had with Freud. Some of my Jungian colleagues still seem shocked by my open struggle.

Freudian psychoanalysis has moved on to whole new horizons beyond Freud's original themes and theories. Critiques of Freud's essentialism and sexism, revisions of his major concepts, and debates about his model have enriched Freudian psychoanalysis enormously. In the writings of many of my contemporary Freudian colleagues, there is a healthy respect for the dialectic of development in their field.

I would like to feel the same openness to conflict and dialogue within the Jungian circle in regard to our major concepts, our transferences to Jung, and our responsibilities for using and revising his ideas. It is in this spirit that I have offered this brief introduction to the multi-leveled relationship that has been my psychoanalysis with Jung.

# Chapter 4

# On the difficulty of being a Jungian psychoanalyst

All that I write here should be read in the context of my own practice, teaching and writing in the field of analytical psychology. In every professional setting in which I've worked – from being a professor at Bryn Mawr College, to being a research psychologist and teacher at a psychiatric hospital, to being an author – I've been *translating* Jung's ideas. That is, I've been communicating with people who have little or no specific interest in Jung, but who are committed to understanding or practicing psychodynamic psychotherapy. From graduate students to psychiatric residents, my typical everyday audience has come to Jung with skepticism. Even in my own private practice of psychotherapy and analysis, I've had, and still have, patients who know nothing about Jung. They come to see me simply because I've been recommended as an effective psychotherapist.

I've never taught in any Jungian training program, and although I've lectured to many Jungian audiences, I rarely face listeners who are primed to hear things described in a Jungian vocabulary. My ambition has been to make Jung understandable, readable, useful and applicable in the world beyond the converted and the convinced, especially in other psychoanalytic circles. Why that's been my aim is more complicated than I can summarize here, but suffice it to say that Freud and object relations theorists have had major influences on my life and work, and I believe that the divorce between Freud and Jung has crippled the psychoanalytic family for years and made all of us feel like stepchildren in one or another context.

I've tried to do something about that. By and large I believe that I've succeeded within the range of my influence. What I write here needs to be understood, then, as the product of a particular person who's been influenced a great deal by the larger world of psychoanalysis and developmental psychology, and who's conversing with, and teaching, mostly those who do not worship at Jung's altar.

Rather than address one of the frequently addressed difficulties of being an analyst (e.g., managed care), I have chosen to address my difficult and confusing experiences with some of my Jungian colleagues who seem unable to sustain the transcendent or dialogical space in reflecting on Jung.

Frequently this has led to incomplete and unsatisfying conversations with my colleagues.

## Rigidities and splits

In my encounters with Jungian analysts, other professionals and interested laypeople in the Jungian world, I've too often found myself taken aback by anti-intellectual, anti-scientific, and anti-rational attitudes. Among American Jungians especially, there's a strong tendency to draw a dichotomy between the "head" (thinking) and the "heart" (feeling) and to believe that the heart should win. False arguments and splits are stirred by fearfulness about thinking through concepts. Some people seem to fear looking too closely at what we're about or want, perhaps in order to protect their turf because they feel it's already been infringed on.

In the popular Jungian domain, I have often encountered New Age hypes about certain aspects of Jung's theories of individuation, typology, astrology or synchronicity. In any popular movement, people want excitement and handy formulas. When analytical psychology is promoted in this way, as primarily a popular movement, naturally it is compromised. This rush to the New Age is a peculiarly Jungian problem though, not a problem in other branches of psychoanalysis.

Sometimes it seems to me that Jungian professionals in the USA turn too readily to the popular domain for their support and recognition. Many are not active members of professional groups beyond the Jungian, such as their own professional disciplines, where they could be reflected and criticized by non-Jungian colleagues. Instead of being in the mix of dialogue and debate with other psychoanalysts and therapists, Jungians may be parochial and isolated, and then vulnerable to whims and biases that falsely promise community or security.

A major way in which I've developed as an analyst and human being over the past years has been through the challenges made to me about my Jungian beliefs. These challenges have emerged especially in conversations and debates about postmodernism, feminism and philosophical critiques of psychoanalysis.

## Postmodernism

Postmodernism has played a major role in the revision of Freudian concepts such as the drive and structural models and the Oedipus complex. Postmodernism is a broad critique concerning the grounds for all and any truth claims. It's been unfolding over the past thirty or more years in all major disciplines from science to literature, from linguistics to psychology, from art and architecture to religion. Many of my Jungian colleagues have reacted to this broad and profoundly important development as if it were a mosquito: they've ignored it or brushed it away or swatted at it.

Before we Jungians could begin to operate intelligently in a postmodern context, we would have to review and justify our claims that archetypes, instincts, and complexes are universal to all human beings, and show how and why this is so. Rooted in Kant, and developed more fully in Hegel, Heidegger and Wittgenstein, postmodern inquiry and theory extend into the present with Quine, Rorty, Taylor, Kuhn, Putnam and many other philosophers whose commentaries are often clarifying for our practice and theorizing. To give you a sample of the kinds of questions raised by these philosophers and their relevance to analytical psychology, I'm going to review a few of my favorite quotations, of the sort I'd like to discuss in relation to Jungian theory and practice. The first is from the philosopher of science T.S. Kuhn, best known for his work on the structure of scientific revolutions. He taught at the Massachusetts Institute of Technology (MIT) and spent his career studying the epistemology of the natural sciences.

Kuhn states in this passage that the natural sciences, just as the human sciences, have a hermeneutical base that is their foundation. His aim is to show that the natural sciences (e.g., physics, biology, chemistry) are not dealing with "brute data" or anything beyond human perceptual and conceptual schemes. Kuhn (1991: 22) says:

> the natural sciences of any period are grounded in a set of concepts that the current generation of practitioners inherit from their immediate predecessors. The set of concepts is a historical product, embedded in the culture to which current practitioners are initiated by training, and it is accessible to nonmembers only through hermeneutic techniques which historians and anthropologists come to understand as other modes of thought.

In other words, the claims of the natural sciences are not independent of bias or concepts, arrived at from raw or descriptive data, nor are they necessarily "more objective" than claims from other fields.

Claims for objectivity depend on exactly what we are trying to study and to say, not just on our method. Kuhn goes on to say that natural science practitioners speak of their work differently from practitioners in the human sciences; natural scientists generally do not disagree much about the interpretations of their findings. "Rather, they put to use the paradigm received from their teachers in an endeavor I've spoken of as normal science, an enterprise that attempts to solve puzzles like those of improving and extending the match between theory and experiment at the advancing forefront of the field." Those of us in the human sciences, however, "appear to be hermeneutic, interpretive, through and through" (p. 22). The human sciences – such as psychology, anthropology, linguistics and history – demand debate to clarify their findings.

Another philosopher of science, Hilary Putnam also of the MIT, argues that no fact, whether from the natural sciences or some other discipline, can ever stand on its own. Although he spent much of his career originally promoting a kind of biological realism, Putnam (1988: 114) has ultimately concluded "To talk of 'facts' without specifying a language to be used is to talk of nothing; the word 'fact' no more has its use fixed by the world itself than does the word 'exist' or the word 'object.'"

When we Jungians attempt to ground our truths in biology, chaos theory, morphological structures, or mathematical formulas, we are not escaping the hermeneutic circle. These methods are not beyond interpretation and they probably distort our truths which are grounded in subjective life.

If we attempt to explain ourselves by resorting to the languages of the natural sciences, as though they are endowed with a privileged status, we make a big mistake. Not only are their truths rooted in a different context, but their methods are so different from our own as to make comparisons highly questionable. When Jung was alive, certain accounts from the natural sciences were taken as self-evident, but the intellectual world has changed since then and has demanded that all truth claims reveal the underlying assumptions on which they rest.

From the perspective of postmodernism, Jung and Jungian ideas are often criticized or dismissed as "foundationalist" or "essentialist." Essentialism and foundationalism make assumptions that some principles or forms reside outside of human experience, and are beyond interpretation and the constraints of human perception. Although some of Jung's ideas, like some of Freud's, *are* essentialist and antiquated, many of his ideas are thoroughly postmodern.

The philosophical contributions of Kant, Heidegger and Wittgenstein have shown us how we, as human subjects, are always agents or authors of our perceptions and our world as we perceive it. We make the world through our thoughts, but the world does not make us. And yet, the constraints of the world resist our projections as well, making an interplay of our projections of form and meaning and a resistance from the world and others that changes us. Once we've firmly grasped this interplay, the epistemological stance of essentialism is automatically undermined. Here's how philosopher Alistair MacIntyre (1977: 455) puts it:

> The most that we can claim is that this is the best account which anyone has been able to give so far, and that our beliefs about what the marks of "a best account so far" are will themselves change in what are at present unpredictable ways.

We can never escape our own perspective, our human embodied engagement, in our investigations of the world or ourselves.

This insight does not lead necessarily to wild subjectivism and solipsism. Once we understand what our assumptions are, then we can speak of facts and truths within the limits of our context. In analytical psychology, this means that we can specify how and why we claim that archetypes are universal, and then allow others to dispute our claim. We modestly acknowledge, then, that we are not omniscient, and that we have understood just what our own project and practices are and what they are not. For example, we practice analytical psychology in a subjective domain in which meaning is established interpersonally. Our objective facts come from comparisons of findings and evidence with others, mostly within psychoanalysis and similar disciplines.

I don't think that Jung would disagree with MacIntyre, and yet I've heard some of my colleagues speak as though they had encountered privileged, almost divine, information or knowledge from the Self, a dream, or archetypal images. At times, this sounds like taking a god's-eye view rather than a human one. And yet, our claims for truth and insight depend on our own interpretive community with its assumptions and historical roots. Broadening that community broadens our base, but claiming physics, mathematics, or biology as a base will tend to distort our context. Freudian psychoanalysts have been guilty of something similar when they attempt to explain their work through a weak version of biology. Postmodern critiques of the sciences, both the natural and human sciences, help us to see our claims more clearly, and remain modest and practical.

## Sexism and racism

Over the past two decades, I have tried to examine the claims and assumptions of analytical psychology in a social as well as philosophical framework. American Jungian analysts have, until recently, included no African-Americans among their ranks. This fact raises a question about whether and how our assumptions might be racist. Jungian accounts of dreams, images, and complexes have been steeped in Eurocentric biases: seeing the world from the perspective of an elite white European. Nothing is wrong with this perspective in itself. Our founders were elite white Europeans and they couldn't have had any other perspective. But this original bias now has to be corrected if we are to apply our ideas beyond their original audience.

We now see how aspects of theory affect our assumptions, even while we create our theory. Jung didn't live late enough into the twentieth century for post-structuralism to affect his thinking very much, and yet he was drawn to developmental and evolutionary theories which are post-structural. But *we* who live in this postmodern era are challenged to examine the assumptions we've inherited, to see them in a new light. When we realize that they were not dictated by some immutable reality "out there" or "in here," we can ask new questions. For instance, why would anyone claim that an image is universal in its meaning? Why would we say that the shadow is dark or black? What does it mean to say that the anima connects a man to soul, but the animus connects a woman to authority? What does it mean to take the hero myth as the basis for individuation? These are questions that must be addressed if our theory and practice are going to survive professionally and culturally.

As a feminist, I've often been shocked at the way women in Jungian groups (myself being one) have been treated in regard to stereotyping. Female authority has been belittled as "animus possession." Female capacities for nurturance or feeling may also be aggrandized through endowing them with goddess powers. Again we need to ask the questions about why we would or would not want to retain a language of universal categories of masculinity and femininity, recognizing that these are not biological imperatives, but rather convenient ways of speaking. We can question whether they are helpful for the context in which we use them to characterize personality styles and to interpret subjective meaning. Feminist and gender scholars from other fields help us to examine the explicit and implicit assumptions about gender that have sometimes led to offensive sexism in psychoanalytic interpretations. Sexism is not a necessity for the practice of analytical psychology or any other branch of psychoanalysis.

I've often needed the help of historians and anthropologists to understand the roots of analytical psychology and its methods. I'd like to feel that my Jungian colleagues are open to acknowledging the complicated history of Jewish and anti-Jewish influences on the development of our field. Because many of my colleagues and patients are Jewish, I want to know if I have unknowingly adopted offensively distorted methods for analyzing their subjective experience. I have welcomed the clarification that Andrew Samuels (e.g., 1993) and others have brought to seeing how and why Jung may have developed some anti-Semitic tendencies during the 1930s and how these have affected our concepts and community since. Knowing this, I can examine and correct my use of theory.

This issue of anti-Semitism bears directly on healing the splits within our larger psychoanalytic family circle. More often than not, my Freudian colleagues have spoken openly about their suspicions of Jung's anti-Semitism only after they've come to trust me. In my view, misunderstandings about Jung's attitudes toward Jewish people and culture are among the greatest unspoken barriers between the Jungians and the rest of the psychoanalytic community.

It is my intent to open up more dialogue with my own colleagues in relation to some issues that have troubled me over time. The liveliness of our profession, in its practice and theory-making, depends on our ability to understand ourselves and the claims we make. I hope that analytical psychology can stand side by side with other branches of psychoanalysis in the twenty-first century, moving forward in revising its conditions for claiming to be true and significant.

# Chapter 5

# Subject to change: feminism, psychoanalysis and subjectivity

As a practicing *Jungian* psychoanalyst I have often been excluded from the mainstream psychoanalytic world. As a feminist, I have been an outsider to the American Jungian community and as a Jungian, I am looked upon suspiciously within the broader American feminist community. Finally, as a developmental psychologist and a constructivist, I am frequently misunderstood by all of the above. But as a feminist constructivist Jungian psychoanalyst I am uniquely embedded in a matrix of relationships that permit me to think about issues of subjectivity that are critical to the practice of psychoanalysis in an evolving gender-conscious world.

## Self as interpretive community

Until only recently it was radical, even perhaps provocative, to critique the individual self of personal autonomy, to consider the self to be a social product constrained by a cultural era. Although such critiques appeared throughout the decade of the 1980s, they tended to be seen as outsider views. At the beginning of the 1990s, though, we came rather suddenly into a new *zeitgeist* in which the insider view is that the self is originally and continually the product of a relational matrix and thus is neither free nor even fully individual.

I offer the following premises for subjectivity among a chorus of voices, although they were spoken by the isolated not long ago: (1) that selves are created and developed in relationships; (2) that the geography (boundaries and domain) of selves is shaped by cultural contexts; and (3) that selves carry the local meanings of the folk psychologies that sponsor them, both on the level of particulars such as gender, class, and ethnic meanings, and on the level of general design such as degree of individuality.

First I will describe these premises and then discuss them in relation to Jane Loevinger's (1976) model of ego development. Let me begin by making a distinction between persons and selves, to show how narrative is especially important for a self.

## *Persons, selves and narrative*

Several philosophers have contributed significantly to the premises of self that I listed above. For me the most prominent are P.F. Strawson (1959), John MacMurray (1957/1978), Rom Harré (1984), and Charles Taylor (1989). From their work especially I have come to define "self" as the set of attitudes, beliefs, images and actions that permit a person to sustain individual subjectivity. Whereas the category "person" can be universally identified by public criteria (such as body form and expected powers), the construct of self is the product of an interpretive community, more local or homegrown, so to speak. Still, certain features are universal in the way persons account for selves.

Charles Taylor (1989: 33) universalizes the role of morality in self-formation. He connects identity to the fact that "we cannot do without some orientation to the good, that we each essentially are . . . where we stand on this". He stresses also that "One is a self only among other selves. A self can never be described without reference to those who surround it" (p. 35). Like Winnicott's famous dictum "There's no such thing as a baby," Taylor can be paraphrased as saying "There's no such thing as a self" – only selves.

Rom Harré (1989) urges us to see the significance of self-making in the development of a person.

> animate beings are fully human if they are in possession of a theory – a theory about themselves. It is a theory in terms of which a being orders, partitions, and reflects on its own experience and becomes capable of self-intervention and control.

Harré challenges psychological investigators, "to look for conversational practices in which a theory of the appropriate kind could be acquired by an animate being who is . . . organized in a strong unitary fashion" (p. 404). I would add that a person is fully human only when she or he can narrate a self as unitary over time, space, and causality.

The state of being a unitary subject is sustained everywhere by coherence in the sense of the integration of complex subjective states into an embodied unit, and by continuity in the sense of narrating oneself over time and space. Harré (1989) cautions us not to universalize a masterful, bounded individuality in our accounts of coherence or continuity. Depending on the forms available within an interpretive community, a person may have a collective self like that of the Copper Eskimo (Harré, 1989: 399): "When one weeps, they all weep; when one laughs, they all laugh" or a powerfully independent self like that of the Maori who view the mana of an individual to be a sort of physical force (p. 400).

Psychologist Jerome Bruner (1990) builds on the claims of Taylor and Harré in seeing narrative as the major vehicle for self-construction.

Narrative refers to a story that links past, present and future. After young children have grasped the basic idea of reference necessary for language, their principal linguistic interests center on stories of human action. The self as narrator is born with the practice of language.

The self as agent, as a personal cause or prime mover, seems to be another universal feature of selfhood, emphasized especially by philosopher John MacMurray and researcher Jean Piaget who discovered the centrality of action in the development of thought. Agency and continuity are linked in narrative, as Bruner shows, because a basic requirement of narrative is to account for the outcome of actions.

From the work of John Bowlby and the investigators of the attachment model, we can fill out the claim that the self is relational by pointing to affective relational patterns that are ubiquitous features of subjectivity, patterns arising from the interdependence of persons, organized by human emotion across the life span.

What is perhaps most compelling about selves is their organizing power, their ability to draw into related meaning much that would be dissociated without them; and perhaps this is why fundamentally and universally persons need selves.

## Ego development and self in psychotherapy

Jane Loevinger (1979: 3) claims that her model of ego development is a master variable that "encompasses the complexity of moral judgment, the nature of interpersonal relations, and the framework within which one perceives oneself and others as people". Ego development is the type of theory specified above by Harré (1989), based on a study of "conversational practices" that progressively organize the subject in a "strong unitary fashion." From my clinical and research experience, I believe Loevinger's nine stages or frames of reference of self–other *are* exhaustive of types of subjectivity among adolescents and adults in North American society.

Each of her stages is a paradigm of meaning derived from peoples' actual narratives collected from a sentence completion test. Each new stage reorganizes all that has come before and thus it is impossible to skip a stage. Typically, a person moves expectably through early stages until a plateau is reached, usually in young adulthood. A majority of Americans appear to stop developing after about the age of twenty-one (at the Conformist or Self-Aware stage) and thus Loevinger's model also serves as a typology of difference among adults. Stages are frames of reference for self–other that are not directly observable (not usually conscious), but must be inferred from respondents' narratives. Loevinger's sentence completion test has been used reliably for respondents from the age of twelve years onward.

I will briefly introduce her nine stages of ego development that fall along a continuum of self from less to more complex, from less to more integrated, from less to more internalized, and from less to more differentiated. As I describe each stage, I will also give an illustration from a recently completed study on the meaning of psychotherapy.

My point here is that patient and therapist form an interpretive community of self. The patient's self puts at least as many limits on this narrative as the therapist's self. A stage of ego development represents not only an individual, but a whole fabric of cultural exchange in which a person validates meanings. If one goal of psychotherapy *is* self-development, then we must pay attention to the interpretive set of the patient's self. For my purposes, I chose examples from people not in psychotherapy. Although their responses are exemplary of their stages, their language is not burdened by the jargon of a particular therapeutic culture.

With the help of graduate students from Bryn Mawr College, I surveyed 210 people using the sentence completion test for ego development and a simple questionnaire about psychotherapy. We were interested in the self–other narratives of psychotherapy that might fall along the continuum of ego development. We asked the question "What is psychotherapy?" and the following illustrations are brief examples of our respondents' answers.

The first stage of ego development (after the nonverbal "Pre-Social") is called "Impulsive." The impulsive person tends to dichotomize the world into nice to me and mean to me, and has difficulty controlling impulses. Emotional expressions tend to be limited to wishes and fears. Adults who remain at this stage usually live within institutions – psychiatric hospitals and prisons – or on the streets. What is psychotherapy at this stage? A fifty-six-year-old man and a woman (of unknown age) at this stage both said it's a "Doctor," "Is a doctor who helps people," defining psychotherapy as a person, a doctor person. What appears to us as a confusion between a concrete person and an abstract process is not really confusion for people at this stage. There is as yet no differentiation of the person of the therapist from the process of therapy.

The "Self-protective" stage signals a new ability to control impulses and stay out of trouble. Luck and other people are to blame for life's difficulties in the self-protective stage. Feelings are expressed as quasi-physical states (such as "pissed off"). Psychotherapy, for a fifty-three-year-old self-protective man is "analiss" in which the therapist is said to "cheat." Preoccupations with the therapist's "advantages" are common projections of the patient's opportunism at this stage.

The "Conformist" stage involves a major paradigm shift from the first two stages because it focuses on a trust in belonging, especially to a group or family. Conformity to rules and norms is expected, simple, and absolute at the conformist stage. Feelings are described in generalities associated with groups: for example, "teenagers are rowdy" and "elders are wise." Identity corresponds to group membership and is usually described in demographics such as age, race, religion. What is psychotherapy? One man at this stage said "Is someone to talk to"; another man said "When you talk about your problems"; a woman answered "A person who listens to your problems" and another man said, "To tell the truth, I really have no idea." At this stage, psychotherapy is described as "talking about problems" and getting advice. Clearly this kind of discourse occurs everywhere, and the conformist respondent may imply that he cannot say what distinguishes therapy from anything else.

The "Self-aware" stage (post-Conformist) is named for its hallmark of self-consciousness and rudimentary self-criticism, but the person is still quite captured by conformity to the group. Feelings are more clearly expressed, but differences in attitudes, interests, and abilities are recognized mostly in global terms. Multiple possibilities are envisioned for the self at the Self-aware stage. The self is often described as "future-oriented," looking for success in the future. Moral values are of the Hallmark greeting card type and people are judged in terms of how nice, good, and polite they are. (This is the modal stage for adults in North America.) About psychotherapy, a self- aware woman said, "It's a study where people's thoughts, actions etc. are studied to try to find a way to help the person understand herself, know what she really wants, why she acts in some ways etc." Another woman said, "The art of helping people through a relationship that allows a person to look at What hurts (?) in his/her life and gives him/her choices (?) on making changes. The relationship is mainly one-to-one and by conversation." Many people at the Self-aware stage describe a form of helping through relationship, a process, or a knowledge base. It seems to me that the Self-aware stage is developmentally the first interpretive context in which psychotherapy per se can really be engaged. At earlier stages, counseling, guidance, and advice-giving are a better match with self–other narratives.

The "Conscientious" stage and the three beyond it include a richly differentiated inner life that matches a psychoanalytic narrative. The notion of self-development (so central to psychoanalysis) arises spontaneously at the Conscientious stage and continues to develop at the later two. Life experiences are savored and appreciated with full awareness of the struggle for control. Intentions, motives, and consequences of action are now differentiated, as is the distinction between appearance and reality. The person is understood as an active agent who holds the origin of her or his own destiny. Psychologically complex explanations replace statements of "reasons" or "problems," and true empathy becomes possible with consciousness of the complexity of human life. The final three stages – Individualistic, Autonomy, Integrated – represent the interpretive community in which all depth psychology is sustained. These stages exist only among a small minority of adults in our society, perhaps an even smaller minority of our patient population. The complexity of tolerating ambiguity and paradox, different levels of meaning, and recognizing that suffering and conflict are inherent in human life is the province of only the few. Here is a voice from a man at the final stage of ego development called "Integrated." He's never been in psychotherapy, but he says "Psychotherapy is a disciplined process of diagnosing, identifying and liberating persons from unhealthy or abnormal ways of thinking about or responding to life, which block a person's development of continuing growth as a human being."

Ego development is an interpretive context of the self which constrains both the narrative and the outcome of psychotherapy. Although the therapist cannot take the patient into paradigms, narratives or attitudes unknown to the therapist's self, neither can the therapist evoke or discover narratives wildly beyond the patient's interpretive context. Given what I have set out thus far, I want now to turn my attention to the narrative of gender and its interpretation within much of contemporary depth psychology.

## Gender and subjectivity

As a feminist and a psychoanalyst, it appears to me that much of the psychoanalytic community is stuck at the Conformist or Self-aware stage of ego development in narrating gender as an aspect of self. Within such a pre-analytic context, people regard gender differences as rooted in sex differences. Biology, anatomy, brain chemistry and body structures are used to explain power, envy, fear and idealization between the sexes. Gender differences are assumed to be as concrete and inflexible as body structures. They are portrayed in greeting card fashion: men are more autonomous and aggressive, women are more emotional and nurturant. These dichotomizing differences are assumed to be built into the nature of things, and this fundamentally narrows the possibilities for selves.

I regard gender categories not as universal givens, but as products of the local interpretive community that assigns meaning to sex differences, primarily to get work done and maintain social structures. In all large organized societies, gender is a dichotomous signifier, as psychoanalyst Jacques Lacan has so well clarified. From birth onward, people are required to join one of two clubs in which membership is exclusive. Changing one's appearance, even one's body, may allow one to switch to the other group, but one can neither be in both groups at the same time, nor ultimately wholly disgard one's original assignment (even though one may change the body and "pass" as the other). Human subjectivity is constrained and divided. This division is a powerful key to unconscious fantasies and meanings of gender throughout the life span in everyday activities in sex, work, and family life. Gender divides not only the human community, but also the human subject. That which is feared, envied, and idealized can be tidily packaged as the Other, the one unlike oneself.

A multiplicity of conscious and unconscious meanings associated with self and other gender should be the stuff of psychoanalytic contributions to contemporary discourse. Multi-layered meanings of gender, and the ambiguity of the actual categories (depending, as they do, on a binary system) make this aspect of subjectivity a rich field for psychoanalytic study. Reworking fixed gender identities, defended through projection, is a central aspect of my own work in dialogue therapy with individuals and couples.

When I turn specifically to Freudian or Jungian discourse about gender, I often find myself mired in a form of concrete realism. In these contexts, gender is frequently treated as though it were fixed by structural , functional, or anatomical properties of the human body or universal archetypes. In discussing the symbolic meaning associated with sexual identity, psychoanalysts of a variety of persuasions are too often realists. They reason from the Conformist stage of ego development: individuals are defined by groups (racial, class, gender) that differ because they were made that way – by biology, God or the universe.

While it is a mistake of concrete realism to see gender as emanating from our brain or biochemistry, it is also a mistake to think that the complexity of gender can be reduced to social factors. Naturally (in the nature of being human) gender is constantly being constructed out of a variety of biological and environmental cues, and its subjectivity changes throughout the life cycle.

As long as the human community maintains a structure of two exclusive genders, the "opposite sex" will always carry the complexity and ambiguity of Otherness, in addition to the biological imperatives of the moment such as erotic drives, sex-typed behaviors, care-giving and the like. Psychoanalysts should certainly embrace this complexity and its fantasies, rather than reduce gender to concrete realism.

# Chapter 6

# The self in analysis: a postmodern account

As I have written in many places (e.g., Young-Eisendrath & Hall, 1991), my theorizing and practice of analytical psychology are strongly influenced by certain branches of contemporary philosophy – hermeneutics and psychological constructivism – that have been dubbed "affirmative postmodernism" by theorist Pauline Rosenau (1992). These are distinguished from "skeptical postmodernism" known particularly in the work of deconstructionists and related philosophers. I find my practice of psychoanalysis has benefited from a prolonged study of affirmative postmodernism. Theories of knowledge and interpretation (hermeneutics) and the branch of constructivism that takes embodied action and relationship to be the roots of our organized perceptions of a phenomenal world (rather than finding a "real world" given "out there") have grounded my thinking about psychoanalysis in particular, and the human sciences in general (e.g., see Hiley, Bohman & Shusterman, 1991).

I don't think it's important here to go into a lot of bibliographical detail about these influences, but simply to say that they arise from a critique of science, history, literature, philosophy and psychology that began with Hegel and Wittgenstein and continues to develop. Feminist epistemology has also been an important influence on my thinking about self, gender and sexuality.

I consider psychoanalysis (whether Freudian or Jungian) to be a *human* science, distinguished from the natural sciences by its goals, preoccupations and methods. Arnold Modell, a Freudian, and I agree on a great deal about what the self is and how it operates, but we may differ on the issue of the province of our study. Modell (1993: 187–188) in his recent book on self says:

> Those who recognize the self as a superordinate agent . . . are divided as to whether that agent . . . is embodied or disembodied. For those who consider the agency of the self to be outside biology must also consider psychoanalytic theory to be outside biology.

For my part I have no question that the self is an expression of our particular human embodiment. But I would like to be careful not to conflate *embodiment* and biology. The concerns and questions arising from our embodiment as they relate to our subjectivity are neither precisely nor adequately captured by the natural sciences, and certainly not by biology whose direct focus is at the organismic level of functioning.

Human embodiment and its complex expression of self – especially through intention, responsibility, reflection, motivation, emotion and memory – are the focus of many of the human sciences, psychology being one of those. We are only beginning to see the difficulty of mapping a self that is at once universal and particular. The problem of finding forms to study, scientifically and systematically, the life of a person and the development of self, without reducing that person to an animal, an organism, or a process, is at the heart of psychoanalysis.

I believe we are better served to enrich and develop our own methods in a systematic way than to look to the natural sciences for metaphors and concepts in order to build the self from the bottom up, so to speak. Let us make use of the natural sciences for support, but not for developing our basic questions and paradigms. The examples of empirical research on which I draw below are fine illustrations of the work already underway in the human sciences to build paradigms for the study of subjectivity.

I have found the reflections of philosopher Charles Taylor to be especially helpful in regard to the importance of investigating subjectivity from within the human sciences. For example, Taylor (1985: 4) says:

> Our personhood cannot be treated in exactly the same way we approach our organic being. What it is to possess a liver or a heart is something I can define quite independently of the space of questions in which I exist for myself, but not what it is to have a self or be a person.

Earlier in the same piece, Taylor remarks on those psychological theories that attempt to model the study of personhood on findings or categories from the natural sciences, that they seem "to be terribly implausible. They lead to very bad science; either they end up in wordy elaborations of the obvious, or they fail altogether to address the interesting questions" (p. 1).

In studying the self through analytical psychology I want to ask the interesting questions: for me, they concern the process of development or individuation as it is revealed or hidden through expressions of individual subjectivity. When I say "individual subjectivity", I mean this term to be a definition of self, and to be interchangeable with self.

## A postmodern Jungian self

The ways I have revised and am still revising Jung's approach to the archetype of Self, I consider to be continuous with Jung's own direction, especially after 1944 when he turned his interests increasingly to evolutionary biology, ethology, and structural processes. He recognized that his notion of archetype, as an innate predisposition to develop emotionally charged images in particular situational states, would thrive in the framework of ethology, the study of human groups and relationships. In his desire to clarify universals in human life, and especially to show how powerfully we are constrained by them, Jung could see that the concepts of an "innate releasing mechanism" and "situational patterns" were going to be useful in studying archetypes and in substantiating the link between emotion and image.

Although Jung lived far into the twentieth century, he did not have the benefit of responding to the critiques of science that have resulted in a thorough reconsideration of what we mean when we lay claim to truth. The critiques of postmodernism have demanded that we psychoanalysts rethink a lot of what we had claimed was true in the period of time when our science was started, when biological realism and philosophical idealism were both expected to reveal objective facts and truths that lie beyond human interpretation, or eventually to lead us to such facts. Philosopher Richard Rorty (1997: 63) says of this earlier "modern" perspective: "This is the idea that inquiry is a matter of finding out the nature of something that lies outside the web of beliefs and desires". Postmodern analyses of logic, science, and history have revealed that we cannot get beyond our own observations and interpretations; we are constrained by them.

I believe that Jung anticipated these critiques of scientific realism, in his stress on subjective factors in the psyche – by which he clearly did not mean anything like solipsism, personal subjectivism or multicultural influences. In many ways, Jung can sound like a constructivist when he speaks of the universal subjective factors in what we take to be our objective reality. In 1939, in his psychological "Commentary on *The Tibetan Book of Great Liberation*," Jung (1939/1992: 58) wrote:

> Every new representation, be it a perception or a spontaneous thought, arouses associations which derive from the storehouse of memory. These leap immediately into consciousness, producing the complex picture of an "impression", though this is already a sort of interpretation. The unconscious disposition upon which the quality of the impression depends is what I call the "subjective factor". It deserves the qualification "subjective" because objectivity is hardly ever conferred by a first impression. Usually a rather laborious process of verification, comparison, and analysis is needed to modify and adapt the immediate reactions of the subjective factor.

And he adds, "The prominence of the subjective factor does not imply a personal subjectivism . . . The psyche and its structure are real enough" (p. 58).

In my work in analysis and teaching, I have been searching for the means to explain the universal phenomenon of individual subjectivity without being entrapped within one or two cultural variants of the self, and without sounding as though the experience of a self is entirely dependent on social or cultural influences. I have found Jung's self psychology, especially his model of individuation, to be useful in formulating a clinically relevant theory of an embodied self.

First, though, I have had to come to terms with the failures of Jungian theory in this domain. Because Jung's earlier theory of archetype was founded on a conception of an *imago* or underlying image standing alone, without an acknowledged situational state or relational dynamic, his concept of a universal self bore a strong resemblance to the concept of an enduring individual soul. In my view, and in the light of many epistemological critiques, there is a great deal wrong with this way of the thinking. For one, many Asian people do not believe in an enduring individual soul. In their beliefs, the identity of the individual subject did not link up with a permanent essence. Obviously we cannot claim that something is universal if it doesn't develop in a chunk of the world's population.

More problematic is the clinical confusion in Jungian theory and practice that has arisen in regard to self as soul. When practitioners write and speak about the influences of this soul-self, they very often speak of it as though it were a person, as though it had a human subjectivity. For instance, in interpreting a dream or transference phenomenon, I have heard many practitioners – analysts and other psychotherapists – refer to the Self as wanting, seeing, intending or guiding. These are actions of a person, not the products of a predisposition to act and perceive, as I noted in my first chapter. Speaking in this manner can easily lead to a mystical authoritarianism that is, in my view, antithetical to an effective holding environment for a therapeutic relationship. Instead of a therapist saying, for example, "The way I interpreted this mandala was as an expression of a needed coherence . . ." (acknowledging the contribution of a human interpretation), the problematic report will sound like this, "The Self spontaneously produced this mandala." This way of speaking conflates the interpretive stance of a human subject with the role of an organizing principle in such a way that sounds as though the Self is acting on a motive of its own when actually this is but one interpretation offered by a therapist about a particular moment in therapy.

In Jung's later theory of self, he clarifies that this archetype (like others) is a *predisposition* (not an imago) to perceive a coherent image in a particular situation or relational dynamic. In the case of the self, the relevant image is of the embodied subject around which an ego complex will form. This tendency to experience oneself as a separate subject also provides an enduring organizing principle for the whole personality to cohere, and an underlying potential (which may or may not be actualized) for greater integration and differentiation of the individual over time. Jung even described this principle as an 'empty center' (e.g., Jung, 1955/1975: 259) around which the multiple centers of subjectivity revolve and evolve.

Jung also thought that this tendency to cohere as an individual subject was expressive of a principle of coherence in the universe or world as we know it – a sort of transcendent coherence that is expressed by the fact that we can explore and manipulate, predict and control, intuit and illuminate the environment that surrounds our subjectivity. Just as developmentalist Jean Piaget held fast to the distinction between what he termed the "epistemic subject" (the structure of structures or the principle of all organization) and the "individual subject" (the person), we need to be extremely careful not to step over into sounding like the self operates like a human subject. Not only are there many epistemological errors in assuming that this self function or action has its own subjectivity, clinically and practically we sound like we know the unknowable in saying that the Self has certain intentions, views, and desires.

At the same time, I find it absolutely necessary to posit an archetypal predisposition to form and perceive a separate subjectivity that gives rise to an ego complex and a process of individuation in people everywhere. What is universal about self, transcending cultures and societies, revealing some of the constraints of human subjectivity as an embodied being? What sustains the state of feeling oneself to be a unitary subject over time, space and causality, and those patterns of organization that form a consensual world "out there"?

I would respond by claiming that there are four characteristics that are invariant in human selves everywhere. The first of these is coherence, the integration of complex and diverse subjective experiences into the unity of body-being. Coherence is that sense of being within this bag of skin and held into its boundaries and influences.

The second universal characteristic of self is continuity, the memories and beliefs that permit one to experience the self as 'going on being' in Winnicott's words, as having a single narrative history. Philosopher Rom Harré (1989) and a number of feminist theorists have cautioned us not to universalize the story of a masterful, bounded self as a necessity for everyone. Depending on the cultural and relational forms valued within one's interpretive community, a person may have a collective self or a powerfully independent self, or some other self narrative.

The third characteristic of the human self universally is the attribute of agency or efficacy, the experience of being the author of one's own actions, of being an agent in the world. Piaget recognized the centrality of human action in the development of thought from infancy through adolescence. Agency and continuity appear to be linked in human narrative as psychologist Jerome Bruner (1990) has shown in his studies of young children's principal linguistic interest: stories of human action. Similarly, Harré (1989: 404) describes the self as a theory of active invention:

animate beings are fully human if they are in possession of a theory – a theory about themselves. It is a theory in terms of which a being orders, partitions, and reflects on its own experience and becomes capable of self intervention and control.

The story of self over time invariably includes accounts of the experience of being and doing, of taking on an identity of someone who makes things happen.

The final characteristic of the archetype of self is the affective relational patterns that are the ubiquitous features of human relationships due to the interdependence of persons in the process of growing selves. The work of John Bowlby (e.g., 1988) and his followers in the investigation of human attachments, and the work of such affect theorists as Izard (e.g., 1977) and Lewis (e.g., 1991b) has conclusively demonstrated that human emotions and emotional dependence, are communicated in recognized patterns the world over. This work also substantiates the claim made by many that the human self is fundamentally relational: as philosopher Taylor (1989: 35) has put it, "one is a self only among other selves. A self can never be described without reference to those who surround it."

These four characteristics of the archetype of self – coherence, continuity, agency and affective relational patterns – are the core issues that I rework and relive with patients in psychoanalysis and psychotherapy. In the abstract, these issues of subjectivity transcend the particulars of a person's psychological complexes, ego and otherwise. But in the immediacy of a transferential dynamic between a patient and me, between life partners, between a child and a parent, these archetypal themes take on particulars that give a personal signature to the sweeping brush stroke of self.

## Individuation through psychotherapy

To conclude I'd like to give my own postmodern account of the self in analysis from a Jungian perspective, a sort of overview of what develops through the ideal therapeutic relationship.

The first step in the development of individual subjectivity, from a Jungian point of view, is to come into possession of an ego complex, a dynamic that is bound to the self-conscious emotions, the experience of individuality, and the image of body-being. This step depends on the adequacy of early relationships and the capacity of the individual to unify multiple perceptions, cognitions and actions into a complex of continuous active embodiment. If early relationships were not adequate for such a complex to develop, or if there was a great deal of confusion and/or trauma in regard to the issue of self-determination, then my analytic work will begin at this primary level of self, the formation of a healthy ego complex.

If development has progressed, within therapy or prior to therapy, then I will enter into the process of individuation in regard to the breakdown of the defenses of the ego complex – the shadow or the persona, in Jungian language. The shadow is a defense of projection and dissociation in which alien and otherwise disowned aspects of the personality are externalized from the ego complex. In treatment, I (the therapist) may become the repository for these devalued or idealized aspects. The persona, on the other hand, is a defense of rationalization, sublimation, passive aggression or reaction formation. In a neurotic patient, it is usually the breakdown of the persona that disables the ego complex and brings the person into therapy.

The developmental movement from the breakdown of ego defenses to ongoing individuation is one in which a person gradually learns to acknowledge a number of subpersonalities or states of non-self or not-I that have been disturbing and/or blocking coherence, continuity, agency or affective patterns in a way that has been destructive or overwhelming. These subpersonalities usually involve dominance and submission, sex and aggression, wish-fulfilling and despairing attitudes and enactments that the person has repeatedly disowned. Many adults in our society, perhaps most, resist taking responsibility for these subpersonalities and instead spend most of their adult lives defending and rationalizing their unconscious motives and desires.

From a Jungian viewpoint, in order to develop into psychological wholeness, one must move into a new self-awareness, consciously claiming and taking responsibility for one's multiple subjective motives and centers as aspects of a complex personality. One becomes a psychological individual when one no longer simply projects one's negative complexes into others, attacking and devaluing, when one no longer primarily blames the world and others for one's suffering.

In a successful, long-term psychotherapy or analysis, both the patient and I come to read her or his history – the complexes of the personality – as an aspect of the self, as fundamentally human. Then we learn to accept and tolerate a range of emotions and images without necessarily acting upon them. The capacity to reflect on the whole personality within a framework that psychoanalyst Thomas Ogden (1986) calls "a dialogical space" is the goal of a successful long-term treatment, as I see it. I believe that Ogden's dialogical space is consonant with Jung's transcendent function, but I tend to prefer Ogden's account because he emphasizes not only one's ability to maintain openness in the face of conflict or opposition, but also the fact that there is always a human subject who stands between an experience (the symbolized) and a symbol (a meaning). Emphasizing the human subject clarifies the fact of our construction of our world. Developing the capacity for complex self-reflection will open the door to empathy and compassion for others and oneself, and finally to an experience of one's interdependence.

What I have just described is an account of the self in analytical psychology that is non-essentialist and does not posit an eternal ongoing Self with views and desires, but rather conceives of this archetype as the predisposition to perceive and experience unity within the context of multiplicity or diversity in inner and outer life. Psychological complexes as multiple centers within the personality are multiple subjectivities, while the archetype of self is a transcendent coherence, providing the possibility for continuing integration through differentiation of psychic life with oneself and others.

At our most complex and integrated stages of human subjectivity, as Jane Loevinger's (1976) research on ego development shows, a person dissolves the defenses around the ego complex that keep one mired in self-conscious (see Lewis, 1991b) emotions – like pride, shame, envy, guilt, and embarrassment. One begins to experience directly the impermanent and fluid nature of self (that has no fixed context) in which one feels essentially connected to others, not only to human beings but to all sentient beings. In this way, one is freer through not being ruled by self-centered desires, not being driven by complexes – ego or otherwise. One is not more independent, but is more mature in one's dependence on others. I think Jung's (1961: 359) own reflection on his life, at the end of his autobiography, captures this complexity of an evolved self:

> This is old age, and a limitation. Yet there is so much that fills me: plants, animals, clouds, day and night, and the eternal in man. The more uncertain I have felt about myself, the more there has grown up in me a feeling of kinship with all things.

This "uncertainty" that Jung refers to, as he makes clear earlier in the passage, is the sense that the self is a gathering of subjectivities, with plenty of contradictions, that exists on the foundation of a particular embodiment.

# Chapter 7

# Jungian constructivism and the value of uncertainty

Constructivism is the philosophical position that human interpretation is primary in what we take to be reality. Thus, both our "outer" and "inner" realities are constructed and constrained through our embodiment. Our knowledge systems cannot reach beyond this fallible stance, and so we can never take a god's-eye view of our experience and come to a final truth about it. Jung (1939/1992: 58) wrote:

> Every new representation, be it a perception or a spontaneous thought, arouses associations . . . These leap . . . into consciousness, producing the complex picture of an "impression," though this is already a sort of interpretation. The unconscious disposition upon which the quality of the impression depends is what I call the "subjective factor."

Like a good constructivist, he went on to say:

> The prominence of the subjective factor does not imply a *personal subjectivism* . . . The psyche and its structure are real enough. They even transform material objects into psychic images . . . They do not per-ceive waves, but sound; not wave-lengths, but colours. Existence is as we see and understand it. There are innumerable things that can be seen, felt, and understood in a great variety of ways (p. 58, emphases in original).

Jung's belief that "material objects" (waves and wavelengths in the example above) might exist outside of our perception shows traces of scientific realism, but his gist is clearly in keeping with constructivism. On many occasions, in a similar vein, Jung refers to psychic reality as the foundation of our experience.

Jung's constructivism has, however, been difficult for his followers to grasp. At times he grounds it in Platonic forms and Kantian categories which make Jung sound like an essentialist who would claim that the ultimate truth of our experience lies in universal forms that are superhuman.

At other times, as in the passage above, Jung grounds his constructivism in human experience, that ubiquitous organization of our world and reality through the constraints of our embodiment. From this standpoint, it is assumed that humans actively organize the perceived environment around us. We don't see, hear, and feel a world that is "out there," but rather we create a world, through our senses, that appears to be outside, existing as a constant.

Constructivism, as a philosophical position, is different from realism, rationalism, and idealism in not assuming that some particular forms or patterns are the ultimate, the infallible, and the transcendent. In this way, constructivism is a postmodern critique of "grand narratives," those accounts that claim to possess sources of objectivity beyond human interpretation. For constructivists, the "really real" is neither the physical nor the mental. It is neither thrust upon us by the stimuli around us, nor imposed on us by eternal forms. Rather, our experiences of self and other, including all of our phenomenal world, are understood as resulting from our own perceptual and emotional systems as these faculties enable us to organize an environment in flux.

Such a view is compatible with the methods and findings of many contemporary scientific studies of perception and experience. For example, we know from many biological studies that other animals organize worlds different from ours. Although we cannot perceive their worlds directly we can infer them from experiments. Constructivists give no privileged status to the human world as the most comprehensive or best account. Rather, the human world is understood by them to be but one perspective on a mysterious universe.

On the other hand, the claim that experience is constructed is not a threat to our ability to establish objective truths about our consensual experience. Many realists reject the interpretive stance because they fear that if interpretation is the basis of knowledge, any individual could make any claim, and all claims would be equally valid. But all fields of knowledge, especially the sciences, establish a systematic body of knowledge that is controlled by agreed-upon methods of observation and interpretation, bringing order, coherence and plausibility to claims about truths. Additionally, these methods are continuously argued, compared and evaluated in conversations within and between fields of study, according to the standards for consensual agreement in any period of time.

Moreover, making the assumption that the commonsense world appears to us out of a strong consensus of human reality leaves plenty of room for theorizing and studying universal aspects and sequences of human development. Universal structures and experiences affirm the shared nature of existence among our species. Thus, a Jungian constructivism includes the study of archetypes, emotions, psychological complexes and mythology as universal occurrences among human beings.

The development of our experience of a physical world of time, space, and causality – Kant's particular interest – is just such a universal. As our individual minds develop, we learn to construct roughly the same consensual world that serves as a basis for our shared physical reality. When the physical world seems normal, with the sky above and ground below, we feel sane and human. If, however, there is a sudden or ongoing shift from expectable norms, whether the shift is painful or ecstatic, we are jolted into something unexpected.

Such unusual states of mind are labeled by names like dissociation, the collapse of time, disembodiment, depersonalization, and paranormal. Overall, we refer to them as "altered states of consciousness" to indicate that they deviate from the norm we agree is "reality." Drug-induced states and shock jolt us out of our usual foundations. In some highly unique cases, such as the "man who mistook his wife for a hat" or the "man who tastes shapes," neurologists have found people who experience worlds quite different from our consensual reality. Such examples remind us that the world is not out there, but is shaped through our sensory and emotional organization of an environment in flux.

Even though the physical world is generally a stable shared reality, other aspects of our experience are not consensual or readily affirmed by others. They reflect the particulars of our development. There is a great variety of emotional patterning among humans, both between cultures and among individuals. Most significantly, emotional image-traces of our earliest interpersonal environments color our lives in highly diverse and idiosyncratic ways. These patterns result in meanings and images that fill our personal complexes of ego, mother, father, and the like.

Because our emotional patterns do not overlap to the degree that our perceptions of a physical world do, human beings disagree between each other about what's true in life. Anyone who asks even ten adults for a definition of self, will see a lot of diversity. Among cultures and languages there is a great variety of selves from the collective to the highly individual. Nevertheless, all people have some symbolic means to represent the experience of individual subjectivity; the experience of being an individual subject is universal, even though the forms that express that subjectivity are diverse.

It seems also that our emotional development and conditioning are conservative: once we have organized certain patterns, we bring them to new experiences. What we took to be normal as self and other in our earliest years will be applied over and over again to the new and different subjectivities we encounter after we leave our original families. Jung has given us the psychological term "complex" to name the imposition of old emotional patterns onto new situations and experiences. Complexes are constructions that lead to reenactments or repetitions of the emotionally charged dramas of childhood in any new situation that seems to us to resemble the original.

Through the lens of a complex, for instance, a spouse may seem to resemble exactly one's parent, and then one feels (and often acts) exactly like a child rather than an adult partner. Although one can become conscious of a psychological complex, and reduce its influence on behavior and responses, the complex will never completely dissolve. Its emotional core, which Jung called "archetypal," is a permanent part of embodied experience.

Jung describes the core of a complex specifically as an emotionally charged archetypal image evocative enough to motivate us to fantasize and reenact our original relational situations, as we experienced them. Archetype, meaning "primary imprint" or "prime imprinter," is a predisposition to form a coherent image in an emotionally charged state. We know, from the work of affect researchers like Izard (1992, 1994) and Tompkins (1962, 1963), that babies are born with six or seven basic emotions hard-wired, and from the work of Lewis (e.g., 1991b) that they develop secondary self-conscious emotions (such as shame, pride, envy and guilt) after about eighteen months. Jung believed that, within our primary attachment relationships, the human personality gets organized into coherent images that are charged with positive and negative emotions. According to this view, our early development is fundamentally organized by images of Great and Terrible Mother, Great and Terrible Father, self, and other archetypes. These affective images are subjective factors that are both personal in their content, and universal in their form. The subjective factor of the psyche, thus, has an "objective" core. The emotionally charged archetypal image is as real and primary as time, space and causality. It is a basic condition of being human.

## Uncertainty and the transcendent function

People come to psychotherapy because they are facing an impasse in their lives, often one in which they are enacting psychological complexes with loved ones or authority figures in ways that endanger someone's welfare. The goal of analytical therapy, grounded in Jungian constructivism, is to develop new meanings from the old dramas represented by the complexes (see Modell, 1990 and 1993 for a discussion of this process in detail; also see Goleman, 1995 for an account of the patterning of "emotional intelligence" in infant and childhood relationships). Although transference and countertransference obviously include both positive and negative complexes (of patient and therapist), it is usually the painful, dangerous complexes (primarily enacted and experienced by the patient, not the therapist, one hopes) that are the most troubling and most essential to be encountered in order for transformation to occur. These painful complexes have compelled the patient again and again to see and react, both within the self and with others, in ways which repeat and evoke the dangers already experienced in the years of personality formation. Inevitably, whole worlds of meaning will have been reconstructed and defended around these most troubling, painful complexes.

To move from a painful enactment of a complex into what Jung calls the "transcendent function" is, in my view, a major goal of analytic work. Jung's transcendent function, similar to psychoanalyst D.W. Winnicott's (1971) "potential space" or "play space," is the freedom to see emotional meanings from more than one perspective. Within the psychic space of the transcendent function, one is free to watch and wait, not compelled to assign meaning prematurely to images, affects, memories or actions. Transcending opposites, splits, and dichotomies through the discovery of a third position – not previously known – we discover a new insight or are able to play with several views at once. In 1916, Jung defined the transcendent function as a "union of conscious and unconscious contents" (1916/1969: 69). In 1920, he said that this function "facilitates a transition from one attitude to another. The raw material shaped by thesis and antithesis . . . is the living symbol" (Jung, 1920/1971: 480).

A major goal of an analytic treatment, in my view, is to secure in the patient a fairly reliable ability to hold onto this function in the face of powerful psychological complexes in therapeutic sessions and in everyday life. Contemporary psychoanalyst Stephen Mitchell (1993: 83) seems to agree when he says, "the capacity to hear, hold, and play with an interpretation, neither surrendering to it as powerful magic nor rejecting it as dangerous poison – [is] . . . a criterion of readiness to terminate" (p. 83).

The transcendent function emerges through an appreciation of uncertainty in becoming cautious about feeling too quickly, too reactively, too certain about what is going on. Ultimately, the transcendent function implies a change in attitude, and a new openness to an ongoing process of discovery based on a dialectic of subjective and objective factors of experience.

Because people are loath to give up their old meanings, on which they base reality and a sense of self, analytical psychotherapy must provoke uncertainty about the value of old constructions, whole worlds of meaning. Effective psychotherapy is transformative on a level beyond talk or interpretation about what is or what was happening. The process of transformation is, to a great extent, dependent on the paradoxical and unknown, even though it is guided by theory, knowledge and expertise. The therapeutic relationship, supported by rituals of time, place, and fee, is itself paradoxical. It is impersonally personal, empathically non-gratifying, erotically non-sexual, provocatively non-aggressive, and welcoming of spontaneous communication within a strongly bound time–fee–space limit. A person coming for help, already in distress, is likely to want to create order – an old order – in such a paradoxical environment. The analyst or therapist, in response to what the patient imposes, is just as likely to impose an old order, in the form of theory, expertise, authority and her or his own psychological complexes. The effective therapeutic relationship is like a Zen koan for both participants: it invites and defies old interpretations.

## The case of Professor L

In the following, I will comment on an analytic treatment of a patient, published in an article called "The analyst at work" by Van Spruiell (1984). The article presents a psychoanalytic case in depth. My excerpts here do not summarize the case as a whole, nor do my comments in any way presume that I could have fared better with this difficult case than Dr Spruiell did. Rather, I am using the case for its examples of analyst–patient communications that appear to be stuck or frozen in a particular world of meaning. My commentary is not intended as a critique of what the analyst actually did, but is intended as an illustration of how old meanings can be imposed and continued in a chronic way in a stalemated treatment.

Specifically, I am pointing to how projective identification can overtake the transcendent function of a treatment. In using the term "projective identification," I am referring to the patient's attempt to communicate unconscious material by projecting it into the analyst and evoking from (and with) him a playing-out or enactment of what is projected. Obviously, projective identification could also be stimulated from the analyst to the patient. Projective identification is both a defense and a communication, but when it is enacted in psychotherapy – and, inevitably will be in an effective long-term treatment or analysis – both patient and analyst are in danger of "going crazy" together and even of spoiling or destroying the treatment. At such times, both participants in the analytic dyad play out one emotional reality, often what is imposed by the patient's repetitive complex interacting with or evoking aspects of the therapist's emotional life, in a way that deadens or deadlocks the therapeutic process. As Modell (1990: 56) says:

> When the analysand projects his inner life into the analyst, it is as if the analyst is an actor who receives stage directions from the patient, but the entire process remains outside the consciousness of both participants. For some patients it seems that their affective experiences need to be placed within the other because language itself is inadequate, and some other means must be found to communicate.

When projective identification occurs between a patient and a therapist and it is not understood and contextualized, it can become a dangerous disruption of psychotherapy itself. In my reading of Dr Spruiell's case, I see such a situation.

A brief history of the patient is necessary for a full understanding of my comments. The patient, referred to as Professor L, reported a "not unusual" babyhood and toddlerhood with some stormy interactions with his parents at around the age of four or five. He also reported a lot of clinging to his mother at that time.

At the age of five, his parents suddenly disappeared, leaving the patient with relatives. He heard nothing from them for two years except to know that his mother was alive. When she returned, just as unexpectedly as she had left, she had a new husband. He saw his biological father only a few times after that. Upon meeting his new stepfather, the patient tried to kiss him, but was told that this was "sissy behavior."

The patient reported that his mother had been indulgent and over-protective after her return and that he had found it difficult to play with other children. He had "intellectual friends, but no playmates" during the remainder of his childhood. He saw this as analogous to his having "sexual encounters, but no authentic partners" in adulthood.

At the time treatment began, Professor L was employed as a university professor, but he was functioning well below his capacity. His life felt meaningless to him. The analyst, Dr Spruiell, reported that the patient "alternated between the manners of an ex-nobleman and a constipated, very miserable, little boy."

The patient smoked a lot of marijuana during the early parts of his analysis, and the interpretations of his analyst seemed to have no effect on this behavior. Finally the analyst told the patient that he could not continue the analysis unless the patient quit smoking marijuana. The patient stopped smoking the intoxicant, but felt enormous rage and distrust for Dr Spruiell.

The analyst found the patient's behavior frequently provocative. As Dr Spruiell (1984: 17) described the patient's attitude: "certain rules were not 'made' for him. In fact, some rules ordinarily shared with others did not *exist* for him in intimate situations . . ." (emphasis in original). This included the general rule to operate in analysis by moving back and forth between observations of subjective experiences and their meanings through analyzing. The patient refused to assume an "analytic stance" even though he followed the Basic Rule of free association.

Professor L seemed to operate as though his analysis was *not* a para-doxical relationship of conflicting meanings, but rather a literal real-life situation in which only one meaning counted: how he felt at the moment. Dr Spruiell says that there was a "seemingly unending set of attempts to manipulate me into a position in which I might take an external part in his life rather than maintain my stance within the analytic situation" (p. 17). This analyst described his patient as "using the analytic situation as a way of being a temporarily complacent baby instead of anything connected with analysing" (p. 18).

In Jungian terms, I see the patient as enacting his "mother" complex. He is enacting the complex through the medium of a projective identification, a drama in which he invites his analyst to play a part. The patient cannot experience his analyst "as if" the analyst were his mother, but instead believes that his analyst is "just as" self-absorbed, unexplaining and unempathic as mother was. The patient sees this as a fact having nothing to do with his (the patient's) own attitude. Consequently, the patient cannot have an authentic relationship to his analyst; rather it is yet another example for him of an inauthentic, exclusively intellectual relationship.

Although Jung did not specifically map out what we would now call "projective identification," he did understand that certain enactments by patients were unconscious pathological invitations to the therapist to join in. He called this phenomenon *participation mystique* and thought it a necessary part of successful analysis, provided the analyst could retain some consciousness of what was taking place. Without such consciousness, Jung realized that the analyst would simply reenact with the patient whatever the original affective situation was.

Before we look at what Dr Spruiell felt and did with his patient, I want to return to the problem of change in psychotherapy. Throughout the treatment process, therapist and patient have strong emotional responses to one another and there are countless situations in which there can be a foreclosure on meaning for either. In a situation such as the one we meet in Dr Spruiell's case, both people tend to experience the therapeutic relationship as "proof" that people "don't change." Dr Spruiell certainly felt this way about his patient when he said that the patient "had a severe limitation on the scope of his worlds of realities" (p. 17).

I believe that the patient felt his analyst was equally limited in his ability to care and respond. The patient says "I just don't trust you . . . Of course I 'really' trust you, but there is a not-trusting too. And that's 'really' too . . . I admire you but don't trust you" (pp. 22–23). In such an emotionally charged standstill, both patient and therapist feel frustrated and each feels "certain" about what's going on.

Modell (1990: 56) describes this kind of standstill in an analytic treatment as a chronic projective identification, saying:

> [it] can be said to rupture the frame of the analytic setting; it can also be viewed as a confusion of the multiple levels of reality present in the therapeutic process . . . This results in a temporary rupture of the frame, with a consequent loss of this level or reality, the reality of the therapeutic setting – a reality separate from that of ordinary life.

What Modell refers to here as the "temporary rupture of the frame" is the inability of patient and analyst (neither one nor the other) to hold the transcendent function, the potential or play space, that permits the movement from one kind of meaning to another without overwhelming anxiety.

Modell's (1990) three (sometimes competing) emotional fields or realities of psychotherapy are summarized here: (1) the dependent-containing transference which is fundamentally the patient's experience that this "is therapeutic and it helps," a transference that is not usually interpreted; (2) the iconic-projective transference which is composed of the psychological complexes discharged by the patient – and occasionally the analyst – into the therapeutic relationship, a transference that must be interpreted and revised in order for the patient (and therapist) to change; and (3) a human relationship, a kinship libido, of two human beings striving together to fulfill the goals of the treatment. There is a great deal to say about each of these realities, but my point here is to show how an enactment of limited unconscious meanings (from either one or both of the participants) can rupture or destroy the dependent-containing transference.

In my view, the dialectic of development, from old to new meanings, is facilitated in effective psychotherapy by the following three conditions:

1    the therapeutic ritual (time, fee, ethical conduct, confidentiality, etc.);
2    the therapist's ability to contain and hold tensions, moving in and out of, but always returning to the transcendent function, and;
3    the patient's belief in the therapist's capacity to help.

These conditions underlie the dependent-containing transference that sets psychotherapy apart from ordinary life. While both patient and therapist may get stuck in unconscious complexes, the therapist has the sole responsibility of paradoxically maintaining the appearance of knowing what's happening while remaining open to not-knowing.

In reviewing the case of Professor L, we remember how difficult it is for the analyst to fulfill the above conditions in times when the patient unconsciously discharges complexes directly into the analyst and refuses to see them as anything but "reality." In talking about a particularly difficult session in which Professor L refused his analyst's interpretations about why he (the patient) had wanted to bring his analyst a cup of coffee (a gesture which the patient had decided against) to the session, Dr Spruiell (1984: 23, emphasis in original) reflects:

> I believe that the *primary* meanings during that particular session had to do with Oedipal fantasies, conflicts having to do with genitals and murder. Stealing penises and having them stolen from him – the terrible and wonderful wishes to avoid all that by becoming my Ganymede. [Ganymede was Zeus's cupbearer in Greek mythology.]

Although Dr Spruiell did not speak these particular interpretations, he held onto them during a difficult session and could not seem to let them go afterwards.

Dr Spruiell himself recognized his inability to hold open any potential space around the meaning of his patient's motives. In reflecting on his mental handling of the case, he quotes from John Keats's famous letter about negative capability: "I was *not* 'capable of being in uncertainties, mysteries, doubts,' I *did* have 'an irritable reaching for facts and reason'" (p. 26, emphasis in original). The analyst, that is, found it next to impossible to step back from his theory of an Oedipus complex to maintain any openness to not-knowing. The analyst's inflexibility confirmed the patient's distrust. In Dr Spruiell's account, the patient says, "I can't let you get in. I can't even let you be an analyst . . . Heaven forbid that I let us do it together!" (p. 22).

Although it might be tempting to believe that a Jungian might have been more open-minded to discovery rather than imposition of meaning, Jung did not describe how an analyst might sustain the transcendent function during times of intense negative enactments, except to instruct us to hold the tension of the opposites. It was really Winnicott (e.g., 1971) and object relations analyst Thomas Ogden (1989) who have filled out my understanding of how to work on this problem. Winnicott, in describing his concept of potential space, speaks of an attitude of playful openness. Practically speaking, this means that the therapist should be alert not to clamp down on conceptual meaning, especially one that comes quickly from dogmatic theories. Ogden has further clarified how this kind of attitude can be sustained through a particular kind of awareness.

Ogden has elaborated the idea of a "dialectical space" to extend Winnicott's original notion of a potential space by emphasizing our awareness of an interpreting subject. Ogden claims that the creative dialectic takes place primarily in the "space" between the symbol (the construction of image or word) and the symbolized (the experience itself). What resides in this space is the active, engaged subject. When something takes place in the treatment situation, such as Professor's L's reluctant confession of having wanted to bring a cup of coffee to Dr Spruiell, a dialectic is instantaneously set up between the therapist's experience (with its immediate affective and perceptual organization) and his symbols (images or words) for it. If the therapist is able to keep this space open, there emerges an interplay of experiences and meanings that can be examined in terms of their subjective and intersubjective possibilities. Some of these may be offered to the patient, and some silently recognized, but in either case what develops in the verbalized and unverbalized therapeutic conversation that ensues will be a discovery process in which one or both people will come upon an interpretation that has an "aha" character and brings relief.

For example, a middle-aged woman who lives alone and came to see me in psychotherapy because she wanted a more "exciting and challenging" life told me that I wanted "too much; you want me to change in ways that I find impossible" such as being able to date or meet new friends or have casual conversations with people she didn't know well.

The patient's mother had experienced very low self-esteem in regard to her own physical attractiveness, and had attributed a "fat and ugly" body image to the patient in childhood and adolescence (an image that seemed to me to be grossly unfounded from viewing childhood photos of the patient). Confusingly, the mother also expected her daughter to have dates and develop a successful social life, even after the emotional disruption of her husband's – the patient's father's – violent and public suicide during the patient's adolescence. Although there are many other levels in both the dependent and iconic transference in this therapy, this is probably a good enough sketch of some of the emotional meanings my patient brought with her to see that her comment that I "wanted too much" from her may contain contradictory elements in the different realities that I described from Modell.

On one level the patient is speaking to me as one middle-aged woman to another, saying something about how really difficult it is to meet suitable male companions at this time of life. On another level, she is also obviously speaking to me as though I were a demanding mother who condemns her to low self-esteem while I encourage her to date. On still another level, that may not be immediately obvious, the patient is also speaking to me about her actual trust of me as her therapist, about whether or not she can believe I have an authentic understanding of her.

In order to keep open the dialectical space, I would have to speak to all three levels of meaning, to move around among them. Gratification of any one level will lead to frustration at another. For instance, if I interpreted her concern about me as only a displacement from her mother complex, she may feel typed and labeled as if I were saying that her complaint about me was "only" a transference problem. If, on the other hand, I tried to counteract her statement and "reassure" her about my motive – something like "I never intended to confine you to one alternative" – she might feel that either I had been confused about what I had said about dating, or that I was afraid of her confrontation and was now backing down.

Morever, if she felt that any psychological interpretation I might make was "the only" way I would look at her statement, she might feel a special need to educate me about, and convince me of the "reality" of the male–female ratio of available partners in today's society. In order to keep open the space around such an emotionally loaded moment, I, therefore, have to speak from a kind of playful therapist perspective saying something to the effect, "As your therapist I'm looking at what you've said with a curiosity and a concern about what my statements about dating have meant to you." If she too is willing to "play" with all of the meanings, then we will likely be able to move into some kind of "aha" discovery – perhaps about how she often evokes from others what she dreads – but if she is not willing to play, then I may have to venture an interpretation of what I am sensing in hearing her statement. Again, I would strive in this instance to say something open-ended about how I feel as a therapist in this situation, letting her know that I feel in somewhat of a dilemma about how to answer because any one answer will be inadequate, and yet silence would also be inadequate.

Sustaining the dialectical space has become a central component of my work as an analyst. Because of the archetypal nature of psychological complexes (i.e., that they seem as real and fundamental as time and space), this is a demanding task. Like Dr Spruiell, I may come up against a deep frustration, and sometimes come to feel that my patients are "unanalyzable" concrete realists. I find such a view especially tempting when my patients claim that their views of me are factually based, and not impressions based on subjective factors.

Of his patient, Dr Spruiell (1984: 17, emphasis in original) says, ". . . all *his* past experiences led him to assume the hatred of me and the fear of any positive contacts were *factually* based. He could not discover that some 'facts' were illusory and some 'illusions' were factual". Yet, in applying the stock rules of interpreting the Oedipus complex from whatever he found that seemed (to him) to smell of it, was not Dr Sprueill also becoming a concrete realist? His account admits that, rather than wonder about what was happening between him and his patient in the moment, he resorted to a dogmatic way of thinking about his patient's unconscious intentions. All analysts of any persuasion can surely relate to this. I, too, can get trapped in a defensive premature "knowing." Such frozen constructions of meaning are often defenses against my fear of a destructive attack on my usefulness as a therapist. Any attack on my ability to help is, after all, an attack on the therapeutic alliance itself.

Here is a description of such a situation by Modell (1990: 54):

> A young single woman who was withdrawn and depressed complained that I was not helping her in her treatment because I was not making useful comments and interpretations. I, in turn, was feeling frustrated because I felt that in her withdrawn, mostly silent, unengaged state, it was not possible to say anything that was meaningful.

What Modell goes on to describe is that he, as a therapist, was being made to feel, through identifying with her projections, the affective memory of the patient in her childhood interactions with her father. In other words, the patient was enacting her father complex in such a way that the analyst felt victimized by the complex much in the way the patient must have felt as a child.

The patient, on the other, also experienced herself as the victim, not the perpetrator, of another father figure who seemed to her to be withdrawn and critical just as her father had been in her experience of him. As Modell says, ". . . we *both* were attacker and attacked . . . What was projected was an encapsulated, specific affective experience – a . . . slice of the analysand's . . .

psychic reality" (p. 54, emphasis in original). Chronic and unresolved projective identification creates a particular kind of *co*-transferential state in psychotherapy. It is a self-fulfilling prophecy, almost like a curse under which both people are saying, "I somehow *knew* it would turn out this way."

This frozen construction is a collapse of the transcendent function or the dialectical space into only one meaning, usually one organized from a paranoid-schizoid perspective, a meaning that seems especially threatening to both people. When projective identification is ongoing and unresolved in a psychological treatment, both patient and analyst will tend to confirm the worst, most cynical, hopeless or painful views of themselves and each other, or alternatively they will defend against the despair through an idealizing or grandiose *folie-à-deux*.

*Therapeutic dialectic*

In order to protect the therapeutic dialectic in which several meanings can be entertained without collapsing into one, the therapist has the responsibility of remaining alert to the implications of the self as interpreter, one of which is the self as trained interpreter. This ongoing recognition of the analyst's subjective responsibility for meaning – that it arises from impressions and is not a given – invites the patient to become aware in a similar manner. Hopefully the therapist's professional training and development (including therapy or analysis) will assist in recognizing her or his own complexes that might be activated in projective identification, including the ability to note and apologize for mistaken meanings, when such an apology is needed to affirm the therapist's authentic presence. Additionally, a manner of speaking modestly about "seeing it this way" or "wondering if this makes sense" also enhances the recognition that meanings emerge from contexts and are not fixed by absolutes.

In addition to self-knowledge, I have found a useful guideline in keeping specifically in mind Modell's three overlapping realities of psychotherapy. Keeping all three of these realities (the dependent-containing transference, the iconic-projective transference, and the ordinary human relationship) in mind assists me in behaving as a good constructivist and resisting any temptation to play out a projective identification by interpreting on one and only one level of experience.

For example, if I respond only from the level of the therapeutic alliance, I am going to formulate things in terms of self-fragmentation, empathy or the holding environment. If I respond only from the level of the projective transference, I'm going to interpret symbolically, conflictually, or genetically about the hypothesized dynamics of what is being enacted. If I interpret only from the perspective of the ordinary human relationship, I may commiserate, instruct, reassure, or guide. I believe that full attention to all three of these levels is important in every session, and that the preoccupation of a therapist at one level or another is always defensive, a way of protecting oneself from the other realities.

As I have observed myself and my supervisees over time, in regard to chronic projective identifications, I have seen that we all have a primary tendency to do what Dr Spruiell confesses to doing: to use the authority of our training in a somewhat pre-emptive way when negative enactments threaten the therapeutic frame or alliance. At such times, consciously or unconsciously, the therapist stakes out a claim to "know" what is going on, and then is drawn into the drama of the enacted complex. Being drawn in temporarily may be a necessity, but becoming chronically locked in is deadening and disastrous for effective therapeutic change.

## Conclusion

Constructivism, as a philosophical perspective, demands that we examine our theoretical and clinical practices to question our certainties. In recognizing that even physical reality is human-sized, we become more modest about making claims to knowing the unknown, even in our consulting rooms. Although Jung many times warned not to believe that we capture the unknown through the names we use (i.e., archetype, transcendence, God, Self), perhaps he also reinforced our human longing to believe "*Now I've got the truth.*"

Modell's tripartite map has assisted me greatly in discovering my own uncertainty principle. When a patient is experiencing me as part and parcel of the problem, I must discover what is going on. I try then to see the issue from at least those three perspectives described above. I want to play with all the possible meanings, but in doing so I am faced with a paradox about my own expertise. The patient and I need to believe in my expertise in order to sustain a therapeutic alliance while at the same time I must remain open to uncertainty about what I know. This uncertainty principle, as I have tried to show, is consistent with practicing analytical psychology from the perspective of constructivism in which the "really real" can only emerge in our active engagement with the mysterious nature of experience, always alert to our limitations.

Perhaps my best expertise is an ability to tolerate uncertainty in the face of emotional demand to enact or join into a psychological complex, old meaning imposed on new experience. For all humans, imposing our emotional realities on others and the world around, as we do, there is a strong tendency to recreate the emotional scenes that we first discovered in our early attachments. People who come to psychotherapy suffer from the worlds they create as much as they have suffered at the hands of those caregivers who initially imposed those worlds on them. My major task as an analyst, as I see it today, is to open a dialectical space around the constrictive and destructive emotional meanings that my patients try to confirm with me.

# Part 2

# Gender and desire

# Chapter 8

# Myth and body: Pandora's legacy in a postmodern world

At the beginning of the twentieth century, psychology was just getting started and it seemed that the study of human development and behavior should focus first on what was universal and then on what might be individual. We seem to be at the other end of the spectrum at the end of the twentieth century, with a pervasive belief that we can only study what is individual, cultural or local, and not even attempt what is universal, except in the framework of biological determinism.

As a practicing psychotherapist and a psychological researcher, I think otherwise. If I didn't know what psychological knowledge forms the backdrop in an individual's case, I'd never know what direction to follow. For example, a twenty-eight-year-old man came to see me because he was uncertain he had chosen the right career. He was in graduate school preparing for a profession and he wondered if it was right for him. But he didn't just wonder; he worried and fretted and was anxious day and night. One thing I know is that young adulthood is ending and adulthood is beginning at twenty-eight in our society. Although the age for this passage varies from society to society, in all societies there is a point after which young people are expected to be adult and join society in the appropriate ways. If they fail, there are serious consequences – explicit or implicit. So I did not consider this young man's anxiety to be primarily neurotic; I saw it as developmental, befitting his age. Many times a day I measure a particular response or image against the background of what I expect from a human being – at this age, of this sex, and so on.

Carl Jung often used the idea of archetype in a way that now seems antiquated, to mean something like a Kantian category or a Platonic idea, a sort of organizing form for our mental life. In his later work, after about 1944, he revised his thinking. He defined archetype to mean a universal inclination (predisposition) to form an image in a highly charged emotional state. The image would have the same form, recognizable the world over, as for example the image of a Great Mother. Jung began to link emotion with his idea of archetype in a new way. His final definition of archetype was of an innate releasing mechanism: if an infant was overwhelmed with needs –

hungry, enraged, afraid – it formed an image of a Terrible Mother (witch, bitch, hag) that was the opposite of the soothing, nurturing, gratifying Great Mother (although both of these images were activated by the same actual mother). This image of a Terrible Mother would recur repeatedly when certain cues were present. Hear certain sounds, see certain things, and all of the emotions that serve to shape the archetypal image would be released. In an adult relationship, say with his wife, the now fully grown-up man would feel the same emotions he did with his mother when his wife said or did certain things. The child who had perceived his mother as a depressed, denying, and demanding Terrible Mother, would as an adult, experience his wife in the same way when she cried, complained, or criticized. The new situation would seem just like the old.

The idea of an innate releasing mechanism linked to universal human emotions has been carried forward by a famous contemporary British psychoanalyst named John Bowlby. He and his followers have developed a theory called "attachment theory" that shows that human beings everywhere are hard-wired to respond in certain ways in relationships with each other: attachment bond, separation anxiety and grief. No matter how rational we try to be, how much we might struggle to overcome our emotions, we will continue to bond and want to protect this bond, to fear separation, and to protect ourselves from rejection.

In addition, there are now many researchers and theorists of human emotion (called "affect theory"), people such as Tompkins, Lewis and Izard, who have shown that certain primary emotions are part of every infant at birth – joy, sadness, fear, aggression, disgust, curiosity – and that later secondary emotions develop in everyone after about eighteen months of age. These later emotions are called "self-conscious" emotions – shame, pride, envy, guilt, embarrassment. All of these occur in everyone everywhere. Universal emotions are connected with universal images that recur everywhere: great and terrible parents, dragons/monsters, magicians, madonnas, whores, heroes and demons/devils. These are the archetypal images that Jung initially thought arose from a substrate outside human experience. We can now say that they arise quite directly from human experience. They are universal because they occur in every human being from a combination of our emotional hard-wiring, our perceptions of a particular world, and our biological life cycle and what it demands of us. Even though we are complex self-recognizing and reflective beings, we are not free. We are all bound by the forms of our bodies, our reproductive systems, our life cycles and the inevitability of our deaths; these are inescapable and non-negotiable.

Over millennia, mythology has developed narratives about these universal human conditions. Although mythology has served many functions for societies and cultures, a major function it continues to serve is that of illustrating the meanings of universal emotions. When a mythology is alive, it forms the basis of what we call "reality." At the end of the twentieth century, our major Western mythology is science. Its most currently captivating forms are genetics, astrophysics, neuroscience, and subatomic physics. The tales that are told from these myths are amazing. Most of us assume they are reality. We often accept biological explanations for our moods and meanings (*Listening to Prozac*, a book by a psychiatrist about an antidepressant, for example, was a huge best-seller) although we long to believe that earlier stories of heroes, witches, giants and monsters will save us from our fates (*Women Who Run With the Wolves*, a book by a Jungian analyst about Native American and other myths, also topped bestseller lists).

For most of us, the ancient myths now function more as metaphors, allowing us to see aspects of our emotional lives as we penetrate their meanings. For a psychoanalyst like myself, though, the ancient myths are still relevant in the postmodern world because they connect to the archetypal meanings of our emotions, the ways in which we perceive and respond because of the universal constraints of human life.

For example, some years ago I wrote an interpretation of the "Hymn to Demeter" – a Greek myth from the Eleusynian mysteries. I had just reread the myth after having had major surgery for a condition that could have been (but was not) life-threatening. In the shadow of my own death, the myth revealed something new to me, not about the meaning of spring and the cycles of nature, or the bond between a mother and a daughter (also legitimate readings of the myth), but about the meaning of death. What I saw was that the mother's (Demeter's) loss of her daughter to the underworld (death) aroused in her all the typical signs of grief: rage, bargaining, searching, telling her story, apathy, and a desire to substitute for the loss. Here in this ancient myth was the exact formulation of grief that John Bowlby and his followers had discovered in studying the behaviors of war orphans and other children whose parents had died. The Demeter story went through all the stages of grief and into the consequences of too quickly substituting for the loss. It was remarkable to me that an ancient myth could be as precise as contemporary scientific research in charting the process of the universal human experience of grief.

From all that I have learned about human development, through research, theories and the practice of psychotherapy, I would say that we must understand our emotions and the images connected to them in order to understand ourselves. Without this, we are likely to feel alienated, unknowable, isolated and adrift – a fairly good description of the existential and deconstructed versions of the human subject. I am not against postmodernism and its effects on psychology and other disciplines. On the contrary, I consider myself to be a postmodernist but I am not a deconstructionist.

Deconstruction is a skeptical philosophy of doubt and dismantling, based on a negative assumption that human lives are governed mostly by power arrangements. It is also a commentary on the fragmentation of our period of time, an era when cherished hopes and beliefs have been undermined repeatedly through insane, hateful or wasteful human actions. We've witnessed atrocities such as the holocaust. We've lived with the threat of nuclear annihilation and the fear that materialism will overtake the delicate balance of our ecological systems. Our cities are crumbling and we confront the miseries of homelessness and disease in ways more visible in America than ever before. Losing faith in human reason may be a necessary step in trying to understand what has led to our current crises and chaos. And yet to undermine the belief in a common human experience is to eradicate the significance of the most obvious aspect of our existence: the human body.

The ways in which we perceive, think and feel are bound to be universal because human beings are embodied in the same form everywhere, with slight variations. We all enter life through birth and leave through death. There are variations on these themes, but the themes are themselves very powerful. If we fail to study or understand what is common to humanity, especially in this period of despair, we reinforce a dangerous belief in stark individualism – that we are isolated from each other, that we are strangers in a strange world.

## The story of Pandora

I could say much more about the importance of understanding universals, but I want to turn instead to a particular myth, one that is still alive in our postmodern world. It is the story of the first woman in Greek mythology and it shows us a lot about how "woman" was constructed in ancient times and how she continues to be known. Exactly like Eve in the Garden of Eden, this Greek first woman is both the first female mortal and the instigator of mortality in the human race. To be mortal means to die, and both Eve and Pandora bring death into the world. This is a curious reversal of the fact that women bring life into the world, but it says something about the meaning of woman within a religion dominated by male gods.

I am using a summary here of Hesiod's account of the Pandora story. Pandora is created as a punishment to Prometheus who was a Titan, one of the old gods. He had made men from clay and given them fire to help them develop civilization. Prometheus had stolen fire from the gods to give to men. Zeus, the Olympian god in charge, enraged at Prometheus for his theft of fire (that should have remained an immortal power), says to him ". . . you are happy that you stole fire, and outwitted my thinking; but it will be a great sorrow to you, and to men who come after. As the price of fire I will give them an evil, and all men shall fondle this, their evil, close to their hearts, and take delight in it." Zeus laughed long and hard as he told the lowly god Hephaestus to mix earth and water and to set in it a voice and strength. He told Hephaestus to shape a desire-awakening maiden whose face would be like the immortal goddess. Athena was to teach this creature skills and weaving, Aphrodite was to mist her head in golden endearment and the cruelty of desire that wears out the body, and Hermes was to put in her mind a treacherous nature. In place of a heart, Hermes was to put lies, flattery and disloyalty. Hermes named this creature "Pandora" (whose name literally means "rich in gifts") since all of the Olympians had created her as a "gift" for men. She was to be the bane of men, a destroyer of civilization as powerful as fire.

Before her creation, men had been living without evil, free from laborious work, and from all sicknesses. Before the first woman, things were going very well indeed. It was a virtual paradise. But Pandora discovered a buried earthenware jar and in her impulsive curiosity, she sprang the lid open. Out of the jar, scattering in all directions, were the contents of death, disease, evil and troubles, all of the troubles of mankind. Hope was the only spirit that stayed in the jar as she closed the great lid and contained this one remaining content. As Hesiod (from Lattimore, 1959, lines 54–105, pp. 25–31) describes it, what woman has brought into the world is trouble:

> troubles by thousands that hover about men, for the earth is full of evil things, and the sea is full of them. There are sicknesses that come to men by day, while in the night moving of themselves they haunt us, bringing sorrow to the mortals.

Pandora released both sickness and death into the lives of men. She introduced the distinction between humans and gods – mortality. We remember her now for having a "box" that released evil things into the world, carelessly through her own curiosity. Although few of us know more than the phrase "Pandora's box," her story says much about the contemporary suffering of girls and women and the unspoken meanings that lie behind the "commodity" of female beauty. I call it a commodity to stress the fact that a beautiful appearance is the only socially condoned power that women are openly encouraged to have as they enter adult life the world over. The power of female appearance is, however, an awful double bind as we can see from the Pandora story.

What are the emotions represented in the story? By and large the Olympian gods play out a drama of self-conscious emotions – pride, shame, envy, jealousy, guilt – in their struggles to rule and to possess. Jealousy, pride and competition drive Zeus to send Pandora to mankind. She is a symbol of the power struggles among men and of the rationale for oppressing females. Her beauty – and all of its meanings – is a pawn in the struggle for male dominance.

Although her beauty is as powerful as fire, it is based on lies and deceit. Men must learn to be wary of it and to control it. Pandora's beauty is a power chip in male society. It is attractive, but empty. She is dangerous. What she brings to mankind is the ultimate defeat, death itself.

### The double bind of female beauty

The myth of Pandora lives among us still. Journalist and author Naomi Wolf (1991: 12) calls our contemporary demands of the female body a "beauty myth." Wolf puts Pandora's story in the framework of contemporary sociobiology and says:

> The beauty myth tells a story: The quality called "beauty" objectively and universally exists. Women must want to embody it and men must want to possess women who embody it. This embodiment is an imperative for women and not for men . . . because it is biological, sexual, and evolutionary: Strong men battle for beautiful women, and beautiful women are more reproductively successful.

Our current biological story of female beauty – that strong men battle for beautiful women and want to possess them – is not so different from the Greek story. Women are seductive through their beauty and men want to bring this power under their control.

For many contemporary women, especially young women, the beauty myth leads to obsessions with slenderness and/or to low self-esteem. Although beauty is neither universal (it's in the eye of the beholder) nor reproductively superior (anthropologists have frequently shown that the more aggressive rather than the more beautiful female is more successful reproductively), female beauty dominates the lives of women and men through the formula that female beauty equals power. Wherever I am and whoever I'm with, I overhear evaluative comments about female appearances (sometimes my own comments running through my head). Both women and men evaluate women according to the shapes and sizes of their faces, legs, hips, and breasts. As a psychotherapist and a feminist, I frequently feel helpless to break the link between female appearance and power.

From the Pandora story we can see that identifying with this "power" is a double bind – you're damned if you do and damned if you don't. If you identify with the image of female beauty, you put yourself into the Pandora box: beautiful but empty. Increasingly as a woman ages, she finds that identification with a beautiful appearance is a losing game. She will lose the game through aging when she no longer looks like Pandora, a "maiden" – youthful, slender, lovely. To identify with a beautiful appearance and to pursue that power leads to depreciation of her other strengths and ultimately to depression about falling short of standards. To disidentify with the power of appearance (and "let herself go") usually leads to feeling like an outsider, feelings of low self-confidence, and fears of failing to find a heterosexual partner or to be the object of a certain kind of male regard.

A double bind, as documented originally by Gregory Bateson and others over the past two decades, is a condition in which there is no right solution. What keeps a double bind powerful, powerful enough to drive a person crazy, is the sense that it is inescapable. When people feel trapped in a double bind, they feel like they're going crazy. The only way to defeat a double bind is to step outside of it entirely and to stop identifying with either side. In order to do this, one must become very conscious of the origins and meanings of the bind.

The double bind of female beauty is a well-kept secret or we could not sustain a trillion dollar fashion and cosmetic industry for women, or continue to enrol women in the 12,000 classes of Weight Watchers across the USA. Female beauty is a commodity, largely a commodity of male dominance.

What's the loss for men in the Pandora approach to female appearance? If we look back to the original myth, we see at once that men are being defeated by the gods when they swallow the Pandora image. When men believe that female beauty is powerful, they will struggle to bring it under their control. Inevitably this leads to competition with other men (to possess beautiful women) and to feelings of helplessness in the presence of beautiful women. Feelings of helplessness can lead to aggressive and dominating responses, even in men who may otherwise be sensitive to women and their concerns. Feeling helpless in the face of female beauty can lead to fantasies of rape and/or to rape itself.

According to researcher and writer Tim Beneke (1982), justification and rationalization of rape are common among men in our society. (We know from studies of college students that they are common among male college students.) Beneke, who investigated men's attitudes about rape after working to rehabilitate male rapists, was shocked to discover that his own attitudes about female beauty fitted with those of the rapist in many ways. The underlying shared meaning was that rape cannot be prevented and is sometimes necessary because men cannot control their sexual urges when under the influence of a beautiful (i.e., powerful) female person (even if she is a child).

Beneke talked with lawyers, judges, and ordinary men (and with rapists) about how they view rape. He began to see that many communications (jokes, media, advertisements) of everyday life are "rape signs," indicating that rape is natural and even necessary. In jokes, ads, movies, and TV female beauty is often portrayed as power over a man.

The following is an excerpt from an interview published in Beneke's book. He is interviewing "Jay," an ordinary guy from Pittsburgh who would never rape a woman because "it's wrong and unlawful," not because he doesn't want to. When asked about how he feels when he sees a sexy woman, Jay says:

> Let's say I see a woman and she looks really pretty and really clean and sexy, and she's giving off very feminine, sexy vibes, I think "Wow, I would love to make love to her," but I know she's not really interested. It's a tease. A lot of times a woman knows that she's looking really good and she'll use that and flaunt it, and it makes me feel like she's laughing at me and I feel *degraded* . . . I don't like the feeling that I'm supposed to stand there and take it . . . It's a feeling of humiliation, because the woman has forced me to turn off my feelings and react in a way that I really don't want to (p. 44, emphasis in original).

Here is the myth of Pandora in an interview with an ordinary guy. Her beauty is powerful and it's humiliating. He sees the trick. He understands her appearance as a kind of deception. She "knows she's looking really good" and she wants to "use that and flaunt it." What Jay doesn't understand is that the secret code that female beauty equals power is a code among men; it doesn't involve women.

When women dress up or look beautiful they are either (1) trying to be themselves in the ways that they were socialized or (2) trying to be attractive, approved, and well-regarded as people, not as power brokers. Female beauty is a scam and women have been its victims, as the Pandora story shows. Young women and girls are encouraged to trade on appearance, to make it a focus. They are openly admired for appearance, in a way they may not be admired for intelligence, and certainly not for aggression or competition. Taking up the challenge of making a beautiful appearance, a young girl or woman does not know that her appearance may be used by men to compete among themselves as a commodity to be bought and sold, or as a dangerous power to be tamed.

Men, on the other hand, know the code. Many have been immersed in the Pandora myth. They've heard that having a beautiful woman brings admiration from other males. They've heard how a beautiful woman can use her power to humiliate a man. They've also heard that "no can mean yes" and that resistance to having sex should be "worn down." Why do men have such suspicion, fear and hostility about female beauty? The legacy of Pandora, as far as I can see. Men are captured and intimidated by the myth of the empty, deceitful, beautiful maiden who brings all kinds of troubles into the world. This is a power-over story that begins with Zeus's power over men, and ends with men's power over female beauty and the female body.

To uncover the Pandora story in contemporary life means to become alert to the ways it still captures us – and to step outside the double bind of female beauty. Female beauty does not equal power. Female beauty means control and subjugation of the female body, control by men and culturally imposed standards. As the Pandora story implies, this myth of female beauty leaves little freedom for men. It is a story about the curse Zeus created to punish men. The curse is a beautiful but deceitful and empty woman. This is an image that brings much sorrow and trouble to men, as well as to women.

What is beauty then? As I said earlier, beauty is a condition that lives mostly in the eye of the beholder. No single standard for beauty reigns among people everywhere. There is no archetype of personal beauty. Also, and you may have noticed this, our perceptions are colored by our emotions so that at one moment your lover may look beautiful (when you're feeling joyful, nurturing, content) and at another moment she or he may look dreadful (when you're feeling angry, resentful, afraid) or even boring (when you're feeling bored). Cultures set standards for beauty that reflect the ways in which people are to specialize and fill roles, particularly in reproduction.

Our society has been undergoing changes in regard to female roles over the past three decades. The beauty myth has not changed along with other cultural forms. Adolescent girls are still introduced to their own sexuality in terms of how they should look. They are encouraged to be the "objects of desire" instead of agents of their own pleasures and desires. Young women feel a sense of control by controlling their appearance and weight. In order to feel sexual they try to look sexy. Naomi Wolf (1991: 157) emphasizes the effects of TV and advertisements in this socialization process:

> Girls learn to watch their sex along with boys; that takes up the space that should be devoted to finding out about what they are wanting, and reading and writing about it, seeking it and getting it. Sex is held hostage by beauty and its ransom terms are engraved in girls' minds early and deeply.

The only way to step outside this process is first to recognize that it's a double bind and then to disengage from it. Once this is accomplished the myth becomes a metaphor, and Pandora becomes a metaphor of the female oppression through beauty.

## Living myths and metaphors

In working with people in psychotherapy, as individuals or couples, I have the task of revealing the myths they live by. I help them to reveal to themselves the assumptions that have been taken to be "reality." Of course, many of these myths are unwritten rules and unspoken fantasies from their families of origin. As Carl Jung put it, we are all destined to live out the unlived lives of our parents, the fears and fantasies that they projected into us. If we take these to be reality, then we are living within them, unaware of their consequences. Like all mythologies, our family myths have archetypal cores that evoke particular emotions when certain things happen. For instance, if you grew up with a mother who desperately wanted a life as a musician or the career of a lawyer, but did not live out this desire, you may find yourself filled with joy and motivation to play Bach or write constitutional law – quite apart from your talents or even your interests. If someone asks innocently "Why do you want to do that?" you will answer "Doesn't everyone want to do that? Isn't it just natural?".

It's the same thing with the Pandora myth or the myth of scientific realism, although these are broad cultural myths rather than unique family myths. People living in these myths feel like they are doing what's natural, merely being realistic. When I work in therapy with women who are bulimic or anorexic they cannot imagine anyone not caring about body weight or slenderness. "Isn't it just natural to want to be thin?" they say.

Obviously we need living myths. We need them to translate our emotions into meaning, especially the bigger meanings of life. All societies use mythology to promote certain ways of living and certain principles of behavior. Underlying these myths are the archetypes of universal emotions and images. Myths only become troublesome when they interfere with emotional development, when they bind us to childish fears and fantasies, when they prevent us from being in touch with our own desires and motivations. Such myths form the dramas of psychopathology, the ways in which we suffer unnecessarily from our own images and emotions.

Much of my work involves confronting and analyzing harmful myths, like the Pandora story, that are the bases of suffering. This is not an easy task because people cannot let go of a myth without having something to replace the lost reality. With most people, I work to replace concrete belief with self-awareness that allows them to see their myths in terms of metaphors rather than reality. This kind of awareness provides a "space" or perspective that encourages us to examine our beliefs from several angles. We come to recognize that our sense of what's real depends on seeing things in a particular way, and that seeing things is always colored by emotions.

When a person recognizes deeply the patterns of image and emotions that have shaped her or his reality, that person can begin to see reality differently. Now it does not seem "just natural," but, "as if" it were the case. If you penetrate the Pandora myth and discover the double bind, you no longer feel that female beauty means power, freedom or control. You will feel instead that being beautiful (if you are a woman) or having a beautiful woman as your partner (if you are a man) feels as if it is powerful. A beautiful woman is a metaphor in our culture for certain kinds of power, but that power also has other meanings and consequences. Once you step outside of the double bind of female beauty and see Pandora as a metaphor for woman's place in society, you can decide whether or not you want to hold onto a belief that female beauty is important to you. A thirty-year-old man that I see in therapy knows that a beautiful woman will not enhance his power nor substitute for accomplishments, but he still wants to have a beautiful woman for a partner because he chooses to feel this is important. He has had the possibility of relationships with a number of attractive and intelligent women, and he has decided on the most beautiful because the symbol of her appearance still means something to him. Mostly he likes to know that he "can attract and keep" such a beautiful woman. Although he acts as if her beauty matters a lot to him, he is also prepared to let go of this as his partner ages, and to commit himself to her person rather than her appearance. He is seeing female beauty as a metaphor of male power rather than a myth of male power.

When we recognize that our most cherished beliefs and desires rest on seeing things as if they were true, we are also open to other meanings. We can hold open what psychoanalyst Donald Winnicott called a "play space" within our imagination. In that play space we can entertain other meanings for these beliefs and desires and see the consequences of playing out one meaning or another. This capacity gives us greater freedom, based on self-awareness, than we have if we live simply within a myth and assume that it is reality. At the same time, ancient myths that are no longer alive among us – myths of powerful gods and magical kings, for example – can be used as metaphors to explore our own emotional states. Sometimes you may feel a surge of Hera-like jealousy or the imperial certainty of Zeus, to use a couple of examples from Greek mythology. When we are not living within myths, their images provide illumination of our emotional experiences.

## Conclusion

Currently, we need to be concerned about how we treat the topic of human universals. If we were to discount our emotions, the constraints of the human body and life cycle, or the worldwide configurations of human relationships, then we would end up with a conviction that we are isolated individuals, difficult to understand or even profoundly unknowable.

I'm completely in favor of our current focus on human differences of gender, race, privilege and ethnicity. We are trying to free ourselves from the old myths of dominance–submission that keep us wanting power over each other and the natural environment. In the midst of this focus, though, we need to hold onto the thread of our common psychology. If we can study mythology and human development in the context of universal human emotions and their archetypal images, we will find new insights into human differences as well. We need to break down the living myths that oppress us with themes of dominance and submission, as the Pandora myth does. When we see these myths as metaphors, we see ourselves in a new light. Some of that light is shed from the knowledge of what is common, shared and unchangeable in human life. Constantly rediscovering the line between the changeable and the unchangeable is what enlivens the work of a postmodern Jungian analyst.

# Chapter 9

# Feminism and narrating female persons

Being a Jungian psychoanalyst and a feminist may seem to be a path to healthy self-awareness, but more often it has been a struggle with alienation. Many of my Jungian colleagues are reluctant to accept feminism as psychological theory, even perhaps to accept any serious concern with the social or cultural meanings of being female. Many of my feminist colleagues are sternly critical of the misogynist or patronizing biases of Jungian psychology. My identity as a Jungian feminist has been mostly a vexing consciousness of my own dividedness. For some years I hid my dividedness; I was a "closet feminist" among Jungians and a "closet Jungian" among feminists. Some time ago, however, I pledged to myself that I would no longer silence my political and social beliefs when writing or speaking Jungian psychology, nor hide my Jungian psychological ideas in speaking with feminist colleagues and friends.

Feminism, as a cultural movement and a personal meaning system, has been basic and fundamental to my discovery of myself as a person. Prior to my acquaintance with feminism, pre-1974, I was nonetheless an enthusiastic person fully engaged in life. I lacked (although I only "knew" it was lacking by the unspoken discomfort it perturbed) a *form of discourse* that included with precision my experiences as a daughter, student, wife, mother, author, professional, and person. The only genuinely female form of discourse that was available to me was gossip in which I wholeheartedly engaged. Gossip, though, was disparaged by others. Even alas by me at times. Ultimately I classed it as "trivial."

Many of my concerns seemed similarly trivial, including such concerns as my love life, my reproductive system and its vagaries, my particular perspective on Western philosophy, my relationships with my mother and other women, my desire to describe the details of kitchen or house work, and many others. Perhaps the most poignant (as I reflect back on my darkest pre-feminist hours) were the dreadful times I spent in remorse and shame, afraid of my enraged and sometimes murderous feelings toward my delightful and beautiful babies. These feelings would overwhelm me at times, especially at night when I would drag myself from bedroom to bedroom, attempting to soothe and nurture and contain what was troubling my children. At one point, when I was about three years into mothering my two little children, I thought I would go beserk. I knew I had these intensely ambivalent feelings about my children, but I could find no reference to these feelings in *any* text or manual on infant care (and I had many). On the absolute brink of desperation, I encountered a copy of Adrienne Rich's (1976) *Of Woman Born* and I had my first feminist awakening.

## A new narrative

Although I had been politically active in the women's movement before 1976, I had not previously had the experience of discovering a new narrative, a form of discourse in which my own experiences were validated. Reading *Of Woman Born* was liberating in a way that I had never before known. What I discovered here was a woman's narrative of her *experience* of mothering and its contrast with the *institution* of motherhood. My eyes were opened for the first time to the possibility that my own experiences were not alien, isolating, or even perhaps unique, but rather that they had not been *recorded* and that they fell outside of institutional truths.

That was the beginning of my search into feminism. My own definition of feminism shares its principal themes with many others' definitions. Feminism is a discipline of thought and action that aims to enhance mutuality and trust; to reveal the meanings of gender differences, especially as these might interfere with mutuality or trust; and to oppose all models or methods of dominance–submission for relationships among people. Feminism is not a "power-over" movement. It is not women wanting power over men. What feminism has revealed, in its many forms from theology to literary criticism to psychology and philosophy, is that the silencing and trivializing of women and their ideas affect all of us all of the time in the way that we expect the world and ourselves to be.

Feminism has awakened an appreciation for the fact that our beliefs influence our perceptions, and that whatever we take to be real – what we assume to be "really true" of ourselves and others – is true from our vantage point at that moment. We do not discover some reality that is out there, but rather we invent our reality from our beliefs. Our knowledge is primarily pattern-matching and we all search for the best fit with the patterns or expectations that we hold. These expectations become biases in the way we expect things to be. We develop our biases largely through emotionally charged influences from family and society, especially through language, what we are told. As feminist psychologists Rachel Hare-Mustin and Jeanne Marecek (1988: 455) say, "Language highlights certain features of the objects it represents, certain meanings of the situations it describes. Once designations in language become accepted, one is constrained by them . . . Throughout history, men have had greater influence over language than women." This is not to say that women have made no contribution to patriarchal language and culture, but rather that men – primarily certain white men – have had privileged status at all levels of cultural participation from education (and literacy) to leadership and decision-making to writing and publication.

I believe that we are just now entering a period in which women are beginning to take control of their own belief systems. Perhaps for the first time in recorded history, enough female people have now entered the cultural record to open an avenue for female discourse – one that is barely open and needs much protection. In the USA, the 1970s and 1980s produced an outpouring of female voices, on every level of discourse, from reports of sexual abuse and battering to accounts of philosophical and theological theory-making. We seem to be in the midst of constructing a "feminist epistemology" – a feminist theory of the nature and grounds of knowledge, how female people come to know and recognize themselves and the world. It is my belief that this epistemological project is an essential aspect of contemporary feminism, especially within the sociopolitical limitations of current partriarchy. A study of the nature and grounds of our knowledge will permit female people to develop narratives of strong and complete women.

## Gender stereotypes

Currently, we are still in the position of being dominated by gender stereotypes that function to limit our experiences, expressions, and expectations of the lives we live. We all necessarily participate in everyday conversations in which the given worldview includes assumptions of female inferiority, inadequacy, and weakness. Inevitably all female people arrive at adulthood with feelings and significant beliefs about their own inferiority. As I have written elsewhere (Young-Eisendrath, 1987; Young-Eisendrath & Wehr, 1988; Young-Eisendrath & Wiedemann, 1987), female persons must identify in some way with the theory of female inferiority in order to survive. Attributions about women's weaknesses and narcissism, about their lack of competence and objectivity, are sustained in ongoing conversations in which both verbal and non-verbal communications are structured by the hard-core belief that female persons lack something. Inevitably all female people develop individual theories of themselves, their families of origin, their bodies, their intelligence, their competence, their nurturance, or the like, that indicate to themselves and others "Something is wrong with me personally."

### In need of stories of adventurous women

What we painfully lack as a patriarchal culture are accounts of complete and strong women. These accounts would be different from any inherited version of heroines, goddesses, or idealized female figures that have been created principally from men's imaginations. As feminist writer Carolyn Heilbrun (1988: 42) puts it:

> How can we find narratives of female plots, stories, that will affect other stories and, eventually lives, that will cause us neither to bury Shakespeare's sister nor to throw up our hands in describing George Sand because we are unwilling to call her either a woman (under the old plot) or a man when she isn't one?

George Sand, a French writer (1804–1876), is a perfect illustration of the problems I am trying to describe. As Heilbrun says, George Sand was an enigma for her biographers and her friends because she lived thoroughly as a woman in a manner that was not permitted for a woman. Although Sand was quite comfortable with the womanly activities of running a hospitable home, delighting in her grandchildren and her garden, she also relished the possibility of social revolution and had many lovers, usually younger men whom she treated well. She refused to live by the gender stereotypes of her day and took a man's name and dress in order to move freely about the cities in her youth.

One of her biographers, Ellen Moers, expresses the dilemma about Sand when she says "She was a woman who was a great man" (quoted in Heilbrun, 1988: 35). The point is made explicitly by Heilbrun throughout *Writing a Woman's Life*; it is simply that we have no narrative, no plot, no paradigm for the life of a strong, adventurous woman. We always speak about such women as masculine or male-identified rather than as wholly women. If a woman refuses the plot that most women live – that is, either explicitly *in* the family or distinctly *out* of the family (as celibate, for instance) – then she would be hard put to answer the question of where she is going or what she wants.

Feminism has taught me to examine the implications of gender, and of difference in general, to help me and others see the ways in which people are expected to be, and to differentiate these from how they are and how they would like to be. This is an exercise in awareness, a bringing to consciousness, of the underlying structures I use to create a *woman* or a *man* from my beliefs and imagination. I have come to be alert to how my prejudices may silence, eliminate, or destroy another's or my own subjectivity – the ability to go on being a self-recognized unity of intentions, desires, and identity.

### Sex and gender

Like many other (but not all) feminist theorists, I draw an important distinction between sex and gender. Sex is the anatomical structure and properties of the human body that signal that a person should be placed in one gender group or the other. In most cases, sex is definite and inflexible and indicates certain structural and functional differences between human beings. Breasts, vagina, vulva, smaller body size, menstruation, pregnancy, lactation, menopause, and greater longevity in the female person. Penis, greater body size, impregnation, and lesser longevity in the male. What these biological constraints might actually mean within any society or family varies by gender categories. Gender is the cultural or familial meaning that has been assigned to sex differences. Gender is flexible and contextual, dependent on the particular society in which a person develops. Sex is concrete and definite. The psychological identification with one's sex is, obviously, the development of gender identity, of the meanings associated with sex within the family, tribe, or culture.

Assignment into a gender group is not flexible in most societies, especially in male-dominated societies such as North America. Sex is typically established at birth from the features of the infant's body; they are read in order to place the infant in a gender group. When the sex of an infant is ambiguous or anomalous, parents and doctors organize quickly to assign a gender and change the body if necessary. Gender serves many cultural and social purposes and we are anxious to get it assigned quickly. In all major societies, there are two gender groups and membership in one is exclusive. In essence, each of us is assigned to one of two clubs at birth and we must practice by the rules of our club for the rest of our lives. We look in at the others as outsiders. This condition of being identified as one gender and constructing the other as an outsider has important psychological implications, as we shall see.

What about the meaning of gender in North American societies? The research conducted by Broverman et al. (1970, 1972), in the 1970s, and replicated thereafter, has shown clear evidence of the collective prejudices we share in our expectations of the two genders. From a broad spectrum of the American population, surveyed via a paper and pencil questionnaire, these sociologists discovered that American women are expected to be weaker, less competent, and more emotionally expressive than their male counterparts. Men are expected to be more intelligent and objective than women. Perhaps most surprising, these researchers have shown that an ideal woman is expected to be more passive and less competent than a healthy adult. (One form of the questionnaire asked for descriptive responses to the category "healthy adult.") Personal responsibility and self-determination, considered to be the cornerstone of American ideals for adulthood, so essential for our democratic valuing of self-initiative, are in conflict with social expectations for an adult woman.

Other research on gender stereotypes (e.g., Bem, 1974; Deaux & Lewis, 1984; Ruble, 1983) amplifies Broverman et al.'s findings and provides a clear and strong profile of the expectations we hold for male and female persons in North America. Psychologist Alice Eagly summarizes these expectations in two categories: communal and agentic. Female people are expected to be more communal, characterized as the following: concern with welfare of others, caring and nurturant qualities, interpersonal sensitivity, emotional expressiveness, and a desire to be at one with others. The agentic category is associated with male people and the following: asserting and controlling tendencies, independence from other people, self-confidence, self-sufficiency, self-expansion, and the urge to master. These are gender stereotypes or expectations that function to assign people to certain kinds of tasks and responsibilities, to limit people to certain roles.

### Psychotherapy's androcentrism

As psychotherapists and educators, we need to be alert to the influence of gender stereotypes on our theories. One such influence has been the problem of androcentrism in the major psychological theories we have inherited. Androcentrism is the tendency to see things only from a male point of view, to accept the male version of experience as "the truth." As a psychotherapist I have been faced repeatedly with theories of female inadequacy – theories like penis envy or the inferior moral and intellectual capacity of women – that arise from the assumption that the female person is inherently lacking something. Once a woman is seen as inherently lacking, then one can reason that she is just "naturally" depressed, enraged, or compensating for this inadequacy. I have called this form of psychological determinism a "Pandora psychology" (Young-Eisendrath & Wiedemann, 1987) from the Greek story of the first woman who was beautiful but empty. As a male version of "woman" she is inadequate simply because she is not a man.

In writing *Female Authority: Empowering Women through Psychotherapy* (1987) with Florence Wiedemann, I reviewed the most prominent psychodynamic theories about women (e.g., those about female narcissism, masochism, and passive dependence) and began to recognize the burden of living in a culture that promotes images of men's experiences of women as though these were images of women. Magazines, movies, TV, novels and poetry are full of men's images masquerading as accounts of female lives. Object relations theory and many of the infant–mother theories of development are replete with men's accounts of the mother–child dyad, even including the experiences of the mother! In order to differentiate the female person, in her own subjectivity, from the male person's "object of desire and dread," we must begin with women themselves. Great trouble and sadness can arise for female people in importing male meanings and imaginings – men's fear and fantasies about mothers and "powerful" women – into the central holding place of female psychology.

I have elsewhere (Young-Eisendrath, 1990) made a critique of the insidious gender stereotyping that continues to be upheld by many Jungian theorists who talk in terms of "universal" principles of Masculine and Feminine. In this chapter, I would like to examine gender bias on a broader basis, using especially the terminology set down by Rachel Hare-Mustin and Jeanne Marecek (1988) in a thoughtful article called "The meaning of difference." They describe two types of errors that are frequently made in psychological theories about gender, especially theories used in psychotherapy.

The first type of error they call an "alpha bias" after the statistical error of inference. This is a view that exaggerates difference. "The view of male and female as different and opposite and thus as having mutually exclusive qualities . . . has deep historical roots" (p. 457). The traditional psycho-analytic theory of different resolutions of the Oedipal conflict for boys and girls is an example of an alpha bias. In a favorable resolution, a boy can idealize his adequate and complete father, and look forward to his (the boy's) eventual possession of a big penis and women like his mother when he grows up. The boy can take initiative to become a man and a father. Even in a favorable outcome for the girl, she is poorly disposed for adult life. She can only partly idealize her necessarily inadequate (no penis) mother and surrender her romantic love for her father. This love will be replaced by the desire to become a mother herself and have a male baby. Because her mother does not possess the penis, however, she cannot be wholly admired nor represent culture and achievement. This notion of a lack of an adequate image of female maturity has been carried over into many psychodynamic theories about female functioning and experience.

Oddly enough, many contemporary feminist theories of gender differences also have an alpha bias. This bias tends to fall along the lines identified by Alice Eagly (1987) earlier, as the "communal" nature of women and the "agentic" nature of men. Nancy Chodorow (1978), Carol Gilligan (1982), Jean Baker Miller (1976), Mary Belenky et al. (1986), and Young-Eisendrath (1984) have advanced gendered psychologies that have an alpha bias. We have characterized female people as more connected, relational, empathic, and caring than male people. We have characterized male people as more separate, rational, and dominance-oriented.

Although I am aware that an alpha bias may replicate the problems of gender stereotypes, I still find it sometimes useful, especially in doing psychotherapy with male–female couples. I am now less convinced of the gender lines of these categories and more concerned simply to describe a new category for subjectivity: one that includes strengths in the forms of attachment, mature dependence, and a relational self.

Also I understand that some of these differences may be more a product of power differentials between the genders than they are a product of any particular socialization of personality traits. Deferring to others and caring for others may, in part, be what is left to those who are not in power in the family or the workplace in a society that undervalues care-giving and rewards status with privilege, which most societies do.

The other bias described by Hare-Mustin and Marecek (1988) is called "beta bias" and it is the tendency to deny differences that exist. Beta bias runs the other side of the gamut in saying that both sexes are essentially androgynous or capable of doing the same things. Beta bias occurs in most theories of family therapy. In structural family therapy (Minuchin, 1974), and strategic family therapy (Haley, 1976), for instance, no distinct differences are clarified regarding the roles played by male and female people in the family. Similarly, in theories of healthy androgyny (e.g., Bem et al., 1976; Singer, 1976), both male and female people are understood as being capable of developing the same traits in different situations. Beta bias theorists ignore the power and status differences between the genders; they underestimate or ignore the effects of gender expectations on people's identities.

The issue here is how we approach the idea of difference and not what perspective we take. If we relegate gender difference to the realm of the repressible or the ignored, or if we assume gender difference is as fixed and concrete as sex difference, then we have made a move to eliminate the other as a subject. If we eliminate the possibility of knowing another in her/his own subjectivity – investigated through understanding and inferring *from* the actual other's account – then we limit the possibility for our own and others' development. Ignoring or stereotyping difference is the obstacle I would like to avoid. Differences of female subjectivity are especially apt to be silenced or trivialized because of the lack of cultural records and accepted forms for their expression.

## How we tell the story of gender

Demaris Wehr (1987) and Andrew Samuels (1989) are two Jungian theorists who share with me the concern to understand gender differences from the point of view of different narratives or experiences of people within society, rather than in terms of stereotyped categories of difference. The danger of rigid categories of gender, such as the ones used by Erik Erikson (1965: 590) in his article "Inner and outer space: reflections on womanhood," is that they confuse sex and gender and lead us to expect gender differences to be as inflexible and concrete as the form of the human body. In general, psychoanalytic theory, even contemporary object relations theory, has insisted on reducing gender differences to universals that depict symbolic states connected with the form and function of the human body. Here is a passage from Erikson's article that illustrates what I mean:

> the girl's scene is an *interior* scene, represented either as a configuration of furniture without any surrounding walls, or by a *simple enclosure*

built with blocks. In the girl's scene, people and animals are mostly *within* such an interior or enclosure, and they are primarily people or animals in a *static* (sitting, standing) position . . . Boy's scenes are either houses with *elaborate walls* or *facades with protrusions* such as cones or cylinders representing ornaments or cannons. There are *high towers*; and there are *exterior scenes* (emphasis in original).

No doubt these structural differences in scenes, built with toys as a part of a study at the University of California for which Erikson is famous, seemed obvious to Erikson and would be to any observer. They are differences that are concrete and observable like anatomical differences.

But what do they mean? Too easily and reductively, psychoanalytic theories have tended to conclude that these are natural and inherent, arising from the differences in body structures. Inferences about these differences have largely been made by adult men who collect their data in psychotherapy with adults or researchers who observe infants and children from the outside. Largely in these situations, meaning is imposed, not discovered.

I see a problem with two assumptions: (1) it is necessary and natural for women and men to fit into proscribed roles and categories because of their biological specializations; and (2) an observer can infer adequately what is fundamentally the experience of another. This second assumption is grounded in the idea that there are universal principles of masculinity or femininity. We need only establish the sex of a person and then certain naturally determined truths will follow if a person is healthy.

Reductionism and determinism are methods that lead us to believe in simple truths. These truths usually serve the purposes of a dominant group – scientists or psychologists or politicians. When someone promotes a particular idea about the "real nature" of human differences, I am skeptical. How might the promoter benefit from these natural categories of difference?

In terms of gender differences, I certainly believe that there are significant differences in the lives of women and men in all known cultures, but what these are and what they mean is still largely unknowable. We do not know what is masculine or feminine except in relation to context; and we will not know until women's experiences are clearly recorded and integrated into many cultural records and mindsets. I think of gender differences as cultural inscriptions on a universal condition of sexual difference. If we talk about gender difference as universal, then we hold that its content is always the same (e.g., Logos as masculine and Eros as feminine). We assume that we already know what the particular patterns of healthy functioning should be. If, instead, we talk about gender in terms of cultural and familial meanings, then we can incorporate the particular images and ideas that derive from a context.

## A new paradigm of female authority

To return to the vulnerability of female persons, in order for us to develop fully, we must claim the legitimacy of our own experience. We must recognize how and why we construct our experiences as "female." Even the most accomplished women among us must practice knowing the categories of their own experiences because these are largely unrecorded.

Here is an example from Mary Catherine Bateson (1989: 54), the daughter of Margaret Mead and Gregory Bateson, who was a dean at Amherst College (and had published several books) at the time she was faced with the following:

> When a new president . . . told me before coming and without previous discussion with me that he had heard I was "consistently confrontational" that I had made Amherst "a tense, unhappy place," and that he would want to select a new dean, I should have reacted to his picture of me as bizarre, and indeed confronted its inaccuracy, but instead I was shattered. It took me a year to understand that he was simply accepting the semantics of senior men who expected a female dean to be easily disparaged and bullied.

I believe that a psychology of gender differences, grounded in cultural relativism, is both a therapeutic and a cultural antidote for the kind of sexism we all experience in ongoing everyday situations. Feminism assists all of us in this process of deconstructing and reconstructing gender meanings.

When I look at the massive work of contemporary feminism, I like to think that female people are working on a large-scale paradigm shift in the Kuhnian (Kuhn, 1970) sense. The feminism of the 1970s introduced and advocated subjectivism ("gut feelings") in contrast to scientific objectivism. In the early 1980s we witnessed the development of relativism in terms of a feminist awareness of gender differences as constituting power differences. In the late 1980s we have seen the formulation of feminist constructivism in terms of the influence of context and pattern-matching on reality-making. I believe that feminism has vastly influenced culture-making, moving us away from reductive arguments about the universal nature of human difference and toward an appreciation of reciprocal valuing of difference.

The reciprocal valuing of difference leads to the possibility for mutual self-revelation, the joining of knowledge and desire, in ongoing conversations from different points of view, different persons. In order for this kind of dialogue to take place between men and women, we must learn about our repressed , dissociated and fantasied gender meanings.

We must also learn to overcome the silence and silencing of female persons. Having female ideals, images, visions, narratives, and life histories is a major move toward real talk in women's voices. When feminism informs psychology, it reveals the gaps, blindspots, and deficits that color female subjectivity within the history of patriarchy. When feminism is incorporated into psychology, it releases girls and women to speak, vitalizing the artistic and creative practices of female persons (from the ordinary tasks of housework and personal decoration to the extraordinary contributions to literature, art, philosophy, and science) permitting the possibility of dialogue between the sexes, revealing new paradigms of thought, and appreciating compassion as a primary human impulse.

# Chapter 10

# The female person and how we talk about her

> For Descartes . . . an epistemological chasm separates a highly self-conscious self from a universe that now lies decisively outside the self.
>
> (Bordo, 1986: 144)

We all come into being within a social context of beliefs about selfhood, intentionality, power, emotion, intelligence, and other personal qualities. We are entirely dependent on each other for our experiences of ourselves as persons, as members of a social group we call "the human body". As John Shotter and Josephine Logan (1988) point out, we feel the influence of this body most frequently and commonly as overt and covert communication about how to "go on being." All characteristics of our personal psychologies are individually appropriated from the communicative practices of our particular tribe. At different points along the life-cycle continuum, the tribe is differently constituted: as parents and siblings, as peers and friends, as spouse and children, as community and mentors, whatever is focal to personal meaning.

In the following account, I will trace a feminist epistemology for how to go on being as a feminist in patriarchy. Although even the activity of epistemology-making is patriarchal in its social origins, I can exploit the activity to assist myself and others in uncovering the assumptions and limitations of ordinary concepts that refer to the female person in North American society.

My desire to study the ordinary assumptions about being a female person arises directly out of my practice as a psychotherapist and educator. In my daily efforts to persuade and influence women to claim the authority of their own experience, I constantly come up against some problematic concepts we use in our knowledge systems about personal being. My desire to increase vitality and life satisfaction in women is assisted by the task of elucidating ordinary gender concepts that I encounter in conversations with friends, students, and clients. Increased personal authority, as the experience of making one's own decisions and having the wherewithal to live enthusiastically, appears to contribute to life satisfaction in people everywhere.

Although human freedom is complex and often illusory, the concept of personal freedom has much meaning in North America. Its meaning must be clarified if we are to support an increasing participation of women in the philosophical, political, and interpersonal systems of the society in which we live. A feminist epistemology must attend both to aspects of personal authority as they are enacted by women and men, and to the fact that we are bound and limited, both by our existence as persons and by our complete dependence on a world of living beings who are not persons. Still the illusion of freedom is central to the experience of being a person in the USA. Our principles and ideals for social participation as valid individuals include most prominently "freedom," "equality," "liberty," and the "pursuit of happiness."

Because epistemology is specifically the study of knowledge systems, in reference especially to limits and assumptions that bind those systems, I believe that epistemology is a worthy topic for feminist remaking. As Emily Grosholz (1988) says ". . . practical deliberation, not scientific theory, is the right model for understanding what we are about when we engage in feminist . . ." activities and methods. By grounding ourselves in practical deliberations, we move away from believing that theories and concepts show us the truth, and toward the fact that theories and concepts are used by particular groups to keep themselves and their projects going.

My approach to unraveling the androcentric concepts associated with female persons has the practical concern of displaying the effects of patriarchy on women's self-concepts. I want to help women become increasingly their own authorities so that we can freely validate our experiences, and in this way make claims to our truths.

Because I am limited by my purposes of enabling ordinary women, I am not immediately and directly envisioning broad social and political reforms. In my practical interactions with women and men, I work on methods by which we may eventually arrive at such reforms, but my current conceptualizations are not directly focused in that way. I believe that we have not extricated a feminist methodology from the languages and theories of patriarchy and it is unclear whether feminism can develop a methodology or epistemology that is beyond patriarchy. An example may help me to illustrate this.

The psychology of separation–individuation is often used by Americans implicitly or explicitly in defense of our individual rights. This psychology is founded on a problematic fallacy of conceiving human life as a specifically individual affair. Concepts such as uniqueness, genius, spontaneity, independence, and individualism are privileged in our society. They are offered as ideals against a background of belief that people are by nature unique individuals. Concomitantly, concepts of ordinariness, shared intelligence, limitation, dependence, and collectivity are devalued or denied. Much of our philosophical and cultural heritage is rooted in a fallacy of individualism, the shared belief that separate physical bodies endow us with separate and unique minds.

The corollary of most ideologies of mental separatism is that some minds are better than others, whether they are better adapted for survival (Darwinism) or for esthetic expression (Kantian idealism). Consequently, people then may imagine that they are in competition for the privilege or the right to have the best, or at least one of the best, minds. The authority of masculinist culture carries the belief that individual men – such as Charles Darwin, Karl Marx, Sigmund Freud, Albert Einstein, Jean Piaget – have been our true visionaries. Although we are entirely ignorant of the contributions made by their lovers, wives, children, servants, neighbors, and others, to their knowledge systems, we believe that we trace the accounts of individual genius in the records of their lives and achievements. How might a historical account read if we assumed that the roles of the people, animals, and objects that were a part of the life context had to be included in accounts of the origins of exemplary knowledge systems?

I have presented this rather elaborate single illustration of the interplay between different kinds of received knowledge to show that we may never be able to extricate a methodology that is uniquely feminist.

## Feminist epistemology

What is the purpose, then, of a feminist epistemology? From my perspective, it should offer both deconstruction and reconstruction. In terms of deconstruction, for example, feminism presents a critique of cultural and psychological assumptions of the inferiority of female gender and all activities and preoccupations associated with women. The assumed inferiority of female gender is the background for much of our received knowledge about women's everyday lives. Less-than attributions (i.e., that women are less intelligent, less objective, less competent, less supportive of other women) imbue our reasoning about women and relationships with women in ways that are remarkably intractable.

Feminist epistemology should provide us with a systematic framework for unearthing assumptions of female inferiority as they recur in our thinking about men, women, society, art, culture, and truth on a daily basis. This kind of epistemology may not eliminate the suffering of women and girls; feminism is not a salvation theology nor a complete explanation of women's or others' suffering. Feminist deconstruction of received knowledge should, however, provide assistance in formulating new visions of community, work, and relationship that are based on non-patriarchal images and ideals, potentially on values of shared existence, such as limitation, compassion, and mutuality.

Changing our thinking about inferiority–superiority and dominance– submission is a discipline of thought and action that requires a constant examination of assumptions and motivations. Is it possible first to change one's actions and then to change one's mind? Yes, indeed, but changed action does not necessitate reconceptualization. For example, a husband may subscribe to the idea that doing dishes and sorting socks is an inferior activity. Having been influenced by feminism, he may engage in these activities resentfully, continuing to believe they are inferior. On the other hand, it is possible that these new activities could convert his thinking in an unexpected way if he could examine his assumption that they are inferior; if he were assigned these tasks at a Zen monastery, he might imbue them with spiritual meaning! The decision to do something considered inferior is likely to result in sabotaged and dissipated actions, eventuating in feelings of helplessness: "I just can't make this work, no matter how much I want to."

Approaching the "inferiorizing" of women's work from a perspective of feminist epistemology, I would examine and analyze the assumptions that determine the work is inferior. Typically, we can conclude some particular work has been given lower status simply because it is done by women. Once the meaning of an activity is freed of inferiorizing attributions, it can be examined in terms of its actual components – in terms of the skills, talents, and shared concerns of the people and the environments involved.

The reconstructive aspect of feminist epistemology is the articulation of a feminist knowledge system through new social contexts, new meanings, and new conversations about female work and identity. Two major belief systems stand in the way of women doing this directly at the moment, as Jean Lipman-Blumen (1983) has shown in her analysis of gender roles and power: (1) the belief that men control the knowledge necessary to direct our daily lives through the political and cultural forms of patriarchy (in which we are all engaged); and (2) the belief that men control the major resources on which we all depend.

Feminist analyses of resources, vitality, agency, and ideals connected to women and their activities must provide a persuasive counterposition to these beliefs. Indeed, we have begun to do this. Luce Irigaray (1985a, 1985b) has provided us with some epistemological guidelines for reconstructing the understanding of female experience, especially for retrieving the meaning of female experience from the records and ideals we currently possess within patriarchy. Briefly, the method of Irigaray includes two steps: (1) analyze the gaps, the missing information, the unspoken meanings, irrationalities, and blind spots in the existing knowledge systems in order to read the text of female experience; and (2) use the method of original analysis to analyze the originator of the method in order to recover his motivation and sympathies in constructing his system. The hidden position of the female and the feminine can be revealed through such analyses.

In my analyses of North American ideals and beliefs about female persons, I will use methods of Irigaray and guidelines offered by other feminists. Additionally, I will use the work of Rom Harré and some other philosophers, such as John MacMurray, who are not feminists but whose conceptual frameworks can be adapted to feminist deconstruction and reconstruction.

### Female persons and gendered selves

The central role of the social environment in providing the framework for being a person-among-persons has been traced by P.F. Strawson (1959), John MacMurray (1957), and Rom Harré (1984), among others. For my purposes, I will define *person* to be a primary first-order experiential construct that refers to a mind-and-body unity, an embodied mind, or a spirited body. Persons are publicly visible and "endowed with all kinds of powers and capacities for public, meaningful action" as Harré said (1984: 26).

A person refers to a human being who is both a point of action (agency, intentionality, movement), and a point of view (cognition, mentality, perception). Through our relationships with other persons we (human beings) become persons. We acquire the meaning that defines us as knowers and doers like other human persons. Through ongoing communication with the world of persons and others, we articulate "personality" that is shared among ourselves. There is no knowledge or experience of being a person that is first learned alone and then attributed to others; in order to see ourselves as persons, we need the reflections, definitions, and perceptions of other persons. Personal experience is originally and continuously a shared existence.

A *self* is secondarily acquired through commerce with a culture of persons. As a theoretical construct or belief about individual subjectivity, the concept of self takes on meanings of the culture in which we develop as persons. Beliefs about self are highly determinate of how persons relate to each other and to their environment. As Harré (1984: 20) described it:

> A person is a being who has learned a theory, in terms of which his or her experience is ordered. I believe that persons are characterized neither by their having a characteristic kind of experience nor by some specific genetic endowment. They can be identified neither phenomenologically nor biologically, but only by the character of their beliefs.

Our ethnocentrism frequently enters into our discussions about self-constructs of other cultures. In America, people tend to believe that individuality, individual freedom, and self-reflectiveness are the truest, most valuable and least contestable aspects of self. In other words, we universalize the aspects of selfhood that suggest personal uniqueness and separateness. As a society (see Bellah et al., 1985), we cultivate and sustain a morality of independent freedoms, self-reflective responsibility, and equity based on balancing individual claims.

Other societies, for example the Copper Eskimo (as recounted by Harré, 1984), attribute characteristics of a collective self to persons. In such a society, there are no unique individuals. People share an identity as a group that is so profoundly collective that, as Harré reports, if one person sneezes, most people sneeze. In such a collectivity, attributions of individual autonomy simply do not exist and no theory of independent individuality – no uniqueness, genius, independence, and so on as we know them – is fostered in the development of self.

In North American society, the concept of self includes an array of attributions that support an ideal of individual autonomy. We are a society that advocates and even hypervalues independence and uniqueness. Our selves are created by our coming to believe that we are independently motivated actors, makers and creators of our own lives. We do not live as participants within a cosmic or social order that sustains us, as we might have done in the Middle Ages of Europe, but rather we share the impression that we sustain our own individual order within a collectivity of other separate individuals. We are each responsible for enacting a morality and an ethic that are typically unsupported by convictions of a larger cosmic or social order.

How does female gender enter into our creation of independent selves and interact with the categories of "basic human rights" that provide a person with validity or legitimacy within the ongoing dialogue of personal life? Women regularly surrender the validity of their own truth in the face of challenges by men and by others perceived to be authorities. Because girls and women receive, support, and are supported in the construction of the female as inferior, they engage in building individual theories about their own inadequacy.

This situation is entirely unavoidable, as long as we all grow up within an androcentric social system in which our elders and peers share deeply held beliefs that men control the knowledge necessary to direct our lives. Individual men are imagined to be geniuses, to have our best interests in mind, to be visionaries for the future, despite their dominance and devaluation of those whose lives they direct. Consequently, all women arrive at adulthood with feelings and significant beliefs about their own inferiority. These are not simply occasional or transitory beliefs; they are pervasive, inescapable ideas of being inadequate with regard to fundamental aspects of being a person. The typical framework of female inadequacy includes women's and girls' beliefs about inferiority of attractiveness, nurturance, strength, intelligence, and competence. These beliefs have been constructed as personal theories built from ongoing conversations about the identity characteristics of being male and female selves.

Individual women and girls unavoidably strive to validate theories of personal inferiority in a patriarchal society. Female persons surrender their personal authority in exchange for being liked or loved or reflected positively; they replace this authority with personal theories of inadequacy and inferiority. Willingness to identify with reflections of female inferiority is a fact of survival; we are socialized into negative self-concepts as female persons. We cannot refuse these reflections because they constitute the basis for our social participation in the world. As individual people, women and girls readily claim inadequacy and evaluate themselves in terms of inferiorities perceived as bad and detrimental to self and others. These evaluations are attributed and sustained in ongoing conversations in which both the social contexts (i.e., verbal and non-verbal communications) and theoretical concepts for human health and welfare support the idea of female inadequacy in strength, independence, health, knowledge, objectivity, and so on. As female persons, we have been shaped by the belief that we lack something. We witness our inability to fill the decision-making and status-holding positions of our societies, and the general devaluation of the work and culture we produce, and we inevitably conclude that something "is wrong with me."

### Double bind of female gender

Until women and girls are offered a feminist epistemology for examining and contradicting the received knowledge about female selves, they are necessarily in a double bind regarding their status as females and adults within a patriarchal society – perhaps even most strenuously double bound in a society like ours, which predicates goodness on freedom and individualism.

The creation of a concept of self (as point of view and point of action) is a product of beliefs about subjectivity in personal life. An individual's self is consequently constructed from the experiences of being a person-among-persons as these are evaluated and explained. ". . . [T]he semantics of the conceptual cluster around the general notion of the 'self' is to be understood as if the 'self' were a theoretical concept like those of the natural sciences, judged by its behavioral and material analogies . . ." (Harré, 1984: 25). Theories of the female self and her subjectivity are built so wholly around assumptions of female inadequacy (widely accepted in many literate societies) that we must wrestle with our basic concepts of being persons even to recognize the experiential difficulties generated by our theories.

Male standards for health, mental health, leadership, culture, competence, judgment, relationship, and personal freedom constitute our recorded and received social reality for the most part. Studies of North Americans' expectations of ideal women and men, conducted by Broverman et al. (1970) and Broverman et al. (1972) in the 1970s are often cited as empirical evidence of the collective prejudices we share about gender identities. These studies show that we expect men to be stronger, more objective, more competent, and more independent than women – results that are obvious in daily life. Perhaps more important, from the point of view of self-constructs, is the assumption that women are less competent and more passive than "healthy adults" when gender is not specified.

This last finding from the Brovermans' research is a fine illustration of the double bind of female adults. Ideals of personal responsibility and self-determination are directly in conflict with ideals for womanly behavior. If a woman behaves as a healthy adult, she will be criticized for being unwomanly; conversely, if she behaves as a feminine woman, she will be considered childlike or worse (e.g., mentally ill).

The double bind of female authority is wholly unavoidable in a society that predicates the individual self on attributes and conditions of which the female is expected to have considerably less than an equal share with males. The categories that support the condition of being free in our highly individualized society – strength, judgment, knowledge, independence, and objectivity – are not expected to be fulfilled for individual women.

Many women oppose the labels of female inferiority in the contemporary USA. They openly fight feeling inadequate and identify themselves with strength, competence, and authority. They will not escape the double bind of female gender until they examine the assumptions on which they are basing their strength, competence, and authority. Such women are frequently described (both by others and by themselves) as compensating or being too masculine or too dominant. Such a woman experiences a great deal of distress when she is acting in an insistent or forceful manner, even when she is simply defending her own beliefs. Paraphrasing Harré (1984), the legitimacy of being a person (the fundamental reality for one's existence) is limited by the right to occupy a space and time in the ongoing conversations of shared reality. This contingent right is closely related to consensual validation or intersubjectivity as truth or worth. Women who oppose female inferiority frequently find themselves in a terrible bind; what they are saying or offering is being questioned simply because they assume a posture or manner of authority or competence. "Persons are embodied beings located not only in the array of persons but in physical space and time. The relation between the consequences of our joint location in both manifolds is mediated by the local moral order, particularly the unequal distribution of rights . . ." (Harré, 1984: 65).

An authoritative woman may be physically present with others, but she may not have the right to occupy a position of contributor, analogous to the female secretary at a male board meeting. She will be seen, but she will not be heard. Because the personal existence of such an individual is threatened in such moments, she will necessarily get the impression that she is doing something wrong. Rather than lose her sanity (experience herself as a non-person), she will tend to accept an explanation that she has not acted in her own best interest. Usually such an explanation will be constructed according to the rules of the female double bind: she is too forceful, overly controlling, demanding, aggressive, rigid, compensating – in short, too masculine.

Women who espouse female authority fall prey to evaluating themselves, both privately and publicly, in terms of their negative subjectivity. They see themselves, as others have reflected, as too intense, too much. Perhaps they even perceive their own personal psychology (family of origin patterns) as inherently problematic. Until a woman wholly understands how female gender is socially constructed to include her individual inferiority, she will be prone to proving and validating the theory of inferior female self whether or not she subscribes to the theory.

Women who do subscribe to the "less-than" female categories and express themselves as more passive and less competent (than men and other women) are perhaps at greater risk. They may be perceived as valid persons under most conditions of their oppression, but they experience their personal validity as grounded in their childlikeness and inherent weakness. Many syndromes of mental "disorders" are descriptions of exaggerated femininity: depression, hysteria, phobia, dependent personality disorder, bulimia, anorexia, and some aspects of borderline psychotic conditions are but a few examples. When feminine-identified women experience life stresses and seek help, they are at risk of being labeled into mental illness categories. With a label such as "depression," an individual may waste most of her life's resources on unintentionally proving the theory of her helplessness.

## New categories for female persons

In the following brief treatment of female authority, I attempt to reverse and exploit some of the received knowledge about female persons that contributes to the disabling ideas women commonly use in constructing individual female selves as inferior. Through a feminist epistemology, I would like to extricate concepts for personal being that are better aligned with women's experiences of themselves and are opposed to the andro-centric constructions of female persons as less-than male persons. I believe that women already operate by such assumptions and beliefs (largely unarticulated and unrecorded) that are both effacious and emergent in relationships with other women.

Three conceptual categories constitute my major focus in this paper: (1) personal freedom as "personal authority" (as distinct from illusions of independence, mental separatism, and individualism); (2) foundational experience as "dependence" (as distinct from self-reflective subjectivity, individual freedom, and social isolation); and (3) beautiful appearances as "personal power" (as distinct from narcissism, compensation, and selfishness).

These three categories of meaning are neither inclusive of all experiences that women bring to self-definition nor exclusive of masculinist influence in my analysis of them. I am using them as case studies of how I apply feminist epistemology in deconstruction and reconstruction of received meaning in my work in psychotherapy with women. By reversing received meaning, analyzing gaps and blindspots in our knowledge systems and validating the "illegitimate" knowledge shared by women, we can extricate new meaning from our recorded cultural standards of patriarchy. Still, our methods require ongoing conversations and revisions through our using them in personal life.

Attributing intentionality and personal responsibility to one's self and others is critical to Western categories of personal freedom. Women's experience of personal sovereignty – as intentionality and the knowledge that they act by free choice – is ambiguous at best, in terms of both their female gender identity and their location in social contexts. Because they are assumed to be less competent and less rational, they are also assumed to be less capable of self-determination; women are often unsurprised to find that other women do not fill higher status and decision-making roles in our society. Idealized passivity (being "taken care of"), lack of validation of female culture, and exclusion of women from the active life of community (women and children are supposed to "stay at home" or at least in the background), all contribute to inhibition of women's personal agency.

Although women routinely make decisions and cope with complex environmental data involved with relational and caregiving skills, they often assume that their decision-making activities are not real because they are dissociated from status and money. When we are offered theories about our "dependency" and our "need for protection," we tend to respond in one of two ways, concluding: (1) that we are individually less than adequate in decision-making skills and responsibility-taking; or (2) that we would achieve the status of being free and independent if we were less inclined to acknowledge our needs for emotional contact or close relationship. Androcentric psychologies of separation–individuation tend to increase women's anxieties about their relational needs *and* to undermine their experiences of personal agency. Because we seek to validate the theory that we are inadequate, we automatically (as a social group) will locate ourselves in explanations about women's dependency needs in such a way that biases about personal freedom and dependence are obscured in conversations.

When women heed the command to "be independent" as a resolution to feelings of low self-esteem and negative self-referencing, they become confused about their experiences of pleasure in relationships. Rather than give up cherished relationships, some women may undermine their motivations to be agents of their lives, and instead believe in a theory about their inferiority. This is a masculinist solution, as is the opposite route of living alone (or being literally "independent") as if social isolation were the path to personal freedom. Living alone has little to do with personal agency, even though people can become more self-reliant under conditions of social isolation. Similarly, repressing one's own desire to express personal creativity and other resources, in order to "protect" one's relationships, does not lead to a useful and satisfying life. Ultimately, evaluations according to any measure of masculinist independence–dependence configurations tend to result in confusion about women's experiences of themselves, especially their decision-making and relational styles.

From women's experiences of their own lives, as illustrated, for example, by Baruch, Barnett, and Rivers (1983), we can clarify a new orientation toward freedom that does not inhibit our desire for relationship, nor obscure our skill and intelligence in decision-making. Freedom is personal authority – the ability to make claims to truth, beauty, and goodness based on one's own experience. Out of this authority people make decisions about their own lives and consider themselves within the contexts of others' lives. Female authority has been repressed and oppressed because of the double bind of female gender identity (see Young-Eisendrath and Wiedemann, 1987, for a fuller discussion of this).

Feminist theologians help us spot new ideas and ideals for female authority. Mary Daly (1978) called our attention to the dominant aggressive structure of patriarchal religious beliefs in a way that reveals an alternative of pleasure, affiliating, cooperating, and imagining with other women. Daly especially validated our pleasures and power in relational contexts as aspects of our own authority, on which we always and everywhere draw in making our own choices. Naomi Goldenberg (1979) directed us to our own images and dreams to find configurations that support our experiences, our own categories of differentiation.

Along the same lines, I find myself opposing common androcentric dictates for success and power in patriarchy, although I am aware of how carefully one must proceed in this activity. When college women query, "Tell me the truth, isn't it really better to become a psychiatrist than a social worker if you want to make a difference in women's lives?" I must study the question carefully. I invite the questioner to enter with me into an analysis of her terms: what does she mean by "better" and how does she view her participation in a profession founded and shaped by men versus one founded and shaped by women? I am making an inquiry about the double bind of her female authority, how she expresses it and how she manages it. In a patriarchal society, we need to protect our access to creative expression, personal power, integrity of our own beliefs and values, and our sovereignty over structuring time and space, as we enter into the world of "success." No false dichotomy of independence–dependence or selfish–selfless can help us orient ourselves to the complexity of the foundation for our own truths.

As long as we confuse personal freedom with an illusory independence, we will have no possibility of validating our experiences as agents and communicators. False talk about independence continues to confuse us in making choices based on our pleasure, mastery, and satisfaction.

Physical and emotional dependence is a primary condition of human life throughout the life cycle. In patriarchy we deny this condition and talk about ourselves as separate individuals. Our misleading fallacy of individualism – that we are uniquely separate beings housed in separate bodies – has led to endless confusion in our philosophies and politics. Every day I encounter people who idealize and promote cultural individualism in a way that supports a phenomenology of mental and physical separatism. They confuse personal agency with the idea that we each live alone and make our own decisions. As organisms and persons, we never live alone. We must have a differentiated dependence on an elaborate environment of physical and social contexts in order to go on being.

Human existence is, in principle and obviously, a shared existence. We are individually vulnerable animals and part-persons. Personal being and the sense of self are elaborately dependent on relationships that provide contexts, reflections, and structures for all our activities from birth to death. Children learn how to be people, male and female persons, through interactions with other persons. There is no human activity that is first learned alone and then noted as corresponding to others' behaviors, yet we constantly speak as though there were such activities.

Women tend to repress their dependence less than men do, probably because women provide more nurturant care as dependable, as well as dependent, people. Our massive cultural and social denial of dependence in North American culture is a product of androcentric knowledge systems. Men repress their original dependence on a "big woman" and they oppose their identification with her. They fight female authority in all of its forms as it is reminiscent of the "big woman" of their childhood life context.

Many cultural by-products of men's repressed dependence confuse our analyses of human relationships. Remnants of the Cartesian epistemology of being – the belief that self-reflective thought brings subjective awareness into being – are with us still. These lead us to the absurd position of asking questions about how minds and bodies can get together and keep on going. Obviously, they were never separated, nor were minds separated from each other. When dependence is freed of its masculinist constraints through feminist methodologies and actions, we may find that much of our Western philosophical tradition since the Middle Ages seems useless and delusional. If an individual person is taken to be the unit of our study, the point of reflection, and/or the topic of investigation, then we are misled into conclusions that preclude the foundation of human experience, the shared existence of our being.

In Carol Gilligan's (1982: 160) study of women's moral reasoning, she discovered that women remember the contextual or relational reality as a foundation for moral principles. She noted that ". . . in all of the women's descriptions, identity is defined in a context of relationship and judged by a standard of responsibility and care. Similarly, morality is seen by these women as arising from the experience of connection . . .".

In order for women to validate their cherishing of relationship and their experiences of ongoing differentiated dependence, they must turn to female friends, and even then they may be loath to call themselves "dependent." Calling oneself dependent has become tantamount to calling oneself a non-person, a child, or a cripple. In order to share in the privilege of being an adult person and to have the right to contribute to the ongoing conversations of daily life, many women choose to see themselves as "independent" and/or to denigrate their dependence in patriarchal terms such as "over-controlling" and "needy." Naturally, women become confused when they have no consensually validated terms for expressing their own dependence and their differentiation of dependent relationships throughout the life cycle.

A feminist analysis of communication practices, in both private (family) and public (communal) life, reveals that women control a valuable cultural resource that is frequently invalidated and referred to perjoratively as "feminine intuition." In mature and differentiated dependence, women accurately perceive the non-verbal and gestural communications of others in such a way as to anticipate others' words and actions. Within a masculinist knowledge system, they cannot legitimately refer to this situation, and sometimes they are hampered in using it as well. Intuition generates what feminists have called empathic regard and what I term "objective empathy" in order to differentiate it from projection, sympathy, approval-seeking, and other forms of feeling undifferentiated from another in one's identity. Objective empathy, as we learn in psychotherapy practice, is the ability to put oneself in an other's perspective or point of view and to accurately infer the other's assumptions and feelings so as to anticipate the other's actions. Under conditions of such objective empathy, the perceiver is able to differentiate clearly between her own desires and feelings and the desires and feelings of the other. For example, it is possible for a thirty-five-year-old woman to infer accurately the frame of reference and assumptions of a two-year-old child without becoming like the child. The adult woman can anticipate the child's actions and even "speak the language" of the child. Putting oneself in another's place and constructing the meaning system of the other is a developmental achievement that appears to rely on blending what we commonly call "objectivity" and "subjectivity."

Critical to claiming the valid authority of her intuition and the potential of her accurate empathy, a female person must have distinguished the authority of her experience from the received knowledge of patriarchy. To achieve this, a woman must somewhat free herself from the desire for approval by the authorities of patriarchy and by its representatives in her immediate life context.

Undoing our rationalizations around internalized female inferiority in order to claim the personal power of our shared experiences as women is a monumental task. Cultural messages about our power must be unknotted and examined in terms of their gaps and blindspots. The hard knots of androcentric reasoning are most difficult to untie with regard to the assumption that women's preoccupations with beautiful appearances (of the body and the domestic environment) are compensations. Female narcissism has been interpreted variously (from the perspective of androcentric reasoning) as compensating for the missing penis, lower intelligence, less access to educational and economic achievement, and for unequal social power. Because women's concerns for beautiful appearances are so widely conceived as trivial and false, even women are reticent to speak among themselves about appearances. Indeed, we often consider appearances to be facades or illusions – the products of patriarchal demands on us – although we have developed considerable skill and intelligence in creating them. We fail to notice that the knowledge and power of these skills belong to us. As Susan Brownmiller (1984) has pointed out, women's appearances – through skin, hair, clothes, etiquette, body shape and body movement – convey essential cultural and social messages. We communicate through our appearances, but we may not understand our messages – but then, again, we may understand them although we believe that they are not valid.

What remains unspoken, hidden, and repressed in our analyses of feminine narcissism? I believe it is the damaging notion that a woman *is* her appearance. Within our patriarchal society, the personal power of woman is conveyed by her appearance. This power of appearance is the only socially condoned power openly afforded to all female persons in patriarchy. Women use that power, manipulate and trade in it, in a way similar to men's commerce in money. Implied in the statement "My, she has let herself go!" (as a criticism of a woman's appearance) is the patriarchal message that a woman is her appearance. It is a social fact that women are encouraged to compete for appearances and win material rewards for that competition; artifice is a social commodity of personal power among women. Women have become skillful and intelligent in using this power, but when they believe that it is merely compensatory, they are serving the purposes of patriarchy. Explanations that invalidate the serious social meaning of women's appearances bind women to approval-seeking and put them under the control of a system that makes their daily concerns seem inferior.

When individual women develop beyond the received knowledge of patriarchy, they may be propelled into an existential conflict of "appearance versus reality." When a woman disavows the compensatory meaning of her appearance – and assumes that she is "more-than" an appearance – she necessarily remains caught in the androcentric knowledge system in which appearance is compensation for something more worthwhile. In her own search for authentic expressions of her self, she will discover ways of appearing that are more comfortable or personally satisfying than her previous bound femininity. In her rebellious freedom, she will make judgments that reproduce patriarchy. She will categorize other women in terms of their appearances, having achieved some personal resolution about her own appearance. Once again, she forces women to operate according to the patriarchal judgment that a woman *is* her appearance. The new feminist-seeking categories then resonate with contempt: women are judged as feminist versus non-feminist, as bright versus dumb, as conformist versus liberated, on the basis of *appearance*.

Recognizing that beautiful appearances are social commodities of power, women can integrate their personal authority into differentiated appearance and skilled beauty without reproducing patriarchy. Appearances provide access to personal power and drama; "dressing up" and wearing "high" heels can lend emphasis of size and color to one's dramatic expression. Decorations, illusions, artifice, and personal esthetic contribute to the creative visions women express in their appearances. We can learn to appreciate the skills and intelligence we have developed in making beautiful appearances when we have freed our conceptual categories from repro- ducing the dictate that a woman *is* her appearance, while not forgetting the social power of this dictate.

In reconstructing the meaning of female authority, my most serious aim is the rebonding of women and the integration of the female community. Competition for appearances has remained a patriarchal arena among women which is often reproduced within feminist groups. As we pull apart the assumptions that lead us to denigrate each other, we continue to discover the powerful projection of our own authority onto male standards for truth, beauty, and goodness.


## Conclusion

We must remember that we are in a critical period for human survival, acutely aware of the dangers of annihilation that face our species. Those dangers arise directly from our repression of dependence, and our desire for mastery and possession of the resources on which we depend. We have adapted to patriarchy principally through repressing our dependence and vulnerability as relatively weak animals. We have acquired enormous dominion over other life systems while we seem incapable of even imagining our existence as shared. Our species may go the way of many other life forms on our planet whose adaption eventually led to extinction.

On the other hand, we are also certainly aware that we are not in control of our individual destinies. Our personal fate is individual extinction, having lived on a small planet, dependent on a relatively small star in a solar system that will eventually dissolve. The psychological condition of our lives as persons – of limited control and limitless dependence – is obscured by patriarchal social and cultural systems that idealize independence. A new model for human existence, grounded in ideals of personal authority and dependence, appreciative of differences and diverse beauty, may contribute to a new vision for personal being. By acknowledging the reality of our limitations and the meaning of human freedom, we may ultimately understand ourselves to be compassionate beings.

# Chapter 11

# Revisiting identity

I must say at the outset that I never warmed up to the psychological term "identity." When I first encountered it as a college sophomore reading Erik Erikson's (1950: 260–261) *Childhood and Society*, I was confused and troubled by what he said because I could not find myself in it. What Erikson described as identity neither clarified a particular cultural meaning, nor helped me locate myself with regard to the developmental continuum he described. In 1950, Erikson defined identity as

> the accrued experience of the ego's ability to integrate all identifications with the vicissitudes of the libido, with the aptitudes developed out of endowment, and with the opportunities offered in social roles. The sense of ego identity, then, is the accrued confidence that the inner sameness and continuity prepared in the past are matched by the sameness and continuity of one's meaning for others, as evidenced in the tangible promise of a *career* (emphasis in original).

Both the character of Erikson's language and the "tangible promise of a career" were peculiar and troubling to my nascent female intellect.

Little did I know then that the culture of psychoanalysis was more responsible both for the linguistic style and the gender slur than Erikson was. I considered Erikson to be a unique identity, as an originator of a theory who molded his language to fit his experiences, rather than a member of a professional community who spoke the common language of his tribe. I held Erikson personally accountable for his theory and his language in a way that I would not now do, since I have a better understanding of what personal identity is. Especially perhaps because I otherwise found *Childhood and Society* to be an inspiring work, I was perplexed that Erikson fell short of helping me in a search for my own subjectivity, my sense of self.

Much later, as a graduate student in a seminar on psychoanalysis, I read Erikson's *Identity, Youth, and Crisis* (1968: 154) and once again I was at a loss to understand what he meant by identity. I got little help from definitions of identity such as ". . . a self-governing as well as a resisting aspect of the ego to emphasize what has to become the psychoanalytic meaning of it, that is, the inner synthesis which organizes experience and guides action".

At that time I had just finished reading two works by Roy Schafer (1978) on a new "action language for psychoanalysis," and believed that Schafer clarified the problem with words like identity. Terms like "identity" and "self" simply are ways of speaking about personal constructions or aspects of experience. Neither identity nor self can "organize experience" nor "guide action." Only people do that. Schafer (p. 87) proposed that we use such terms to describe actions of people rather than to describe part-aspects of people who are doing the acting. For example, "Self and identity are representational actions of a person; ego, divested of its mechanistic trappings, is a class of actions and modes of action or aspects of these, that a person performs".

With this kind of help, I began to understand identity as a particular class of self-reflecting and self-narrating actions of a person, beginning usually at about age thirteen or fourteen in our society, and continuing throughout adult life. This orientation to identity opened up for me a major new interest in psychology: studying reflexity or "metacognition" especially in its early stages of development in middle and late adolescence.

Let me extend my revisitation with identity in two other directions before we leave it for higher grounds. In my first years of teaching life span development at Bryn Mawr College, I discovered a wonderful text called *From Instinct to Identity* (1974) by Louis Breger. In this work, Breger traces the development of identity as an endeavor to deal with the anxiety of "core-conflicts" of attachment–separation, aggression–love, and dependence–independence as these recur at each new phase of the life span. Just as Harry Stack Sullivan (1953) had done with his theory of "self-system," Breger encouraged me to read identity not as something neutral and necessary, but more as something defensive. At the time I was first teaching Breger, I was also reading some of the new material on psychological and cultural narcissism. The work of Heinz Kohut (1977) and Alice Miller (1981) especially prompted me to see the ideal of individual identity as a product of a society that hypervalues individualism, uniqueness, and specialness.

Finally, now I have come to believe that individual identity, or identity over against our dependence on others, is a very recent cultural invention. It is not even as old as Harvard University! Jim Swan (1985: 150) in an essay on difference and silence in John Milton's poetry provides some intriguing facts in this regard.

> *Identity* . . . is first recorded by the OED (Oxford English Dictionary) in 1570, while 1638 marks its first use in the now familiar sense of individuality or personality. Moreover, the OED's use of the word

individuality as a modern synonym for identity is an especially fine coincidence, because that word, too . . . was undergoing a change . . . For individual as an adjective, two related meanings . . . became obsolete during the last half of the seventeenth century: (1) One in substance or essence; indivisible; (2) Inseparable. Then two modern meanings were introduced . . . (3) Existing as a separate indivisible entity; numerically one, single; particular, special; (4) Distinguished from others by attributes of its own (emphasis in original).

There is a radical transition in meaning from being inseparable to being separate and distinct. This transition also depicts an experiential shift (beginning with the Renaissance in Western culture) from a more collective sense of self to the distinctly personal sense of identity (from the seventeenth century on) that is part of our modern experience. Our modern emphasis on individuality is obvious in Webster's *Ninth New Collegiate Dictionary* (1985) definition of identity that says ". . . the distinguishing character or personality of an individual: individuality" (p. 597). The character of self experience in our society is now distinctly colored by ideas and ideals of individualism.

## Self-identity and self-narration

In order to connect this aspect of modern individualism with some clinically useful application I need to take a brief philosophical detour. Bear with me. We will get back to more common ground by way of a few abstractions that will finally be clarified in understanding features of adolescent identity development.

From many different psychological and philosophical influences, I have gradually come to conclude that the development of a self is a process of construction of the experience of subjectivity that eventually becomes a narrative. Selfhood, as a construct, is culturally embedded and concerns the nature of individual subjectivity or the meaning of psychological individuality within a particular society. Prior to engaging in self construction, individuals must be able to function as persons. In this sense, personal being is primary because it comes prior to the experience of identity or individuality. In another sense also, personal being is primary in that we expect certain powers and qualities of persons everywhere without reference to their indigenous theories of self.

We expect all persons to be embodied in a particular form that provides the basis for being a point of action and for having a point of view. That is, we expect that all people will be able to do things and to know things in relatively similar ways.

A self, on the other hand, is acquired within a specific social context. Self comes into being with the experience of being an individual subject. This

experience initially happens to everyone, provided development is pro-
ceeding normally, within the second half of the second year of life, roughly
between eighteen months and two years of age. The meaning of psychological individuality comes from the context of family, society, and culture.
Beliefs about self serve critical functions in the ways people relate to each
other and expect the world to be. As Rom Harré (1984: 20) says, "A person
is a being who has learned a theory, in terms of which his or her experience
is ordered".

Beliefs about individual self become critically important in preadoles-
cence and adolescence. From the work of Jean Piaget and other researchers
and theorists who have followed him in studying the character of self-
reflection, we now recognize that Erikson's identity crisis is ushered in by
the achievement of a special form of thought: the ability to reflect on one's
own thinking, to operate on one's own "operations." The final maturation
or specialization of the cerebral cortex in the period from about twelve to
fourteen years of age allows for the possibility of what Piaget called
"formal operations" or "formal thought." Formal thought is characterized
especially as the ability to perform abstract reasoning – to deduce and
induce, to reason backward and forward, to reflect on a process as moving
from past to future. Self-reflection comes into being in adolescence for the
first time, and it signals a paradigm shift for the individual and a cultural
watershed for the society.

Other psychologists have expanded Piaget's work on formal thought to
include clinically useful applications. Adolescent egocentrism is the preoccupation of early and later adolescents with their own thoughts and
feelings, accompanied by an apparent inability to move outside of the hall
of mirrors they have recently entered through formal thought. Psychologist
David Elkind (e.g., Elkind & Bowen, 1979) has studied adolescent egocentrism and has come up with two useful terms for seeing its effects of
personal functioning. The first he calls the "imaginary audience": it is the
experience that "everyone is watching me" and especially my personal
manner or appearance. Because of our social emphasis on appearance as
power for adolescent girls, girls often become preoccupied with clothes,
body weight, and makeup. They try desperately to live up to images that
are cast by the media and adopted by their peers to "look good" and to "be
accepted." Boys frequently assume that they are being watched more for
their athletic prowess and macho poses than for their physical appearances
per se. The imaginary audience is probably the result of both the new
cognitive capacity to think about one's own thoughts and feelings *and* the
societal emphasis we place on unique personal identity and individualism;
everyone is watching *me* because I am special, unique, can invent myself.
Girls seem more vulnerable to the effects of the imaginary audience on their
self-esteem. Preadolescent girl "cliques" are a cultural product of the
imaginary audience when this process is externalized and girls review each

other carefully for every fault or flaw. Preadolescent boys don't appear to suffer as much from the imaginary audience unless they are unable or unwilling to participate in athletics, the major external audience for male gender development. When boys do not adapt to the dictates of male initiations, in athletics especially, they may experience some lack of gender confidence over many years.

The second form of adolescent egocentrism described by David Elkind is the "personal fable" and it is the belief that one is unique, special and exempt from the ordinary conditions of human life. This way of thinking also seems to be related to both formal thought and our cultural expressions of individualism. The early experiences of formal thought give the impression that one "is thinking up" one's being. That is, the child is able to reflect on her or his own cognitive processes and so has the impression of "inventing oneself." The child then seems to believe that she or he is unique and different from anyone who has ever lived. This includes having problems that are so unique that no one could understand them. Girls may believe that they are exempt from the conditions under which their mothers have lived. They may believe, for example, that *they* will marry, please their husbands, have careers, rear children, never scold their children, *and* keep their weight under control! Preadolescent girls have little humility when it comes to criticizing their mothers because they can now review their mother's faults with the impression that *they* are exempt from those faults and conditions.

For adolescent boys the personal fable may take the form of risky behavior – fast driving, athletic stunts, drinking – assuming that they will be exempt from the consequences. In the extreme, the personal fable can result in engaging in frankly dangerous activities with no anticipation of the outcome: heavy drinking or smoking while believing that one cannot be addicted; having sex without protection and believing one won't become pregnant; binging and vomiting while being certain one is not bulimic, and the like.

The two aspects of adolescent egocentrism – imaginary audience and personal fable – may be "symptoms" of formal reasoning or they may be cultural by-products of our emphasis on individualism. One way or the other, they are an important contribution to adolescent identity formation – by which I mean the capacity to reflect and conceive of oneself in the form of a personal narrative that has past, present, and future, and that provides one with reasons and motivation for "going on being."

Adolescence, more than any other period of the entire life span, is a time for gender stereotyping and a most rigid maintenance of gender roles and meaning. Research has supported the notion that gender-stereotyping increases in adolescence during the period of middle school (grades 6–8) (Guttentag & Longfellow, 1977; Hill & Lynch, 1983; Urberg, 1979). Moreover, several researchers – most prominently, Elizabeth Douvan (1970) –

have discovered that standards for female appearance and behavior are more restrictive for adolescent girls than for younger girls or older women. That is, adolescent girls especially are at risk for believing that they must give up their earlier strengths (and especially aspirations, achievements, competitive manner, and/or tomboyishness) in favor of attracting boy-friends or simply fitting in with the other girls.

Adolescent boys are at risk in another way. They may develop psycho-logical inflation and later feelings of depression in early or middle adult-hood. Several studies of late adolescence (sixteen to eighteen years of age) have shown that girls *underestimate* their ability in setting their aspirations for adult life, whereas boys *overestimate* theirs. The privileges that seem to accrue from simply being male in adolescence – greater freedom (to roam and wander), greater power, more access to adult males through athletics, and so on – appear to mislead some boys into believing that their chances are better than they are for success in adult life. In his work called *The Seasons of a Man's Life* (1978), psychologist Dan Levinson stressed the significance of the "dream of youth" for the later development of male identity. Through interviews with younger and mid-life men, Levinson showed that failures to meet this dream were significant in their contri-butions to later depression and difficulties in mid-life. It is possible that the gendering influences of adolescence on the personal narrative may result in many boys overestimating their potential lifetime achievements.

## A brief review

Revisiting identity has meant an examination of its meaning from several angles. First, in terms of its roots in psychoanalytic metapsychology and further back in the birth of individualism in the seventeenth century. Next we visited that origin of self-examination: the beginning of self-knowledge in the birth of self-awareness. Formal thought and its attendant attitudes of imaginary audience and personal fable are the stuff of identity formation. Such stuff is much influenced by relationship and gender expectations. We have come round to the end now, and a brief quote from Jerome Bruner (1986: 130, emphasis in original) to emphasize once again that identity is a narrative that depends on self-reflection:

> I think of Self as a text about how one is situated with respect to others and toward the world – a canonical text about powers and skills and dispositions that change as one's situation changes from young to old, from one kind of setting to another. The interpretation of this text . . . by an individual *is* his (sic) sense of self in that situation.

# Chapter 12

# Gender and contrasexuality: Jung's contribution and beyond

> Sexuality belongs in this area of instability played out in the register of demand and desire, each sex coming to stand, mythically and exclusively, for that which could satisfy and complete the other. It is when the categories of "male" and "female" are seen to represent an absolute and complementary division that they fall prey to a mystification in which the difficulty of sexuality instantly disappears.
>
> (Rose, 1982: 33)

The universal division of the human community into two sexes, marked by signs and symbols of gender, has enduring and powerful effects on our psychological functioning as individuals, couples, and groups. Not only are we born into ongoing stories about our own and the opposite sex, stories that constrain and engender possibilities for action and identity, but also we form strong internal images of femininity and masculinity. While we identify with one, we develop an unconscious complex around the Other (I capitalize the subjective Other to distinguish it from the interpersonal other).

Gender is a central organizer of interpersonal reality. It carries so much meaning that we feel compelled to get it established quickly, both at the birth of an infant and in any instance in which we encounter a stranger. "What is this person's sex?" is a question that opens the way to fantasy, symbol, and speech. Any confusion or obscuration of a person's gender creates anxiety. How can I address, act, or engage this person unless I am sure about the category that will determine so much of what I shall expect and perceive?

There are many fertile conscious and unconscious consequences of the division into two genders. Rarely have they been treated seriously within depth psychology without being tied to some biological and/or essentialist argument that women and men are "born that way." Then the mysteries of sexuality are reduced to formulas about differences that should be or just are. This leads to psychological theories about what is missing, left out, or diminished in one or the other sex. Since most theories of depth psychology have been androcentric (taking male people to be the standard for health and success), most theories of gender and sex have described female people in terms of deficits – *lack* of penis, power, moral fiber, cultural strivings, or intelligence – and have assumed that female people are "naturally" depressed, narcissistic, envious. Although there have been exceptions to this, particularly among object relations theorists and feminist psycho-analysts who may see envy belonging to both sexes, most psychodynamic theorizing about gender has been flawed by reducing sex differences to a formula that imitates stereotypes.

Jung's psychology is in some ways an exception to this. Jung loudly calls our attention to one important theme in regard to sex differences: the opposite sex as a projection-making factor. He invites us to see aspects of ourselves that are denied to consciousness (because they are intolerably awful or idealized) through our projections into others. His theory of contrasexuality, that everyone has a biologically based opposite-sexed personality derived from genetic traces of the other sex (hormonal, morphological, and the like), *is* tainted by essentialism but clear about its psychological domain. This condition creates an Other within, an unconscious subpersonality. That subpersonality has a life of its own, usually dissociated, and often projected onto the opposite sex, a fetish, or an aspect of the world, in order to defend the self against anxiety and conflict.

Jung's theory of anima and animus (the Latin names he gave to these subpersonalities) as archetypes is both a cultural analysis of universal opposites, and a psychological theory of "projection-making factors." The anima of Jung's theory, the feminine subpersonality of a male person, and the animus, the masculine subpersonality of a female person, are biologically driven natural evolutions of contrasexuality. Although they develop throughout life, they come into play especially at mid-life because of the shifting nature of identity development in that era. Expressed as emotionally laden images, these archetypes structure what is latent of the opposite sex in each of us, a sort of soul-mate of both ideal and devalued potentials. Jung's contrasexuality is a contribution to depth psychology that problematizes the "opposite sex," tracing the shadow of Otherness back to its owner. In contrast to Freud's narrowly focused theories of castration anxiety and penis envy (which centralize the penis, the phallus, and the power of the male), Jung's gender theory is fluid and expansive in its potential uses in a postmodern, decentered world. Long before object relations theorists (such as Melanie Klein, Ronald Fairbairn, or Wilfred Bion in the earlier group, or Thomas Ogden, James Grotstein, or Stephen Mitchell among contemporaries) conceived of personality as decentered into autonomous suborganizations, Jung had developed a dissociative model of personality with a major emphasis on the split in identity between the conscious gendered self and the less conscious (or unconscious) contrasexual Other.

In my practice and theorizing (Young-Eisendrath, 1993; Young-Eisendrath and Wiedemann, 1987) of analytical psychology, I have revised the definitions of contrasexuality and anima/animus in response to contemporary critiques of feminism and constructivism. In my view, as in the view of many other psychoanalysts, these critiques have effectively undermined beliefs in universal gender differences, in ways of being that are biologically "masculine" or "feminine." Instead of archetypes of masculine, feminine, anima or animus, I focus on the universal opposition or dichotomy of a split-gender world. The two sexes imagined as opposites, as carrying complementary potentials, are spun out into many psychological, cultural, and social fantasies and symbols. As psychologist Gisela Labouvie-Vief (1994: 29, emphasis in original) says of the cultural constructs of gender:

> They not only *reflect* certain inner self-identifications and outer social realities, but they also come to *create* those very inner and outer realities. Thus, the resulting language of gender attributions becomes a framework within which developing selves define themselves, attempting to validate their "appropriateness" as men and women in culture.

Before exploring some cultural and clinical applications of this revised Jungian theory of gender and contrasexuality, it's useful to specify some definitions.

## Sex and gender

I differentiate between sex (as in sex differences) and gender. The "sex" we are born as and the "gender" we are assigned at birth do not add up to being the same thing, although one flows from the other. Sex is the difference of embodiment, the structural and functional properties of the human body (including hormones and brain structure) that provide both possibilities for and constraints on who we can be. Most of these relate to reproductive life in some way, although there are biological differences between the sexes – such as mortality differences at birth and longevity – that stand outside our reproductive period.

Gender is the identity club, the social category, that we are assigned at birth (and now sometimes sooner, thanks to ultrasound tests) based on the sex of the body. Whereas sex is inflexible, gender identities vary from culture to culture, even from family to family. In some societies, for example, men are expected to be more nurturant and home-oriented than women, taking care of the young (see Sanday, 1981, for description of a West Sumatran tribe). In our North American and European societies, men are usually expected to be more autonomous than nurturant, but in some subcultures in North America that may vary. Young Iranian males (even in America), for example, as anthropologist Mary Catherine Bateson (1994: 60) describes them, separate from their parents much more gradually than Americans, are often expected to sacrifice for their mother's care, and are respected by older males for doing so, and as she puts it, "American culture has gone further than most in valuing the autonomous self, downplaying the importance of relationship. It was once virtually unique, for instance, in the preference for having infants sleep alone."

The way a culture plays out the opposition of autonomy and dependence is often reflected in the roles expected of the two sexes. When the arenas of nurturance and relationship are not highly valued, they tend to be assigned to female people. When they are more valued they belong to both sexes and individuality is often downplayed (see Sanday, 1981, for a full discussion of this).

There is also evidence that people may have different gender expectations in different contexts, depending on whether they are making judgments about themselves or others (Spence and Sawin, 1985). North American men, for example, tend to use categories of strength or size to evaluate their own gender whereas women use roles, such as mother or wife, to evaluate theirs. And yet both sexes tend to regard gender as a "fact of life" – not as a construction based on their socialization. Most of us confuse the immutability of sexual characteristics with the variability of gender. From all available studies of sex and gender differences, it appears that *no* longstanding personality traits are connected to any consistent differences between female and male people (MacCoby, 1990; Unger, 1989: 22).

Once we see gender as culturally constructed – as female and male people assigned into roles, identities, and status – biological explanations of sex differences lose their explanatory force. Not only are we not "born that way" but roles and identities of women and men are shifting almost by the moment in all major societies – with one exception. Men continue to have more power than women, both status and decision-making power, in all major societies. To threaten this power dichotomy (that men are more powerful and women less) is to threaten the fabric of civilized life. Major economic systems of the world depend on the unpaid and underpaid labor of female people (see Young-Eisendrath, 1993, Chs. 1–3 for a full discussion). Most of us, both women and men, feel uncomfortable about women out-earning men in the workplace, women playing major political roles, and females being the majority (as they are) in today's world. The relative flexibility of gender roles and the power difference between the sexes have to be acknowledged in any contemporary account of gender, inside or outside the therapeutic consulting room. The changing meanings of gender, the recognition that it's constructed, and the enduring effects of male dominance are as significant in doing Jungian analysis as they are in revising Jung's theory to be applicable to contemporary life.

When people insist on a strong division between the sexes, and assume that women are naturally more relational and men naturally more autonomous, they risk losing parts of themselves forever. Externalization of these parts through projection, envy, and idealization can become a way of life. Romantic partners may be consciously or unconsciously chosen because of their willingness to carry idealized or devalued parts of the self. As psychoanalyst Evelyn Cleavely (1993: 65) says,

> In . . . choosing a partner who for reasons of his own is willing to receive certain projections, it is possible to have unwanted aspects projected outside oneself and at the same time remain in vital contact with them in the other. What is projected into and rediscovered in the partner is then treated in the same way as it was treated in the self. What you cannot stand in yourself, you locate and attack (or nurture) in the other.

Projections into those close at hand are played out through the internal theater of projective identification, an unconscious *participation mystique*. The mystique of projective identification is its uncanny capacity to evoke in another, often an intimate other, the most dreaded or idealized aspects of the self.

## Projection, projective identification and splitting

Although Jung did not fully understand projective identification, he noted the power of mixing up two people's unconscious dynamics in analysis, psychotherapy, and marriage. Using the sociological term coined by Lévy-Bruhl, *participation mystique*, to name the condition, he was undoubtedly referring to the same phenomenon that was later called "projective identification" by object relations theorists from Klein to Ogden. Bion (1952) was probably the first to emphasize the interpersonal component of projective identification. He described the feelings of the recipient of the projection as "being manipulated so as to be playing a part, no matter how difficult to recognize, in somebody else's phantasy" (p. 149). The recipient feels almost kidnapped or coerced into carrying out the unconscious fantasy of the projector. Only through a struggle to be conscious and differentiated can the recipient resist the pull and symbolize the experience, essentially making the projection available to be recognized by the projector.

When gender is strongly dichotomized, in an individual or a group, people lose parts of themselves by "proving" that the others are exclusive owners. For example, if I see myself simply as a giving, feminine person, then I am likely to project my more demanding and aggressive aspects into others, especially men if I believe stereotypes about men being naturally aggressive, and self-interested. By implying that my motives are *never* self-interested, I can evoke in my male partner an annoyed or aggressive statement, "showing" myself that *he's* the aggressive one.

Men may fail to recognize their own nurturant and relational capacities if they "see" them as merely natural to women. Women may silence the voice of their own authority if they assume that men are more rational, decisive, or objective by nature, and so on. The effect of projection is to externalize aspects of oneself and "meet" them in other people, animals, or things. The effect of projective identification is to evoke in another what has been externalized from the self, and then to "prove" that the quality or aspect belongs to the other and not to the self. As psychoanalyst Jacqueline Rose (1982) says in the opening quotation, the mystery of sexuality, as a contrapuntal play of opposites, is obscured and even lost when the two sexes are seen as absolute and complementary divisions. Then the content is set and nothing new can be evoked, nothing new can be discovered, and aspects of both sexes are forever lost to themselves.

Too often Jungian theory has portrayed the sexes as a complementary division of the masculine and the feminine. This has led to a defensive splitting of interpersonal and intrapsychic worlds, both in theorizing and in practice. Each sex then seems to represent a preset part of the human experience. The meaning of "masculinity, men and maleness" in this kind of theory is Logos, rationality, independence, and objectivity. The meaning of "femininity, women and femaleness" is Eros, connectedness, and subjectivism. This is the picture of the two sexes that Jung painted, reflecting the biases of his cultural era.

Stretching beyond those biases, though, he added the concept of contrasexuality, the potential of each sex to develop the qualities and aspects of its opposite in the second half of life, through the process of individuation, the completion of the self. Accordingly, each sex could integrate its opposite at a time in life when reflection and personal creativity might be enhanced, after one had taken one's place in society and attained one's "appropriate" gender development. Critiques of Jungian gender-splitting have been written by many Jungian theorists: Demaris Wehr (1987); Polly Young-Eisendrath and Florence Wiedemann (1987); Mary Ann Mattoon and Jennifer Jones (1987); Andrew Samuels (1989); Claire Douglas (1990); Deldon McNeely (1991); and Polly Young-Eisendrath (1993), among others. Several strategies have been proposed for revising Jung's theory of anima and animus: (1) assume that gender identity is flexible and that everyone, male and female, has both anima and animus, recognized as unconscious prototypical femininity and masculinity; (2) assume that gender identity is flexible, but that biology is the greater determinant of sex differences, and that anima and animus are archetypes related to biological substrata of sexuality, leaving males exclusively with anima, and females with animus; and (3) assume that gender is flexible but that the division into two sexes is not, and hence keep the idea of anima and animus as unconscious *complexes* of the "opposite sex," affectively charged images of the Other(s) as they arise in an individual, family, or society.

I subscribe to the third strategy. Because of its yield of theoretical richness in considering the effect of projection and projective identification, and its clinical usefulness in helping individuals and couples change, I use Jung's concepts of anima/animus as a theory of contrasexuality: psychological complexes of the opposite sex in each of us. This theory includes accounts of sex differences in embodiment (inherent possibilities and limitations) that lead to envy and idealization of the opposite; of the universal division into opposites; and of gender as fluid constructions that change over time and contexts. In my approach, the term "animus" refers exclusively to the contrasexual complex of a woman, and "anima" to that of a man, highlighting the exclusive nature of gender and sex: no one can be *both* genders or sexes, and there is no third possibility.

The division of the symbolic order (that is, language, image, and expression) into opposites leads to an intrapsychic division between a conscious identity of female or male, and a contrasexual complex of its opposite. Both ego and Other are emotionally charged psychological complexes organized around archetypes. The core of ego is the archetype of self; the core of Other is the archetype of contrasexuality (opposite sex). Ego and Other are expressed in images, habits, thoughts, actions, and meanings that arise and are sustained in a matrix of relationships. Thomas Ogden (1994: 95) in depicting Ronald Fairbairn's theory of "internal objects" describes the way in which psychological complexes (internal objects, in his language) operate within the overall personality:

> When Fairbairn says that internal objects are not "mere objects" but dynamic structures, he seems to mean that . . . internal figures are not simply mental representations of objects, but are active agencies whose activity is perceived by itself and by other dynamic structures to have specific characteristics.

These characteristics are easily ascertained in regard to the ego complex, the most conscious subpersonality, but recognizing the "active agency" of animus or anima is difficult. It usually requires self-awareness and a psychological understanding: the capacity to recognize and claim what has been projected into a partner, lover, friend, parent, child, or therapist.

What makes contrasexuality such a powerful emotional determinant of development is its unique relationship to the ego: the contrasexual Other constrains and defines what the ego can be. The way I act and imagine myself as a woman carries with it a limitation in terms of what I consider to be "not-woman," male, masculine, not-self. The contrasexual complex is paradoxically the product of a gendered self. What for a man is anima, or in the term I (Young-Eisendrath, 1993) used elsewhere, his feminine "dream lover," in its positive or negative aspects, is the product of that man's masculinity, what he permits himself to be as a man. What for a woman is animus, her masculine dream lover, is similarly a product of her femininity. Our fantasies of the truly opposite sex are based on what we exclude from the self.

When gender is strongly dichotomized and the world is split into two, masculine and feminine, then an individual is likely to defend the self by splitting off the contrasexual complex entirely, seeing it exclusively in others. There are many symptoms of this on a broad cultural level. Witness fiction, movies, and visual arts in which female people are portrayed as powerful madonnas, whores, overwhelmingly seductive or destructive mothers, bitches, witches, hag mothers-in-law, and so on. These images are legion and they are mostly the product of male contrasexuality, the emotionally charged images, habits, thoughts, actions, and meanings that arise from being a male in a society that fears female power. They depict little about what it means to be female, and yet they may be internalized by female people through a kind of cultural introjection. Female identity has been culturally created as emotionally powerful (often in a negative way), in which female people are expected to lack authority and decision-making power. Images of men's dream lovers tap into familiar feelings and identity issues in female people, but they are not authentic portraits of female lives.

What about female dream lovers? Because women's impact on culture has burgeoned in the last twenty-five years, we now have access to female contrasexual complexes in movies, fiction, and art. Witness demonic and overpowering bully men, developmentally and relationally incompetent lost boys, sensitive erotic heroes, and androgynous lovers. To some extent men are internalizing these projections of female contrasexuality, especially the "they just don't get it" component of the incompetent lost boy. Many adult men come to couples therapy with the complaint that they "just don't get it" and can't seem to figure out why their partners are complaining and/or why their (the men's) methods of communication fail. When contrasexuality remains projected, it permeates the world around and creates barriers to further development, barriers that may never be crossed if strong dichotomizing of the sexes persists over a lifetime.

## Individuation, self-awareness and transcendent function

Jung described individuation as a recognition and integration of inner conflicts, conscious and unconscious complexes, including contrasexuality. This awareness of self-division brings with it a new kind of freedom, a knowledge of the complexity of one's own nature, and an ability to "disidentify" with aspects of it. By disidentify, I mean to see, label, and acknowledge aspects of personality *without* enacting them. This involves developing self-reflection to include both knowledge and choice about one's motives. Although everyone has the potential to develop self-awareness, and to become relatively freed up from childhood and other complexes, only some people actually do. Everyone's invited, but few arrive at individuation – the experience of "psychic totality," in Jung's words.

The door to individuation often opens through the experience of neurosis: self-dividedness in its first bold sweep. Relational disillusionment, lack of agency, the inability to meet one's goals no matter how hard one tries, and painful enactments of negative complexes (e.g., acting like your aggressive father, your depressed mother, or the child who was victim) are the usual wake-up calls. Our wishes and fantasies depose realistic goals and our decision-making seems impossibly impeded. So long as our childhood complexes are the structures on which "reality" rests, either by unconsciously identifying with being children and projecting the parental image, or by identifying with being the aggressive parent and projecting the powerless child, then we are unable to feel our own dividedness.

A person unable to feel self-division is not a "psychological individual," in Jung's terms, not capable of self-reflection and personal meaning. Such a person believes that meaning comes entirely from "the way things are" and "the way we were born." Ask such a person, even a symptomatic person (an addict or an eating-disordered person, for instance), why she believes what she does when the belief seems patently irrational, and you will hear "because it's true." There's no awareness of the frame of reference, the assumptions, the emotions that color the "truth."

Many adults in North America and Europe live without self-awareness; they are not psychological individuals. They develop instead through tradition and ritual. Although its possible to become a psychological individual on the path of tradition and ritual (certainly in some traditions, such as Buddhism, this is a part of the design), many who conform to traditions remain as psychological children throughout adulthood. They are not aware of the subjective factors of their experience, nor do they feel responsible for the lives they've lived.

Some cultures seem to invite neurosis. They value diversity and individuality, rather than homogeneity or community. The individual code is more salient than the collective and people are likely to encounter a lot of conflict about what is ideal, true, and desirable. This kind of society, such as North American democracies, produces social chaos and hierarchical individualism, but it also engenders individual freedoms and felt inner conflict. People are regularly confronted by *differences* of ideals, desires, and the like, and those differences are validated by the culture. By contrast, other societies value sharing and non-competitive community in such a way that neurosis is less likely to develop. There may be no acute awareness of self, self-division, individual needs and truths in such a communal society.

Collective traditions provide the means for orderly development across the life span. Perhaps the only readily available means of development for those of us without clear traditions is psychological awareness. Through such awareness, we gradually create order from inner chaos and begin to take responsibility for our own subjective states.

What happens to people who never fall into self-dividedness or never resolve it? According to Jung, identification with the "persona" both precedes experience of self-dividedness and may prevent the experience altogether. Jung's persona, the defensive mask that presents oneself in a role or "social look," comes into being with identity formation in child-hood. One appears as one is "supposed to act." In adolescence, among those in cultures of individuality, the persona takes on the function of *appearing* as a psychological individual at a time when *uniqueness* is hyper-valued but as yet a complete mystery to the individual. The persona then functions as a pretend-individuality, as a posture of uniqueness that has been imitated. Psychoanalyst D.W. Winnicott's concept of a "false self" (defense of a true self core) is comparable in many ways to Jung's persona, but the false self is originally and primarily pathological. The persona is originally adaptive, a function of imitating or enacting a way of being prior to understanding it. The persona only *becomes* pathological if it prevents the development of self-awareness, authenticity, and other capacities after early adulthood.

When self-searching adolescents ask themselves the question "Who am I?," they answer in terms of the persona: either imitating or opposing received values and ideals. Under ordinary conditions, without childhood trauma, the persona of late adolescence is "only a mask of the collective psyche, a mask that *feigns individuality*, making others and oneself believe that one is individual" (Jung, 1917/1966a: 157, emphases in original).

In order to become self-aware, a person must break the identification with the persona and take responsibility for the multiple voices of sub-jectivity in the self. As Jung (1917/1966b: 20) sees it, neurosis is often the first opportunity to make this developmental move:

> Neurosis is self-division. In most people the cause of the division is that the conscious mind wants to hang on to its moral ideal, while the unconscious strives after its . . . unmoral ideal which the conscious mind tries to deny.

Neurotic conflict leads to loss of self-control, and this loss often brings the individual to question her or his motives or ideals.

The goal of individuation is the power to draw on the transcendent function, the tension and interplay of opposites, in everyday life. In order to reach this goal, one must develop "metacognitive processes" – the capacity to think about and entertain one's own subjective states from different perspectives. To do this, one begins to see oneself not merely from the perspective of the conscious ego complex, nor merely from a complex-related hyper-emotional ("gut feelings") perspective. Instead one can find a "third" point of view from which both of the others can be entertained and looked at without impulsively enacting them. This third perspective is the transcendent function (comparable to Winnicott's "potential space") from which one can engage in a dialectical relationship with aspects of oneself. Theoretically, Jung believes that this function illustrates the existence of an underlying self that is a "supraordinate subject" (Jung, 1917/1966c: 240). Experientially, one comes to witness and accept a range of subjective states without blame and with a certain playfulness or lightness of being. The usual outcome of this process is greater courage, insight, empathy, and creativity – means for uniting the opposites, as Jung would say.

## Gender and contrasexuality in neurosis and individuation

> Just as early development is experienced in terms of different primary paths for boys and girls, so later development is experienced differently for men and women. The primary issues of identity and development for men revolve around a sense of loss and disempowerment as they upgrade modes of knowing and ways of being that they previously experienced as "feminine." In contrast, the main focus for women's development is a deidealization of the "masculine" as they struggle with issues of personal empowerment.
>
> (Labouvie-Vief, 1994: 18)

The all-important persona of adolescence includes roles and identities of masculinity and femininity that are powerful and often consuming for young people. Female people are encouraged to evaluate their worth in terms of appearance, and to believe that they are secondary to male people in strength and intelligence. Even these days, when some young women may be encouraged to see themselves as "equals," they are still more fully rewarded for their appearances (slenderness and beauty) than for their performances in athletics, academia or human service.

Journalist and author Naomi Wolf (1991) calls our contemporary demands on the female body a "beauty myth." She reminds us that adolescent girls are socialized to become objects of desire, rather than subjects of their own desires. In the midst of the gains women have made in claiming and developing their own authority, the beauty myth is still recited as an essential truth based on biological ideology, as Wolf (p. 12) describes it:

> The quality "beauty" objectively and universally exists. Women must want to embody it and men must want to possess women who embody

it. This embodiment is an imperative for women and not for men . . . because it is biological, sexual, and evolutionary: Strong men battle for beautiful women, and beautiful women are more reproductively successful.

This mystifying gender dichotomy of "strong" men and "beautiful" women holds sway over adolescence, and carries major implications for later developments in neurosis and individuation.

The double bind of female authority comes into play for the first time in adolescence. If young women claim their authority too directly they will be regarded as "too much" – too emotional, too pushy, too intellectual, too aggressive, or too masculine. If they disclaim their authority, on the other hand, they will be treated as "too little" – too dependent, weak, immature or even emotionally disordered. No matter how a woman deals with her authority, she will inevitably get it "wrong" because the whole issue is a double bind (for a fuller discussion, see Young-Eisendrath and Wiedemann, 1987). As female people are socialized to be marginal or secondary to men, the contrasexual complex of strengths, intelligence, and competence is dissociated or projected into male people and institutions. Then young women identify themselves as being flawed, problematic, weak, or incompetent. Overall, adolescent women underestimate their strengths and abilities, and rely on the resources of their appearances for self-esteem (if they feel the resources aren't there, then their self-esteem drops).

Adolescent boys, on the other hand, are encouraged to overestimate their abilities and possibilities. They tend to see the world as "a man's world," and often fall into an inflation of the persona based on an identification with being uniquely athletic, strong, intelligent, or creative. Discouraged in feeling their weakness or failures, young males may believe they are exempt from the ordinary constraints of life and pursue activities that are obviously dangerous and foolhardy. The persona of a young white male is shaped around themes of success, competition, strength, and independence. The dissociated contrasexual complex of weakness, limitation, dependence, personal need, and vulnerability is viewed as "feminine" and often thought to belong exclusively to females. Even when young men see themselves as sensitive, creative, and expressive, they tend to believe that these qualities are powerful and unique in a way that reflects their differential privilege and status in the symbolic order.

Often it takes a decade or two of adult life before the male persona begins to erode. In mid-life especially, many men become painfully disappointed in what they have not achieved: the recognition and friends they have not amassed, the status and power they have failed to collect, the money and material goods that have slipped through their fingers. Some men are confronted by family members at this point about what is missing in their relationships.

In otherwise healthy men, the neurotic breakdown of the persona usually includes depression in the face of what seems to be missing in the self. Men who earlier fell prey to an inflation of the persona will have become narcissistic, defending themselves absolutely against feeling their dependence on others. Other men may have experienced an inflation of the ego, and suffered manic, compulsive, or anxiety states in demanding success from themselves. When the youthful persona cracks, most men experience a profound despair about ever finding the missing qualities or abilities in themselves because of the adolescent inflation of the persona or ego. Rather than *blaming* themselves (as women will do, as I discuss in a moment), they feel helpless. The gap between the previously inflated persona or ego and the current recognition seems impossibly large.

For women, the situation is usually quite different. Because women have so many confrontations with the double bind of female authority and the impossibility of "getting things right," they often come to neurosis earlier as a kind of identity crisis precipitated by problems at work, in child-rearing, in romance. They see themselves as the reason things have gone awry. Self-blame and feelings of inferiority are the two most common neurotic symptoms I see in women who come for psychotherapy. In the case of otherwise healthy women, without childhood trauma, the double bind of female authority is often the door leading to neurosis.

The developmental tasks for a woman are to recognize the disclaimed and dissociated authority, competence, goodness and/or power that she has seen as belonging to others, and to dissolve the persona of adolescent femininity. Although the traditional psychoanalytic jargon is "increasing ego strength," I find the Jungian concepts more useful clinically. The persona of appearance-as-worth (or the "unattractive" self as inferior), the contrasexual complex of disclaimed abilities, and the mother complex are, more often than ego strength, the issues of psychotherapy with adult women in my practice. Such a woman has often justified and defended her feelings of inferiority and self-blame through an unconscious identification with a depressed or unfulfilled mother, and the projection of her own (the woman's) strengths into others. She cannot use her own aggression, anger or authority confidently on her own behalf, nor can she count on her intelligence or knowledge. A typical example is a woman in her early thirties with a college degree, rearing two children, working in a profession, who finds herself to be completely devoid of abilities and unable to make decisions for herself. She often feels dissatisfied or angry, but cannot decide what she wants. The integration into conscious subjectivity of the disclaimed contrasexual complex, the dissolution of the adolescent persona of female inferiority and the analysis of the depressed resentful mother complex clear the path for individuation. The goal is to be able to recognize the various subjective complexes of her personality, to know something of the biography of each one, and to keep a perspective that is flexible and creative.

What happens in psychotherapy with a despairing mid-life man? Often the experience of depression and loss must first be encountered in terms of the projected and dissociated feminine complex. Being able to feel and see one's dependence, personal needs, and weaknesses is a liberating but not uplifting experience. In recognizing and expressing these, though, a man is gradually able to find in himself the missing parts or resources that originally seemed impossible to envision. Often these resources lie within his relationships with others as well as in his ability to treat himself more gently with less expectation to be perfect, successful, ambitious, constantly able, and the like.

Accurate empathy and mirroring of vulnerability and need are especially important for allowing the contrasexual complex to emerge in psychotherapy with mid-life men. The mother complex may have colored a man's experience of his contrasexuality for the years he's been identified with the persona. A great sensitivity to male experience is required of the female therapist who is likely to be seen as a powerful (either seductive or punitive) mother within the transference. One man I saw for some years, who was reworking his narcissistic, demanding, but indulgent mother complex was startled when I said something about the *difference* between admiration and love. "Are they really different?" he asked innocently. I quickly alerted myself to hear this question, not as defensive, but from a person who had deeply and genuinely confused the two. He'd been greatly admired for his athletic and intellectual abilities in adolescence, and had identified with an invulnerability to failure or defeat. He was now facing open-heart surgery at a relatively young age, and couldn't imagine how this had come about. He distrusted any statement of affection if it sounded too close to sympathy, and he frequently echoed his mother complex in saying he couldn't tolerate incompetence. His contrasexuality was split between a "beautiful but demanding" bitch and a "feminine, admiring" young woman whom he found erotic. The integration of the contrasexual complex in this case included his ability to feel his own dependency needs, to express his weaknesses and fears, and to sense very clearly how emotionally powerful he was in his relation to his wife and children.

Encounters with the contrasexual are the stuff of couples psychotherapy, especially with heterosexual couples, where projective identification is frequently the major suffering of a wounded couple. Each member enacts the most ideal, dreaded, and primitive aspects of the other in a way that drives both partners crazy. With the knowledge of contrasexual complexes, especially their social and cultural connections to gender, a psychotherapist is able to assist couples in transforming deadening antagonisms and painful attacks into effective dialogue (see Young-Eisendrath, 1993, for a full discussion).

A Jungian approach to psychotherapy with couples is an unusually rich psychoanalytic approach to resistant unconscious dynamics between partners. Lifting into consciousness the Others within, Jungian therapy with couples creates a space, a dialogical space, in which partners can encounter the transcendent function in conflicts. By containing the tensions of projected "opposites" and reflecting their meanings to each other, partners discover that their marriage is a "psychological relationship," as Jung (1925/1954: 187) called it in an essay published in 1925. By this he meant *not* a therapeutic relationship, but a sacred space in which each partner encounters both the dreaded and the ideal through the other's reflections. Then an intimate relationship is a place of individuation for both partners as they reflect each other through mirroring transformations, and discover a playful attitude for dealing with the demons and whores of contra-sexuality. The goal is to protect the safe, committed space of an intimate friendship while taking responsibility for primitive destructive and creative demands of contrasexuality. Although conflict and difference are always components of any intimate friendship, especially a marriage or committed partnership, they take on new meaning when they become a progressive uncovering of truths about oneself.

## Conclusion

By recognizing that the experience of being a person consists of multiple subjectivities, Jung has been prescient in providing contemporary psycho-analysis with an understanding of the projection-making factors of oppo-siteness in sex and gender. Still, Jung's cultural biases and tendencies to universalize gender differences need to be revised in the light of contem-porary findings of developmental and anthropological research on the sexes.

With this revision, his theory is freed to be more fluid and to move beyond the stereotyping of the sexes according to Jung's own cultural norms. This stereotyping has sometimes led Jungian therapists and theorists to assign preset formulas of masculine and feminine to people's experiences in place of discovering the meanings actual people have assigned to gender.

While theories are themselves only stories, and never more than particular stories, the theory of contrasexuality is particularly rich and fluid for understanding how people play out in their erotic relationships and fantasies what is most dreaded, desired, idealized, and excluded from the self. Integrating the meanings of contrasexuality, drawing on them for creative development and responsible partnership, is a major component of life-long individuation.

# Part 3

# Transference and transformation

# Chapter 13

# What's love got to do with it? Transference and transformation in psychoanalysis and psychotherapy

The song made popular by Tina Turner in the 1980s, which is also the title of this chapter, "What's Love Got to Do With It?," engages its listeners with clever and poignant lyrics that speak of ambivalence in love. "Who needs a heart when a heart can get broken?" is the rhetorical question posed in the refrain. This question naturally arises among certain lovers and parents and spouses and grown-up children who are skeptical, even cynical, about the effects of love in their lives. In both individual and couples psychotherapy, I have often heard a similar rhetorical question "Why should I say *I love you* when I don't even know if love exists?"

Outside of a psychotherapist's office, if stopped on the street, most people would casually claim more enthusiasm about love as a form of affection: they would say that they love their children, their pets, a warm sunny day, a new car. But when faced with the demands of a long-term intimate relationship, negotiations with a teenage child, care for an aging parent, disappointments with grown-up children, competitive relationships with siblings, many of those same people would become aware of ambivalent, perhaps even cynical, tinges around the edge of the warm glow of love.

Many North Americans would, I think, admit that they are skeptical about anything like "unconditional" love. This is the case, I believe, because of the widespread cultural influences of psychoanalysis in our society over the past one hundred years or so. There is both good news and bad news about these influences. On the good side, we are becoming more conscious of how difficult it is to be accountable for our own subjective experiences, to contain our impulses to react rather than respond to others. Increasingly, we see ourselves more realistically as the complex, conflicted, well-rationalized beings that we are. We may, for example, recognize how much parents and children both resent the long dependency of a human childhood. Some of us may even openly acknowledge how we entertain fantasies of complete control of others, especially those we try to love.

Psychoanalysis, our Western science of subjectivity, has shed light on the hidden ways in which human love is laced with ambivalence and with dominance–submission, abandonment–engulfment, attachment–separation, and dependence–independence struggles. From my perspective, it's good news that we are becoming more aware, and potentially more responsible, for the array of contrasting feelings that ride with us on the journey of love. The bad news is that we seem to be losing faith in love altogether. Many find little reason to commit themselves to the goals of love, particularly love for our own species, our families, our communities, and our partners – often much harder to love now than other species, other families, other communities, and other partners.

The influences of psychoanalysis have showed the ideal of unconditional human love to be false. This revelation invites a less romantic and more discerning psychology of love, but it also opens the door to cynicism, and even despair, about the surety of deep bonds between us. I, for one, vote for a more discerning psychology of love rather than cynicism about love itself. In this regard, I offer the following account of a transformative love that is part of the therapeutic action in a long-term psychoanalysis or psychotherapy. I will argue that our newly acquired analytic understanding of love can ease our doubt and cynicism by helping us understand more clearly the challenges of enduring love. Before I go into these particulars, I want to outline one extended example of differing contemporary views of love in order to give you the opportunity to see where your own feelings resonate. I will use the example of maternal love.

You may or may not know that in various branches of Eastern Buddhism, especially in branches of southeast Asian Buddhism and Tibetan Buddhism, maternal love is used as a metaphor to help practitioners cultivate the kind of love that is associated with a bodhisattva. A bodhisattva is a saintly figure who has sacrificed her or his own liberation in order to save all beings, knowing that no one can be truly liberated until *all* are freed from suffering. A bodhisattva dedicates her or his efforts to vast and expansive compassion, love, and concern. A particular Tibetan meditation for cultivating this attitude is called "Recognizing all beings as mother."

It begins by considering that whatever the present situation, in the course of infinite rebirths, every living person has been a mother. Focusing on the role of mother is said to help the meditator develop compassion. A meditator then recalls how mothers are evocative of kindness, reflecting then on one's own mother as an example of such kindness, how she "rocked me on her ten fingers," and how "though my birth itself caused her great suffering, she was as glad as if she had found a precious gem," and so on (described in Klein, 1995: 96–97) in paying tribute to one's mother's selfless love. From this reflection on one's mother's clear and pure love, there arises in the meditator a natural desire to repay her kindness and to give to others this loving kindness, especially because all persons have been mothers themselves.

When an American practitioner of Buddhism hears this traditional practice on the metaphor of maternal love, often there is a kind of cognitive dissonance. What? Reflecting on *my* mother's pure love will stir a natural desire to repay her kindness? Americans quite naturally regard a mother's love with more ambivalence, more awareness of the self-interests of the mother that are reflected in her love. Knowingly or unknowingly, we have been influenced by Freud's original theory of parental love as fundamentally narcissistic, a theory he argued very convincingly in a 1914 essay, "On Narcissism" (Freud, 1914/1963). Here Freud claimed that a parent's love, which seems so selfless on the surface, is both self-promoting and self-protecting. This theory has been extended and developed by many other analytic thinkers in these last eight decades. Both Alice Miller and Heinz Kohut have popularized psychologies of parental narcissism that have broadly affected our ways of thinking about mothers.

Indeed, we have become so skeptical of mother-love that many of us more readily empathize with the following passage from the diary of writer Sylvia Plath than we do with the Tibetan meditation on maternal love. Plath wrote in 1958 (see Kukil, 2000: 113):

> Doctor, can I still go on hating my mother? Of course you can; hate her hate her hate her. Thank you, Doctor. I sure do hate her . . . I don't imagine time will make me love her. I can pity her: she's had a lousy life; she doesn't know she's a walking vampire. But that is only pity. Not love.
>
> On top she is all smarmy nice: she gave herself to her children, and now by God they can give themselves back to her: why should they make her worry worry worry? She's had a hard life: married a man . . . who was older than her own mother . . . She suffered. Married to a man she didn't love. The Children were her salvation. She put them First. Herself bound to the track naked and the train called Life coming with a frown.

We have come to believe that the "selfless love" of a mother for her child is a far more complicated and problematic affair than the delight of finding a precious gem, as the Tibetan practice described.

## Transformative love

So how would I define love in this age of skepticism? Very much like the contemporary poet Octavio Paz who is quoted by the psychoanalyst Otto Kernberg (1995: 45) in his book about love. Kernberg comments on the "overwhelming conciseness" of the poet who states that, "love is the point of intersection between desire and reality. Love . . . reveals reality to desire and creates the transition from the erotic object to the beloved person . . .

Love is the revelation of the other person's freedom." This passage speaks of erotic love, but I believe these conditions hold for all forms of love – from erotic to maternal to spiritual.

In contemporary American society, love is often confused with romance, but it may also be confused with desire, wish, admiration and idealization. Whether it is maternal love for a child, childish love for a parent, erotic love, or transcendent love for whatever is perceived as divine, real love reveals reality and defeats the destructive aspects of mere desire.

Here is how I understand the process of transformative love that I will describe in relation to transference in a moment: it begins with desire or need and is expanded through idealization of the beloved, especially in regard to the resources the beloved will bring. This idealization is inevitably challenged by the reality of the other. The beloved will not supply what is desired. The recognition of this fact brings disappointment, bitterness, even rage or hatred. These destructive and hostile residues of desire are often expressed in negative projections and/or attacks on the other – or alternately on oneself, on the bonds of commitment, or on love itself. If the containment of commitment, or of the bonds of affection, repeatedly defeat and revise these destructive residues of desire, then *true* love emerges.

It emerges with the knowledge that the beloved (who is irreplaceable) is beyond one's control and command, especially with regard to one's own wishes, needs, whatever. Replacing the destructive demands of desire is the appreciation of the mystery, wonder and discovery in an ever unfolding relationship. Revealed in this unfolding are both the darker meanings of one's own desires, as well as one's responsibility and accountability for one's actions. Self and other are clarified as never fully predictable nor finally grasped. All the same, one feels one's dependence on the bonds of love and gratitude for love's survival.

### Transference and transformative love in analysis and therapy

This gratitude for the bonds of love is a particular experience of our interdependence. We humans have difficulty feeling our interdependence directly because of our universal tendency to experience ourselves as separate individuals, autonomous agents. Many methods and arguments in Buddhism, of which I am a long-term practitioner, are meant to lead to an experiential realization of our absolute interdependence, our interbeing. Effective psychoanalysis or long-term psychotherapy will, I believe, lead to a similar experience of interdependence through transformative love. I will now attempt to explain how this happens in terms of two kinds of transference, and a kinship relationship, that comprise the psychoanalytic enterprise.

By "transference" here, I mean the sustained projections of certain states, images, and feelings into another, in a way that prevents the recognition of the other as distinct from the projections. The first type of transference – which I call the "containing-transcendent" transference – is most crucial for the patient's experience of love in the treatment process. I have dubbed it the "containing-transcendent" transference, modifying the name used by contemporary psychoanalyst Arnold Modell (1990: 42–52) who called it the "dependent-containing transference". The importance of this transference cannot be overestimated in the therapeutic action of the treatment. It is filled with the hope for renewal, for the transformation of symptoms, and for the transcendence of suffering.

The containing-transcendent transference is first experienced as the patient's belief or hope that *this* particular therapist or analyst is knowledgeable and caring enough to be helpful and effective. Eventually, or sometimes even at the beginning of treatment, the patient may also imagine that the therapist is a highly developed or powerful person. I regard this as the transference of the patient's *own* unknown or unacknowledged potential to transform or transcend suffering. Everyone has this potential, but for most it is undeveloped, and tends to be projected onto others (who are seen as more authoritative or wiser than oneself) or felt only in moments of awe or inspiration.

In psychoanalytic psychotherapy and psychoanalysis, this transference is especially engendered by, and continues to be supported within, the constraints of the ethical commitments and therapeutic ritual of psychotherapy. The commitment to act ethically is usually encoded in various principles of the professions that therapists practice. The ritual is the regularity and predictability of the time, fee, and space for meetings. The ritual also entails ground rules that include confidentiality, the relative anonymity of the therapist, the intention of the therapist not to retaliate against the patient, and the absence of social chatter. Most therapists also have certain ways of speaking and acting that are part of their therapeutic manner. These constraints inherently endow the therapist with a certain power and image of being wise, compassionate, insightful enough to help the patient transcend symptoms, and transform suffering.

Indeed these constraints also assist the therapist/analyst in behaving in ways that are more *ideal* than she or he behaves typically at home. Psychoanalyst Irwin Hoffman (1998: 203, emphasis in original) says the following about what he calls the "mystique" of the analyst:

> the analyst is an authority whose regard for the patient matters in a special way . . . that . . . we do not try to analyze away, nor could we, perhaps, even if we did try . . . Regard for *the analyst* is fostered partly by the fact that the patient knows so much *less* about him or her than the analyst knows about the patient . . . The analyst is in a relatively protected position . . . that is likely to promote the most tolerant, understanding, and generous aspects of his or her personality. I think

of "idealization" partly in interactional terms (as in "making the other more ideal") because the analytic situation and often the patient actually do nourish some of the analyst's more "ideal" qualities as a person.

I believe that the *hope* fostered in this kind of transference matters more to the overall therapeutic action of a treatment than the specific technical proficiency of the therapist/analyst.

Hope is, I believe, what is called the "placebo effect" in studies of recovery from all sorts of illness and trauma. From these studies we know that hope is as powerful and effective as medicines and other physical interventions. The psychotherapy patient's experience of this containing-transcendent transference, connected specifically to a well-managed therapeutic set-up, may be her or his *first* encounter ever with someone or something that truly promises hope, a relief from symptoms, and the possibility that life is meaningful.

If we think of this containing transference as the outermost frame of three nested frameworks of analytic therapy, the next level inward is a second type of transference – the type we would usually call "transference." With Modell (1990: 46–52), I call it the "iconic-projective" transference. It refers especially to the ways in which people unconsciously project images, feelings, and other states from their early emotional self–other developments. Projecting these, they may unknowingly invite another to identify with and play them out in familiar ways. Such "projective identification" can be understood as a preconscious or unconscious communication that cannot be fully experienced or expressed by the initiator of the projection. A lot of everyday communication contains significant projective identifications in which people feel emotionally kidnapped and swept up into one another's internal psychic dramas in a way that is uncomfortable, exciting, and/or overwhelming.

In psychotherapy, projective identification can be made conscious, understood, and studied. It begins with the therapist having a distinctly strong sense of being invited to play out some kind of enactment that would be exciting, damaging or humiliating to the patient. If the therapist is able to put into words what is being invited, without arousing too much defensive resistance in the patient (who, after all, simply takes this to be part of "reality"), both patient and therapist will transform their perceptions of each other. In this way, an aspect of the patient's suffering will be opened to insight and the possibility of change. Within the iconic-projective transference, the patient's childhood complexes will be re-experienced in the therapy as though they were happening in the here and now. The therapist will gradually, but inevitably, seem to the patient to possess the habits or qualities of one parent or another, of an older sibling or a spouse. As the most vexing of these projections are interpreted, analyzed and understood, often more subtle and sometimes more powerful ones emerge. Eventually both therapist and patient are able to trace the emotional history of the patient's suffering through the themes of the iconic-projective transference.

The therapist's interpretations of unconscious themes, put into words, phrases, sentences, and gestures bring out into the open the emotional meanings that have been hidden from the patient's awareness. Therapeutic interpretations reflect especially on the ways the patient unknowingly creates suffering through engaging with others to reproduce certain dangers and excitements of childhood complexes. The therapist's ability to be helpful in uncovering these things is, of course, at the heart of the technical and professional training of all psychoanalytic approaches. The timing and technique of interpretation is often considered most critical in the trans-formative process because of the gains in personal accountability, aware-ness, and subjective freedom. And yet, the efficacy of interpretation is always grounded in the trust of a secure containing-transcendent frame.

The third level of the therapeutic encounter, at the center of the nested model I am using, is what I like to call a "kinship relationship" drawing on Jung's term of "kinship libido." It is often called the "real relationship" but all levels of the therapeutic encounter are real in their own ways. Of this kinship component, Jung (1946/1966: 233) says:

> To the extent that the transference is projection and nothing more, it divides quite as much as it connects. But experience teaches that there is one connection in the transference which does not break off with the severance of the projection. That is because there is an extremely important instinctive factor behind it: the kinship libido.

This kinship engenders "a satisfying feeling of belonging together" says Jung later in the same passage.

Within the kinship relationship, patient and therapist experience each other as equals, as human beings struggling together to try to bring about the amelioration of suffering in at least one of them, and more profoundly in both. The patient has hired the therapist to do a job that the therapist has been educated to do. The therapist, like any person, will be more or less able to perform satisfactorily on any particular occasion, relevant to the therapist's state of mind and body, and other factors.

Over time, both therapist and patient deeply appreciate the discovery process in which they are engaged, and recognize how they have depended on each other in the most unlikely moments when things have felt especially tense or frightening. This recognition of interdependence leads to the awareness in both that they suffer not alone, but with each other and others. I want to note that the effective therapist sometimes, perhaps often at times, feels confused and uncertain about the task of transformation.

Awareness of this vulnerability should allow the therapist to express interpretations and other interventions with openness and questioning.

The therapist feels and should convey the fact of her or his own unconsciousness and ignorance, as well. As Hoffman (1998: 216) says, ". . . analytic therapists in general can safely assume that they do not have privileged access to their own motives, nor are they able, despite their advantageous position, to know exactly what is best for their patients." The therapist's tolerance of uncertainty and respect for the interdependence of the therapeutic inquiry imply the therapist's acceptance of her or his own blindspots.

A realistic acknowledgment of the limitation of "expert authority" in the kinship relationship counterbalances the powerful forces of the containing-transcendent and iconic-projective transferences, showing how the therapist is open and unashamed in acknowledging human foibles. And yet this kind of realism must be handled skillfully so that the therapeutic setting also allows plenty of opportunity for experiencing the two forms of transference.

In everyday life, we are constantly immersed in iconic-projective transferences and kinship relationships with friends, family and strangers. These may provide opportunities for transformation through love, but only in an effective therapeutic relationship do we encounter a special situation in which we have framed the human condition, and its projective tendencies, in a way that tends to "nourish some of the analyst's more 'ideal' qualities as a person" (Hoffman, 1998: 203) and promote hope and a desire for self-understanding in the patient.

The "containing" function of the outermost frame of transference (that this relationship specifically serves a therapeutic function, and will not become romance or friendship) guarantees that both patient and therapist will encounter the ambivalence of love. All of the struggles of dominance–submission, abandonment–engulfment, attachment–separation, and dependence–independence, that I mentioned at the beginning, will ripen into major themes in the development of an effective long-term psychotherapy or analysis. These conflicts necessarily occur as part and parcel of the therapeutic set-up and are not derived primarily from the patient's past, although they may take the forms of iconic-projective transferences.

An effective psychotherapy or analysis moves through all of the stages of love: desire, idealization, challenge, testing, reality, acceptance, and continuing commitment and hope. Reality plays an important role in conflict with desire at all three levels of the therapeutic encounter: at the transcendent level, reality is present in the restrictions and rules of the set-up; at the projective level, reality enters with insight into the meaning of the patient's emotional past played out in the present; and at the kinship level, reality is the full acknowledgment of human imperfections in both therapist and patient, as well as the uncertainty of our knowledge about ourselves.

The patient's desires are sometimes framed by transcendent hope and sometimes by childish feelings and erotic wishes or a mix of these. These will have been transformed and tempered by insight throughout the process of therapy. Love for the therapist, however, even eroticized transcendent love, may increase, rather than diminish, over the course of treatment. Even long after the end of a successful psychotherapy or analysis, the patient's feelings will continue to be colored by the mystique of the transcendent-containing transference.

For this reason, the effective psychotherapist seems a little bigger and better than ordinary people in the eyes of her or his successful patients. The glow of transcendence will not have been extinguished through interpretations or empathy because it is partly in the nature of the therapeutic ritual and constraints. Generally speaking, it will have increased over time in an effective treatment because it tends to strengthen as the iconic-projective transference is interpreted and felt to be understood. To put this in other language, love for the therapist grows because the patient's suffering has been ameliorated.

The therapist's desires for the patient (to change, to succeed, and the like) will also have been transformed through the course of treatment, in part because of the effects of the therapist behaving ethically and compassionately, and in part because of insight into the patient's habits of mind or complexes. All sorts of encounters and discoveries will have revealed the patient to be a human being much like the therapist. This engenders love for the patient in the therapist, but of a different flavor from the transcendent love that colors the patient's feelings about the therapist.

## The demands of love in therapy and life

Psychotherapy was designed to transform individual pain and suffering, not specifically to engender love. And yet love, in the pattern of desire–challenge–reality–commitment greases the wheels of interpretation and empathy for both patient and therapist. In the development of compassion for the patient's suffering, both patient and therapist discover together what Jung (1916/1969: 67–91) calls a "transcendent function": the ability to contain tensions, conflicts, and other pressures. Even deciding whether a particular feeling, image or insight is "good" or "bad" gradually becomes unnecessary because the transcendent function creates a "space" in which meaning emerges and can be played with (see also Horne, 1998 and Young-Eisendrath, 1997c). This function allows both patient and therapist to keep an open mind in the face of unconscious impulses, desires, and needs.

Both patient and therapist make use of the containing-transcendent transference as a protective space in which to develop the transcendent function as well as other skills. In 1916, Jung (1916/1969: 74) wrote that this kind of transference portends a "renewal of attitude" and the patient:

seeks this change, which is vital to him, even though he may not be conscious of doing so. For the patient, therefore, the [therapist] has the character of an indispensable figure absolutely necessary for life. However infantile this dependence may appear to be, it expresses an extremely important demand which, if disappointed, often turns to bitter hatred.

If the promise of renewal is betrayed or trivialized, the patient may fall into a serious psychological illness or come to hate the therapist, or in the worst-case scenario, even commit suicide over this bitter disappointment.

The inchoate spiritual yearnings of a patient can be disrupted and even permanently betrayed through the rupture or dissolution of the containing-transcendent transference. This can happen through an ethical violation or gross mismanagement on the part of the therapist.

On a more subtle level, effectiveness can be breached through a chronic, sometimes unacknowledged, suspicion that this therapist is yet another inadequate, uninformed or unempathic authority figure who has broken the promise of renewal. If the patient regularly feels that she or he cannot speak truthfully or must protect the therapist, the containing-transcendent transference is compromised because the therapist is experienced as too weak or vulnerable to be idealized.

The transformative love that develops in the course of effective psychotherapy or analysis never really ends; it lives on forever in the hearts of both people of the therapeutic dyad, but more powerfully in the patient because of the lingering nature of the transcendent-containing transference. Even when idealization of the therapist has been "fully analyzed" in terms of envy and other aspects of the iconic-projective transference, this analysis will not have included the mystique of the role of therapist because this role cannot be deconstructed while therapy is going on.

Some people who have seen me in treatment over time will spontaneously confess to me, often during the termination process, that despite all of our analysis, they believe I *would* be a better life partner for them than the partner with whom they live. I take this privately to be a good sign that we have traveled the journey of transformative love. Usually I say something about deeply appreciating the feeling, recognizing it as being about the process of therapy, not about me personally. I know the feeling cannot be interpreted or explained away. I always say that I am honored and grateful that they have placed so much trust in me, and convey that I return the love, that our bond is important to me too. And it is: I often feel like the mother whose grown child is going forth into the world.

Handling this transcendent transference effectively is a great responsibility for those who take on the role of therapist or analyst. On the other hand – and this is critical – its power is not a *personal* matter. It arises spontaneously from the universal hope for the transformation of suffering.

This hope is, I believe, the source of all transformative love. Mistakenly identifying oneself personally with the power of the containing-transcendent transference leads to destructive errors and actions of which there are innumerable examples among therapists brought to attention for ethical misconduct.

Some of the charismatic leaders of therapeutic "movements" have unknowingly become identified themselves with this transference. A leader's demands for maintaining omnipotent control, or beliefs in being exempt from ordinary requirements, are symptoms of such an identification. Jung (1917/1966d: 133) referred to the containing-transcendent transference as a "god" transference and wrote, "Could the longing for a god be a passion welling up from our darkest, instinctual nature, a passion unswayed by any outside influences, deeper and perhaps the highest and truest meaning of that inappropriate love we call 'transference' . . ." I would put it more broadly and identify the hope for renewal and transformation as the root of the love inherent in the god transference.

## Love outside the consulting room

What about love outside the consulting room compared to love within? As I showed at the beginning, we have become skeptical consumers of love. Perhaps the effects of psychoanalysis have permanently cracked open our tendency to idealize love; perhaps we can stop love from masquerading as desire, wish, and admiration. Perhaps we can understand that love merely begins with desire and need. But perhaps we need also to understand that even these beginnings express a hope for renewal that "if disappointed often turns to bitter hatred." Perhaps our current cynicism about love is a collective expression of this very hatred. Because we have not known how to transform our desires and needs into love, we have been losing the hope of renewal that love promises. We have become unnecessarily cynical about love's ways.

Love, whether erotic or therapeutic or spiritual, demands our commitment to hope in the face of disillusionment, to reality in the face of our wishes, and to freedom for the individual in the face of our desires for omnipotent control. Psychotherapy creates an artificial environment so that people can study their emotional habit patterns in a framework of relative trust and openness. It helps us understand how containment and right conduct can contribute to the transformation of desire into love.

I believe that we can begin to take this more discerning psychology of love out of the consulting room, and into our lives, by recognizing the importance of containment and right conduct in coming to terms with the hope that love seeks. Psychoanalyst Otto Kernberg (1995: 44) says it like this, "Love is the revelation of the other person's freedom. The contradictory nature of love is that desire aspires to be fulfilled by the destruction of the desired object, and love discovers that this object is indestructible and cannot be substituted".

Within the therapeutic set-up, we preserve a space in which both patient and therapist develop the freedom of personal responsibility and the acknowledgment of human limitations. We deal with the conflicts of love by keeping hope alive. In psychotherapy, only one person is fully revealed while the other is somewhat veiled and idealized. In psychotherapy, there are rules for how to behave in order to protect hope. In life, none of these protections is automatically provided. But perhaps we can learn to bow to the potential for renewal and compassion that exists in every human being. Perhaps this potential deserves our respect whenever desire is directed our way. And if we are very careful, we may all become more discerning lovers rather than more cynical people.

# Chapter 14

# The transformation of human suffering: a perspective from psychotherapy and Buddhism

In my view, there are two main objectives that are shared by Buddhism and long-term analytic psychotherapy: the gain of a perspective and skill that alleviate personal suffering in everyday life, and an increase of compassion for self and others. Although my training as a psychoanalyst is Jungian, I have for many years been associated with institutions and settings that were mainly Freudian, object relational and/or intersubjective. Here, I mean to speak of the goals of psychotherapy and Buddhism in ways that are common to all analytic approaches to psychotherapy.

Clarifying the ways in which Buddhism and psychotherapy are both similar and different in their goals and methods should assist the practitioners of both in addressing the concerns of people who seek help for their suffering. Tracing the boundaries and domain of subjective distress, specifically *dukkha* as it is described in Buddhism, may also assist us in making scientific investigations of certain well-established methods and processes of the transformation of human suffering.

Throughout my development as a psychologist and psychoanalyst, I have been sustained and renewed through my own practice and study of Buddhism – first as a student of Zen and now of Vipassana. I became a Zen Buddhist in a formal ceremony in 1971, nine years before I received my Ph.D. in psychology in 1980, fifteen years before I received my diploma as a Jungian analyst. Recently, I have attempted to refine some of the concepts of analytic psychotherapy and psychoanalysis (e.g., Young-Eisendrath, 1996, 1997a, 1997b, 2000, 2001) drawing on my experiences in, and understanding of, a Buddhist approach to the transformation of suffering. Buddhism and feminism, the latter especially with regard to the effects of gender stereotypes and inequality, have assisted me in my work as an analytical psychotherapist over the past twenty years. Feminism has made me alert to the ways in which both Buddhism and psychoanalysis, like other institutionalized traditions, can oppress and oppose women and others through intentional or unintentional hierarchies and biases. Buddhism has helped me appreciate the importance of concentration, equanimity, and compassion in psychoanalytic work. Without Buddhism and feminism, I could not practice psychotherapy and psychoanalysis as I do. These two other practices have allowed me to see how human suffering, rooted in ignorance, can teach us compassion when we understand the meaning of our own suffering.

In my work as a Jungian psychoanalyst and psychotherapist, I have many opportunities, in both individual and couples therapy, to engage in the struggles of human suffering, and as many opportunities to test my compassion. In the following, I attempt to reflect on my own current encounter with the problem of suffering in my field of work. Prominent for me is the North American fear of even the topic of suffering. An American dread of suffering, based on ignorance about what suffering teaches and how it can be transformed, has recently led to more and more physicalistic and materialist explanations of our pain and adversity. Instead of recognizing the role of subjective distress – the ways in which disappointment, anguish, fear, envy, pride and hostility, for instance, contribute to our suffering – the American anti-suffering campaign now addresses people at the level of neurotransmitters, organ transplants, genetic engineering and biological determinism. This cultural movement has already had massive ill effects on the practice of psychiatry and psychotherapy over the past two decades in the USA, as I shall illustrate.

Particularly significant for me is the medical context that has come to surround the practice of psychotherapy. This context demands that therapeutic interventions be brief and assumes that long-term psychodynamic psychotherapy is of little benefit, especially for those people who have severe psychological difficulties. Only medication, electroconvulsive treatment, and/or brief behavioral interventions are promoted as truly effective. This cultural mood in America is especially the product of the decade of the 1990s and the dominance of the pharmaceutical industry in medical practices.

This mood is now expressed as a demand that human miseries be treated as quickly as possible. So-called "managed care" (*who's* managing and *who* cares?) and other stripped-down services for the ill and emotionally troubled have derailed both psychodynamic and humanistic therapeutic movements. In the twenty years prior to these influences, psychodynamic and humanistic psychologies had begun to encourage Americans to look into their suffering with a kind of interest that leads, inevitably I believe, to spiritual yearnings with regard to the concerns of suffering. Psychodynamic and humanistic therapies have now lost their ability to persuade the public, to acquire any substantial funding for systematic research, and to be fully included in most medical settings. In our current cultural *zeitgeist*, a new form of scientific materialism – biological determinism – has taken hold of the public imagination.

At the same time that this has been unfolding, Buddhism has become a major religious and cultural movement in North America in a way that no one could have easily anticipated in the early 1970s. As a result, Buddhism (especially in its popular Western forms of Zen, Vipassana, and Tibetan

Buddhism) has, perhaps surpisingly, opened up the possibility of a renewed appreciation of psychodynamic practices of psychotherapy. Because Buddhism presents a spiritual argument for the transformation (not the medication) of suffering, as well as specific and systematic methods of analyzing subjective distress, it now assists me in being able to address audiences about the priniciples and uses of analytic psychotherapy. Buddhism has much to offer psychotherapists and those who seek help from them. Buddhism has myriad time-tested approaches to understand and transform human misery. Psychotherapy also has something to offer Buddhism, especially in our study of personal unconscious emotional habit patterns or "psychological complexes." At this unique moment in history, North Americans can witness the powerful influx of ancient Asian teachings into our society when our own psychological sciences are being eroded by biological determinism and the economics of managed care.

## The spiritual problem of the end of the century

Carl Jung (1939/1992: 50) more than once said that science is the "spiritual adventure of our age". Science, with its skeptical and objective methods, allowed us to see that many powers we had projected into an animistic world were, in fact, our own. Jung described this as "the last step out of humanity's childhood, out of a world where mind-created figures populated a metaphysical heaven and hell" (p. 49). Science did not transcend metaphysics, however. It created its own metaphysics with widespread cultural consequences. For example, (1) science has awarded the names of "matter" and "energy" to the ultimate principles of existence and (2) this has led to radically different modern beliefs about human life – as for example the "scientific" conclusion that afterlife does not exist. Whether or not individuals actually understand this new metaphysics, we are all constantly influenced by it. For instance, the ways in which science has permitted humankind to explore and manipulate our phenomenal world (including our own bodies) leads us to speak of "miracles of science" that have largely replaced the miracles of religion in educated societies. Renowned geneticist and zoologist Richard Lewontin (1991: 8–9) of Harvard University says the following about how we have elevated scientific beliefs:

> Not only the methods and institutions of science are said to be above ordinary human relations but . . . the product of science is claimed to be a kind of universal truth. The secrets of nature are unlocked. Once the truth about nature is revealed, one must accept the facts of life.

Lewontin goes on to discuss Darwin's theory of evolution as a case in point. I would like to address this briefly as a prime example of a particular spiritual problem that marked the end of the twentieth century.

Much of our reasoning about human life and other beings on this planet now rests on the theory of natural selection. Most educated people believe (at least vaguely) in the scientific principle that the living organisms on earth have evolved over billions of years from other organisms that were unlike them, and are now mostly extinct. When this story is told of humanity, it wholly eliminates the role of personal meaning and human intentions in the development of societies and the lives of individuals. The "master molecule" of the gene, falsely endowed with an autonomous power, is most often used to explain personal desires, intentions, and actions. The term "gene" or "adaptation" has replaced intention, purpose, and meaning in most psychological accounts of the ways in which people thrive or fail to thrive in their everyday lives. All of our struggles, such as finding a mate or becoming a compassionate person, can now be recast in terms of their supposed "advantages" of leaving the greatest number of offspring.

When people seek psychotherapeutic or other kinds of psychosocial help, they now come with vague theories of biological determinism such as "I am depressed because I inherited depression from my mother's family." These people often continue to feel hopeless even after they have taken the appropriate medications, and comfort themselves with the company of their ancestors, because they do not understand why they suffer. Of course, this can be addressed through effective psychotherapy, but for those who never consider psychotherapy, and most people do not, these vague organic explanations only block any desire to understand the personal motives and meanings that lead to much or most of human suffering through our emotional habit patterns.

The belief that our own intentions and attitudes can change our actions, thoughts, and moods is now considered outmoded in many training programs for psychiatrists and psychologists in the USA. Many of the psychiatric residents that I have supervised in the past five years have no idea of how to talk with a patient about motivations and intentions, whether conscious or unconscious. These residents learn only how to diagnose symptoms and determine appropriate medications, and to conduct brief symptom-oriented counseling. Moreover, the suffering people who come to the offices of these newer psychiatrists are asked to believe that they will be cured by some form of biological intervention, not through a change of awareness or attitude.

A great deal of harm has already occurred as a result of embracing biological determinism as a fundamental explanation of human suffering. This is not to say that we should disregard the important advances that genetics and biochemistry have provided, both in understanding ourselves and in medicating serious psychiatric conditions. But we need to become acutely aware of the consequences of embracing a widespread ideology of biological determinism.

Unique among religions, Buddhism has developed systematic methods for investigating the roots of suffering and other psychological responses in ways that are valid and reliable. The methods of Buddhism are objective and empirical and do not contradict the metaphysics of science. Buddhism also possesses an extensive psychology of unconscious processes. Buddhism and depth psychology stand side by side in helping us to diagnose and treat the spiritual problem that emerged wholecloth in the final decade of the twentieth century: secular self-interest reinforced by the metaphysics of scientific materialism. Biblical scholar Miles (1999: x, emphasis in original) describes the problem this way:

> Enlightened self-interest seems to hold as a necessary postulate that the world is real and the world's goods really worth acquiring. A stock portfolio, a law degree, a flat stomach, an art museum membership card, a foreign vacation, a sex life, a baby – the list is long, and each item on it seems to have generated an advertising campaign, a market strategy, an expert adviser. *Materialism* is too narrow a word for the army of cultural imperatives that both preserve and besiege the . . . self.

Buddhism teaches that our suffering arises from the illusion that the individual self is enduring and needs to be protected. The schools of depth psychology warn of our tendencies to repeat experiences of fear and gratification through our psychological complexes and repetition compulsions. Defending ourselves against events and feelings that we evaluate as negative makes us desire only those things we believe to be in our favor – and to abhor what we believe is not. These conditions naturally lead to overwhelming experiences of despair, anxiety, and envy, as well as compulsions and addictions. All of these ordinary forms of human suffering are now further complicated by a metaphysics based on vague notions of biological determinism.

Biological determinism is clearly no help with the burden or boredom of a demanding self. It cannot answer questions about subjective meaning, nor address the compulsions that arise from personal insecurity, without reducing them to organic processes. If you explain suffering only in organic terms, then you exclude the possibility that you can change your life through changing your mind. If you further believe that the world's goods are worth acquiring, you will eventually face the fact that individual and collective resources are depleted. What I have outlined here is a unique problem of our times: human suffering without interest in its origins or knowledge about its causes.

## Dukkha

The First Noble Truth taught by the Buddha is often translated into English as "Life is suffering." I find myself in agreement with those translators who prefer the terms "discontent" or "anguish" as a definition of *dukkha*. The First Noble Truth then becomes "Human life is filled with discontent" or "Our lives are mired in anguish." The Sanskrit word *dukkha* refers to a vast range of phenomena from the inevitable aspects of illness, decline, and death to the ordinary discontent of everyday life. And yet the word itself conveys a specific metaphor that sheds light on what it means to be a human being.

*Dukkha* refers literally to a state of being off-center or out of balance, like a wheel riding off its axle or a bone riding out of its socket. This off-centeredness is most often experienced as negativity and restlessness. Most of us tend to notice *dukkha* more acutely at times of adversity such as loss, illness, or difficulties in intimacy or parenting that confront us with our limited control over the circumstances of our lives. But *dukkha* occurs countless times in an ordinary day.

Contemporary psychological research on "flow experience" (engaged, unselfconscious activity that eliminates the experience of a separate self) gives some interesting scientific evidence of the First Noble Truth. After years of researching the character of flow experience in everyday life, the psychologist Mihalyi Csikszentmihalyi (1993: 35) says:

> when attention is not occupied by a specific task, like a job or a conversation, thoughts begin to wander in random circles. But in this case "random" does not mean that there is an equal chance of having happy and sad thoughts. [T]he majority of thoughts that come to the mind when we are not concentrating are likely to be depressing.

Perhaps this hyper-alertness to negativity – what's missing or not going our way – has prepared us to protect the interests of ourselves and our species, but it has also created repetitive anguish and destructive tendencies. Ultimately, an unchecked desire to constantly improve our situation has led to endless evils, wars, greed and hatred as our species has come to dominate and overpopulate our planet.

### How therapy transforms dukkha and awakens compassion

Much of our suffering originates with our sense of separateness and fear, through our evaluations of ourselves and others. Our psychological complexes, ego and otherwise, form our basic habits of mind that develop first in our early relationships, eventually becoming the trigger points or reactive cues for our personal emotional patterns of reaction and defense. These complexes are major aspects of what Buddhism calls *karma*: consequences of our conscious and unconscious intentions expressed through our actions. As Buddhist scholar G. Dharmasiri (1989: 37) has said:

> Although a bad thought may seem to disappear . . . it does not com-
> pletely disappear but goes . . . to the unconscious and starts forming
> a complex around the original nucleus . . . [T]he complex becomes
> charged with more and more power as it grows bigger . . . This is the
> maturation of karma. When the complex is fully matured, at some
> point it explodes into the fruition of karma.

Such complexes, derived from universal emotional conditions of being
human, are driving forces in generating and regenerating images of self and
others, through distortions and delusions of fear and desire, dominance and
submission, and power and weakness. From a Jungian perspective, psychological complexes develop universally through archetypes or innate predispositions. "Archetypes" are innate tendencies in humans to form coherent
emotionally charged images in states of arousal. The perceptual and
emotional systems of human beings everywhere are organized by archetypes
around which we form our emotional habit patterns, at first in adapting to
the emotional and interpersonal demands of the conditions we are born
into. Later, in adult life, these complexes are played out with others, in our
families and worklife, as though our emotional meanings were reality.
Negative experiences from our childhood are especially powerful. For
example, if a child was treated aggressively and unfairly by a parent or
older sibling, as an adult that child will have a strong tendency to recreate
both the roles of victim and aggressor, sometimes identifying with one and
projecting the other, and other times reversing that.

Not only the complexes of the unconscious, but also the ego complex of
conscious awareness can throw us off balance through defensive emotional
patterning. The ego complex forms around the core of an archetype of self,
the universal human tendency to form a coherent image of being an individual embodied subject who exists over time. The experience of individual
subjectivity first comes into conscious awareness between the ages of eighteen months and two years in normal development. No wonder the "terrible
twos" are known as the "me me me" period! Once the ego complex is
formed, the self-conscious emotions such as jealousy, shame, pride, self-pity,
embarrassment, envy and guilt – as well as fears and desires – can trigger
defenses of the ego. Then we experience ourselves as separated and isolated
from others and the world around, the pervasive root of subject–object
duality.

Jung believed that modernity engendered a revolutionary self-
consciousness in human development: a new awareness that allowed for
self-investigation and accountability that gave birth to psychoanalysis
among other things. He regarded this development as a mixed blessing
because excessive self-consciousness can result in the alienation of the ego
from the rest of the personality. All of the complexes of the personality –
including those that are typically unconscious such as mother, father and

child – have a certain degree of autonomy or intentions of their own. Excessive self-consciousness of the ego can lead to the denial of other complexes and their motives, believing that our actions are guided only by our conscious intentions.

Because humans all have universal features of emotion and embodiment, Jung postulated a collective unconscious – a shared common ground of unconscious experiences – in which individuality is embedded. When someone projects an unconscious complex into another, it is thus likely that the other has had emotional and conceptual experiences for receiving and identifying with that projection. Projection of alien states into others is an unintentional invitation to another to enact those states. In intimate and hierarchical relationships, people often project and enact each other's darker feelings and images, making for a great deal of pain and confusion in human relationships.

In a successful long-term psychotherapy or analysis, the two people – therapist and patient – come to witness directly how and why this happens. Investigating the projections of the patient, the therapist and patient together will see how the patient has needed to place aspects of her or his motives or feelings or ideals in others. Patient and therapist need each other to make this kind of study, and through witnessing what has taken place between them, they come to feel a deep gratitude for their unique work together, a gratitude that transcends even the insights gained.

Through the specific meeting of these two people, each discovers in the context of their relationship how the self-centered self-conscious subject mistakes the world and others to be separate, passive, external and permanent. In place of this separateness, the therapeutic partners come to see and experience their mutual fluid self–other constructions that are rooted in the emotions and desires of the moment. Both people – especially the patient because the therapy is focused on her or him – see clearly how the ego complex constructs others and the environment to be reflections of its own wishes and needs. The technical terms for these mistaken projections and perceptions are "transference" and "countertransference." Transference means one person seeing and believing that another is a particular way, or feels a particular way, that the first has unknowingly imposed from an internal state of pressure, feeling, or image. One person transfers a whole context or story, or a particular feeling state, to another and believes that it originates with the other. Countertransference is simply the reaction of the second person to the transference of the first, especially in the feeling states and images of the second person. As these are witnessed and interpreted within the safe bounds of effective psychotherapy, the two individuals begin to awaken to greater compassion and wisdom through their knowledge of how suffering is created. In the process of such an awakening, the two people of the therapeutic dyad feel deeply grateful for their interdependence is this process.

## Aspects of interdependence in Zen and Jung

In one example of how this interdependence can be traced in psychotherapy, Gordon Kopf (1998) compares Jung's account of the transferential phenomena of therapy with the account of *katto* (vines) from the medieval Zen Master Dogen's analysis of the master–disciple relationship. Dogen exhorts the Zen student to attain the face of the teacher, and vice versa, while averring that the interwovenness of master and disciple still includes the individuality of each. "The self attains the other" and "the other attains the self" while the self never abandons itself to the psyche of the other. Self and other are not one and they are not two (summarized in Kopf, 1998: 282–283). If it is possible for the self to attain the other without dissolving its individuality, argues Dogen, then the traditional concept of a separate self does not apply to our subjectivity. Dogen maintains that self and other are ultimately interdependent; the self does not exist prior to, or outside of, the other; we only have the possibility of experiencing self or other through relationship.

Both Zen discipleship and long-term psychotherapy demonstrate this interdependence to the practitioners when the relationship is effective. Psychotherapy was designed specifically to respond to personal pain and suffering, not to spiritual questions per se, while Buddhism offers a theory and many methods to respond spiritually to universal aspects of human suffering, not personal suffering with its unique familial and emotional patterns. I will give a brief example of the ways in which interdependence underpins each of these, including a short commentary on how compassion develops in such circumstances.

The core process of transformation in the long-term psychodynamic therapeutic relationship includes encountering difficult feelings, desires and impulses, and investigating their origins and meanings with the therapist. Some of this takes place in the transference of sexual, aggressive, or other frightening feelings experienced as being caused by, or reactive to, the therapist. The effective therapist provides a gentle matter-of-fact attention (often called "bare attention" or "neutrality") that encourages the patient to explore such states, even though both patient and therapist may be somewhat self-conscious or uncomfortable. Both patient and therapist *are* initially ambivalent about such stressful encounters involving the transference, but in the course of therapy they come to feel deeply grateful, even freely creative, in their ability to explore together the patient's most difficult feelings and impulses within the transference, as well as with regard to other people in the patient's life.

Long-term psychotherapy achieves the transformation of suffering by leaving certain kinds of things unsaid – for example, most if not all of the therapist's hostile, erotic, aggressive, or hateful feelings toward the patient – while putting other things into words. The therapist's interpretation of unconscious meaning is one of the methods of achieving insight into the patient's troubling emotional habits. The therapist will use words, phrases, sentences, and gestures to communicate emotional meanings for what may have been unknown or hidden from the patient's awareness, but has been repeatedly implied or unknowingly expressed to the therapist. For instance, the patient may have frequently said to the therapist "I believe *you* are critical and judgmental of me" just when the patient is unconsciously feeling that way toward the therapist. The response to this type of projection of affect may be anything from a silent noting by the therapist that she or he does not in fact feel this way to saying openly something like "Perhaps you are feeling this way about me at the moment?" or something similar. Over the development of a successful long-term treatment, such inquiry becomes quite ordinary. It is an opening to explore a whole context or narrative surrounding the patient's feelings (or occasionally the therapist's feelings) that will inevitably connect to the patient's troubling habits of mind (assumptions and emotional dynamics) that are at the root of a lot of her or his suffering.

Other therapeutic interpretations may respond to a patient's reports of daily life, silences, gestures, claims to truth, postures, and night-dreams. A therapist's ability to be truly helpful in making interpretations, and not humiliating or belittling the patient, depends on the therapist's training, expertise, self-awareness, and confidence in relying on the therapeutic relationship for the discovery of meaning. Within this relationship, patient and therapist are also two ordinary human beings who are working together to try to bring about the alleviation of suffering in at least one (the patient), and more profoundly in both. The patient has hired the therapist to do a job that the therapist has been trained to do. The therapist, like any other trained professional, will be more or less able to perform satisfactorily on a particular occasion, relevant to the therapist's state of mind and many other factors. The periodic expressed acknowledgment of such limitation is a requirement for any therapist to be effective. Sometimes the therapist feels confused, afraid, reactive, and ignorant about the task of the transformation of suffering. Acknowledging these limitations allows interpretations and other interventions, such as empathy, to be made with an openness and questioning, a kind of uncertainty or not-knowing. Within the effective therapeutic relationship the therapist will convey the sense that she or he also suffers and may not always know the way of transformation. This realistic acknowledgment of constraint on "expert authority" will counterbalance the powerful forces of transference, and also invite the patient to be more open and unashamed in exploring her or his human foibles. Yet this kind of realism must be handled skillfully so that the patient has plenty of opportunities to experience the therapist as an authority figure and a trusted expert – conditions that are necessary for transference and trust.

In everyday life, we are constantly immersed in transferences and projections in our ordinary human relationships. Only in the therapeutic

relationship do we encounter the special condition of being able to study the creation of such suffering in the moment. The requirements for effective psychotherapy – ethical conduct and non-retaliation on the part of the therapist, certain ground rules for meetings and payment, the relative anonymity of the therapist, and so on – nourish possibilities for self-understanding and the development of compassion for self and others.

Eventually the patient discovers what Jung (1916/1969: 67–91) has called the "transcendent function": an ability to contain tensions, conflicts, and other opposite pulls without prematurely deciding that they are "good" or "bad" or mean this or that (see, e.g., Horne, 1998). This function allows the patient to keep an open mind in the face of momentary impulses, feelings, pressures, and so on. Eventually the patient finds that the skill of the transcendent funtion can be used in many life situations in which the patient had previously reacted through old destructive emotional habits. The interdependence (of patient and therapist) in the discovery of meaning through the therapeutic relationship, and the skill of the transcendent function, together eventually allow the patient to "suffer with" self and others. Suffering-with is the essence of "com-passion" (literally, suffering-with) in its ability to witness pain, trouble, difficulty and adversity with a sincere desire and ability to help. True help, and not pity or sympathy or sugar-coating, requires a matter-of-fact toleration of the demands of pain and suffering without becoming hopeless. This is the path that patient and therapist follow in the course of an effective long-term psychotherapy.

Buddhist methods, in contrast to therapy's focus on personal relational and identity themes, are designed to alleviate suffering and increase com-passion in terms of broader universal themes. In all of its methods, Buddhism focuses attention on craving, aversion, and ignorance as experi-enced particularly through creating, sustaining, and defending the illusion of a separate, stable, independent self. All methods for transforming our delusions of separateness rely on both theory and experience in Buddhism. A teacher's job is especially to guide the process of awakening to the reality of interdependence and compassion through methods that have already been mastered by the teacher.

The Buddhist student–teacher relationship is transformative from the outset because it carries a belief in the teacher's perfected spiritual state (enlightenment, liberation, satori, etc.). The student initially sees this par-ticular teacher as spiritually advanced, and wants to attain this for herself or himself, and so decides to follow the teacher's instructions. In Zen, a teacher who has been sanctioned to teach by her/his teacher *has* theoretically equaled or surpassed the teacher. So there is a reality to the student's belief that the teacher is well beyond the student in spiritual attainment. And yet, true and deep spiritual attainment should not set a teacher apart from others; the most spiritually adept teachers are often known for being very ordinary people. Paradoxically, then, a spiritual master in Zen (called a *roshi*) is both an especially enlightened or realized person and an ordinary person.

Such a teacher speaks from an authority that the psychotherapist or psychoanalyst lacks. Whereas the effective psychotherapist may still be almost as neurotic as the patient – although able to use insight, the transcendent function, and compassion to continuously transform neurotic habits – the Zen teacher is certainly not as ignorant of the nature of spiritual reality as the student is. In short, the realized Zen teacher is fundamentally unequal, spiritually speaking, with her or his student at the beginning of the transformation process.

This difference in status effectively eliminates the sense that the two are, on some level, just two human beings struggling together to discover meaning. The developed teacher has mastered her or his mind and not merely the knowledge of Buddhism and its methods. Many roshis would say that they definitely know what is best for their students without the kind of uncertainty that an effective therapist feels and expresses. In order for teacher and student to "intertwine" in the way that Kopf (1998) describes, the student must learn the ways and means to her or his own True Nature or Mind. By the end of this process – if the process fully evolves between a particular teacher and student – the student will have fully realized her or his spiritual nature that was originally projected onto the teacher.

In Zen, the actions of the teacher in the process may be harsh and seem hostile, as well as openly caring and compassionate. These extremes are aspects of Zen teaching and not considered a personal matter. The student's reactions to such expressions by the teacher are not interpreted as they are in psychotherapy, and yet they will stir rather extreme transference feelings and fantasies in the student. The dependence and trust that are necessary in the effective Zen teacher–student relationship guarantee that there will be struggles with dependence–independence, trust–betrayal, and engulfment–abandonment between student and teacher. These often repeat or react to the student's parental or other familial patterns. The student feels vulnerable, dependent and deeply concerned about the teacher in a situation that is unpredictable with regard to the extremes of the teacher's responses. Without the benefit of therapeutic insights into specific personal habit patterns, the student must stop behaving and feeling like an omnipotent or victimized child. This happens through the student mastering the reliable spiritual practices offered and guided by the dedicated teacher.

At the point that the student awakens to the reality of Buddha Mind or True Nature, the student and teacher are one although they remain two individuals. This intertwining is very different from the therapist–patient relationship of working through the projections of transference in the discovery of meaning. For the therapist–patient dyad, appreciation of interdependence emerges especially from the sense of being "only human" in the context of difficult feeling states encountered and successfully under-stood and digested during therapeutic sessions. In the case of Zen teacher–student, the experience of interdependence arises in the student's awakening to the reality of impermanence and interdependence through eradicating the delusions of a separate self.

## Conclusion

Through the transformation of our suffering in long-term psychotherapy and Buddhism, we learn that apparently negative experiences open our hearts. We cease experiencing self and others as wholly separate, permanent, stable and independent. And we no longer experience ourselves simply as passive victims of circumstances we did not create.

Through the methods of psychotherapy and Buddhism we encounter the paradigm of our subjective world: the basis for our meanings and percep-tions. Gradually we come to see that as we shift our subjective perceptions, the perceived also changes. Subject and object are joined in the ground of our perceptions. When we conceive of the human self as wholly interdepen-dent and impermanent, as a function rather than a thing, then we appreciate more deeply the freedom that we have in this world. It is the freedom of opening ourselves to our constraints and limitations, and exploring these into the roots of our suffering. Our suffering has a purpose: it gives rise to our deepest compassion when it is transformed. This is a discipline that cannot be captured by any form of biological determinism and must be explored on its own terms – personally, spiritually, and scientifically – in the new millennium.

# Chapter 15

# When the fruit ripens: alleviating suffering and increasing compassion as goals of clinical psychoanalysis

The transformation of suffering, through a psychoanalytic treatment, should lead to gains in psychological well-being that last a lifetime. Knowing how to alleviate one's own suffering presumes some insight into human suffering in general, and an ability to hold open certain experiential moments of emotional meaning that would otherwise trigger impulsive reactions that may be expressed internally, externally or both. Such impulses are felt as pressure or anxiety and are experienced in adults as habitual patterns of action, thoughts, and affects. These habit patterns are largely the product of early relational and emotional conditioning, trauma, abuse, or other adversity.

Jung called these emotional habit patterns "psychological complexes" and regarded them as the fundamental structures of personality. The ego complex (activated by the self-conscious emotions) is the most conscious among multiple centers of subjectivity. Less conscious complexes may be dissociated from conscious awareness or be partly conscious; they may be projected into others or wholly identified with at a particular moment (for a further discussion of these ideas from my perspective, see Young-Eisendrath, 1997c and Young-Eisendrath, 2000). When a person identifies with an unconscious complex, we say that she is "beside herself" or that he is "not himself," and most people recognize this kind of not-self state in their own emotional landscape. From time to time, anyone can lapse into such a state, filled with unconscious or semi-conscious emotional meanings, and unknowingly invite another or others to play out aspects of the first's inner emotional drama. If another person unknowingly takes on the projected or implied meanings, and acts on them, or plays them out, or seems to play them out, the original initiator of such a "projective identification" may feel temporarily relieved of unconscious pressures and fantasies. Jung's term for this was *participation mystique*, a term he borrowed from the sociology of his day.

Projective identification is, in my view, a ubiquitous form of proto-communication that causes a great deal of suffering in individuals, relationships, families, groups and communities – both in terms of what is projected and what is identified with and then played out. And yet, projective identification is also a healthy and ordinary component of human relationships and family life, necessary for certain merger states of sex, care, and love. It is probably also a contributor to the development of emotional attunement, sympathy, and empathy, as well as a component of hatred and alienation. Momentarily or temporarily losing aspects of oneself can be a healthy part of relational life with other people. Permanently or regularly losing parts of one's identity or experiences through chronic projection, identification or dissociation is a major component of most psychopathology and creates suffering in relationship, work, and meaning-making.

The goals of alleviating suffering and increasing compassion depend on an ability to recognize one's own habitual impulses to dissociate, project, and/or identify with some alien emotional meaning, and then to sidestep or hold open that impulse so that something new (that is not part of the old emotional script) can emerge. The capacity to hold open one's subjective experience, in a moment of habitual pressure to react, is called "the transcendent function" in Jung's terminology, "potential space" or "play space" in Winnicott's vocabulary, and "dialogical space" in Ogden's (e.g., 1989). As I say below, this capacity to hold open emotional meaning becomes a skill of the patient's in the course of a successful psychoanalytic treatment. In order to achieve such a skill that can be used in everyday emotional engagements with oneself and others, a patient must have gained more than insight. She or he must have developed compassion for self and others; without such compassion, there tends to be confusion and self-condemnation about the insight gained through analytic treatment.

The capacity to transcend and transform one's suffering in the moment of its occurrence is the fruit of a therapeutic endeavor that interprets transference and countertransference, as well as other relational patterns and dream imagery, and achieves insight into harmful habit patterns. The context in which this insight ripens into an on-going skill of using the transcendent function or dialogical space is a vital, empathic and creative relationship between a trained and well-attuned analyst/therapist and a suitable patient. In such a case, both patient and analyst will come to experience new freedom from old emotional habits, while the two concentrate their primary commentary and attention on the habit patterns of the patient.

All forms of psychotherapy share the common aim of alleviating human suffering, a term I will define momentarily. The effects of therapeutic interventions will, however, be transient and unreliable if the patient is unable to use the therapeutic skills gained at times when complexes and/or projective identifications become troubling in daily life. Analytic forms of therapy – designed to study unconscious motives, conflicts, impulses, drives, and repetitive affectively charged complexes *in the moment* – offer the unique possibility of cultivating self-reflective skills in the face of emotional pressure. These skills, as I will describe, depend on self-knowledge, the ability to analyze oneself when triggered into a troubling habit, and compassion for self and others. All of these are outgrowths of expectable changes in the conscious attitude or perspective of the patient, but also include expectable shifts in the attitude of the analyst. I will describe this process in detail after I define and describe suffering and compassion in light of psychoanalytic (to include Jungian) methods.

## Suffering and insight

As I've stated many times, in many places, I define human suffering as a state of being off-center or out-of-balance that is experienced as anguish, distress, discontent, anxiety or agitation. This kind of subjective disturbance may be as mild as a momentary frustration (e.g., frustration over a hangnail or traffic jam) or as severe as a depressive or psychotic state. In the way I am using it here, I mean "suffering" to refer to mental anguish that may be expressed physically in somaticized symptoms and/or interpersonally as disturbances in relationships and/or intrapsychically through distressing images and fantasies of self and other, or self and world.

We (human beings) create this kind of subjective distress through perseverations, distortions, fantasies and internal commentary, much of which is linked to our omnipotent longings and desires. We suffer a good deal when things do not go our way – the way that we believe they should go – from the resultant feelings of fear, humiliation, shame, rage, and despair. An adult's longings for omnipotence and omniscience will have been profoundly, but unknowingly, shaped by the conditions in which she or he grew into a conscious person. These longings will have been affected particularly through ongoing emotional conditioning, as well as trauma, abuse, loss, illness, accidents and other things that were authentically outside of personal control.

For purposes of my discussion here, and because I otherwise also find it useful, I draw a distinction between suffering as a state of being that can change through a change of awareness, and inescapable pain or adversity over which we may have no or little actual control. Of course, suffering and adversity interact in our experience: often we increase our suffering by wishing, wanting or trying to stop situations or events that lie outside our control, and then find ourselves locked into shame, rage or despair because we cannot. On the other hand, we may fail to carry out, or avoid, effective intervention in situations that cause pain and/or adversity because our suffering prevents us from feeling ourselves empowered and able to intervene on our own behalf. The confusion between pain and suffering, in the way that I am using the term here, can also result in anxiety and depression over the constraints and limitations of one's life.

Ordinary examples of these arise in everyday relationships with family members or life partners whom we long to control. All of us – but perhaps especially those who have already endured overwhelming insults and adversities – find it difficult to accept the limitations of human life. We also find it difficult to understand the responsibility we do have, and to feel and be accountable for our own intentions, feelings and actions. Roy Schafer writes (1992: xiii, emphasis in original) about the distinction between human action and "happenings" in the following way that I find helpful:

> In its broad sense, [human] action refers to far more than overt behavior; it refers as well to whatever it is that people may be said to do, and in this respect it stands in contrast to *happenings*, those events in which one's own human agency plays no discernible or contextually relevant part (for example, a rainstorm or receiving a misaddressed letter a week late). Among the things that people do is perceive, remember, imagine, love, hate, fear, defend, and refrain from overt activity. In psychoanalytic discussion, special emphasis is . . . placed on what people do unconsciously and conflictually (fantasize, remember, love, defend, and so forth).

I believe that insight into our own motives, memories, and actions, as well as knowledge of our early emotional conditioning, gradually allows us to discern the differences between our actions (and hence our responsibility and freedom) and happenings or events that lie wholly outside our control. This insight eventually clarifies the boundaries and domain of suffering that can be affected by a change in our understanding and attitude, as distinct from pain and adversity that cannot.

In a successful analysis, patients come to recognize what they have generally, although not perfectly, under their own control, as well as what they do not. Once this distinction is even somewhat clarified, the patient has a new freedom: the freedom of personal accountability. This includes an acknowledgment that one's subjective life – images, feelings, thoughts and actions – is complex and malleable, as well as responsive to various kinds of reflection. One sees that one can choose to act in this way or that, that one can choose to regard things in this way or that, even when one is strongly drawn into an old destructive habit.

After such insight is fundamentally secured, it appears that a patient (with her or his analyst) faces two major emotional challenges: the challenge of living in the present with these new degrees of freedom, and the regret and sadness for not having seen and lived this way sooner. For example, a woman in her late fifties sees that she has, over many years, unknowingly blamed others – especially her husband, her children, and her mother – for her (the patient's) lack of career achievements. She has rationalized the blame and resentment through idealized images of her children and their potential accomplishments. When her children seemed unable to satisfy their mother's hidden desires for power and success, this

woman sought psychotherapy with me, saying she was "depressed" and
"lacked interest in life." Eventually recognizing her ideals for her children
as compensating for her sense of lack in herself, and her attacks on her
husband and her own mother as projections of aspects of her own inner
conflicts, this woman faced the problem of having "wasted years." She felt
in a double bind: damned if she accepted responsibility for her own development (condemning herself for not having "seen it sooner"), and damned
if she didn't (continuing to feel like a victim of her life circumstances).

Refining this encounter with her own responsibility, she and I came to see
that her double bind was, in fact, her attempt to destroy some of what we
had discovered together in her treatment. Throughout, she had assumed I
was a "career woman" who never struggled with personal doubts about my
abilities or powers. From the beginning, this account of me (one that her
mother would have also given) set me apart from her, and expressed an
unconscious desire to keep me under her control, to make me be someone
different from her. She finally saw that the alternative to her envy and
idealization of my career was not to become alienated from me, as she had
feared, but to trust that I could be supportive of her in her own career
development. And yet, neither of us could know what would happen until
she tried to go out into the world herself. Eventually, she did just that and
was remarkably successful.

She eventually saw how her suffering was created through her own
desiring, fantasizing, aggrandizing and diminishing both objective and
subjective events and experiences she encountered. When suffering extends
beyond momentary frustration, it seems to swallow up our satisfactions,
hopes and interests. Often this kind of anguish is experienced as self-
loathing, self-hating, and/or revenge in the form of dominance/submission
fantasies or enactments.

Freud and Jung and other early psychoanalytic practitioners and theorists spent the better parts of their careers investigating transient, repetitive,
and permanent states of human suffering, and other seemingly irrational
aspects of everyday life (e.g., dreams). They discovered something that now
seems to be largely forgotten in our contemporary era of biological psychiatry and genetic reasoning: that even seemingly meaningless actions
(e.g., the compulsion to repeat self-destructive experiences) could be best
understood as intentional and purposive from the perspective of implied,
but hidden, desires and motives. The strangest and most troubling of
human actions can be rendered meaningful when certain developmental
facts are known. As contemporary psychoanalyst Carlo Strenger (1991: 62)
has said:

> the fundamental step which Freud took at the beginning of his career
> was to radicalize the principle of humanity and to apply it to phenom-
> ena which were previously exempt from it. Neurotic and psychosomatic

symptoms began to be seen as humanly intelligible rather than as phenomena which were only amenable to physiological explanation.

It is the hallmark of all forms of psychoanalysis to show that a close study of any human action will lead to a knowledge of its causes and purposes that can be eventually understood in the present moment, often in terms of emotional themes from the past.

I agree with Strenger when he says that psychoanalysis is committed to the idea that human behavior is "intentional action all the way down" and that by correctly understanding the meanings of our thoughts and actions "we help the patient take full responsibility for who he is, and give him the freedom to change if he truly wants to" (p. 63).

Accurate insight into the causes, purposes and consequences of our suffering opens the door to freedom through the knowledge of our conflicts, deficits, complexes, and other unknown or split-off parts of ourselves. This insight, when it is refined, is not a catalog or list of damages and misattunements or traumas and abuses, but rather is a method of examining our moment-to-moment subjective experience. It is a method for studying our subjective responses: when we feel ourselves emotionally triggered, where is this felt in the body, what images accompany, and what thoughts emerge, what are the themes, etc.? As the analyst (in the role of participating observer), I may be the first to have useful words for what I perceive to be taking place, as I examine my own thoughts, images, and feelings, but this primacy changes over the course of a treatment as the patient typically finds words and other expressions more available in shaping insights. Some patients are so deeply despairing, or very confused, about their own ability to transform their suffering that they need much more than well-timed interpretations and accurate empathic attunement. They seem to need the hope that comes with a broader understanding of human suffering and its transformation.

For instance, a man in his early fifties came into a three-times per week on-the-couch analysis with me after almost thirty-five years with several different, mostly Freudian, analysts in mostly on-the-couch analysis. Three and a half years into the analysis with me, he feels a terrible despair because he now sees with some regularity what is going on in his subjective life. His emotional habits have kept him locked into a deadened interpersonal life at home with his wife and children, and various perverse sexual obsessions and enactments with strangers. He has had a very successful academic career and has paid a lot of money to enlist the help of some of the "best analysts" in every city in which he has lived, and he counts me as one of those.

What can he gain from insight into his habit patterns when it inevitably leads to still more shame? he wonders aloud. He believes that real insight would mean that he would have to separate from his wife of many years (who is the mother of his children and who was pregnant with the first one at the time of marriage). This would be an unbearable change, he believes, although rarely voices. This patient was placed for adoption as an infant; this "abandonment" (as he feels it) has mixed with a story he tells himself about his being fundamentally flawed and set apart from humanity. He assumes that his biological parents were young and irresponsible and did not want him. "Leaving his children" (although they are grown up), which is the way he describes a divorce, would repeat the abandonment trauma that he himself has suffered, he believes.

This patient unknowingly invites me silently to dismiss him (as I tend to think his earlier analysts have done), if I take seriously his belief that he cannot change and will never leave his unhappy marriage. In this case, I feel *I* am in a double bind: should I call an end to this "interminable" analysis and recognize that his life is as "good as it gets," endorsing his alienation? Or should I continue with the idea that he can change and that he could leave his marriage if he so decided, and bear the brunt of the responsibility for him "leaving his children"? Either way I would seem to increase his suffering: unhappy in his marriage and unhappy with his perversions, he uses both to affirm his conviction that he is inferior to anyone who has grown up with biological parents (and he assumes that almost everyone has, including me). Countless times in our sessions I have put into words the above insight about feeling caught in a double bind. I am also certain, and have said so, that I feel (through identifying with the projection) as he did as a child: damned to feel alone and alienated when he did not express his feelings with and about his adoptive parents (who were not cruel, but were emotionally unavailable and narcissistic), or damned to feel bad and mean for expressing them. No choice then, but to find ways to control his unhappiness, to feel omnipotent in doing so, to have a hidden sexual perversion in which he is harshly punished, and cruelly dominated, by a severe woman like his mother.

With this particular patient, I have found it helpful to take a few steps back from clarifying and interpreting all of this. When I look at the process by which we become trapped in certain meanings (both as analysts and patients), I do not feel so tempted to either call it quits or become cynical about "taking his money" as though I were the dominatrix he had hired. Warmth and humor and openness to new discoveries, in the face of old rigidities, have all helped. Sometimes I recall certain stories that reflect our dilemma, like the well-known Taoist story of the farmer. Although I rarely share whole stories with patients, I told him this one:

> One day a farmer lost his horse because it ran off and his neighbors came to console him, saying "Too bad, too bad." The farmer responded, "Maybe." The next day the horse returned, bringing with it seven wild horses. "Oh, how lucky you are!" his neighbors exclaimed.

"Maybe," the farmer said. On the following day, when the farmer's son tried to ride one of the new horses, he broke his leg badly. "How terrible!" the neighbors said. "Maybe," the farmer replied. The following day, soldiers came to conscript the young men of the village, but the farmer's son wasn't taken away to war because of his injury. "How wonderful for you!" the neighbors said and the farmer said "Maybe."

The point of the story – to be open to uncertainies and not-knowing – is a vital one (see, e.g., Young-Eisendrath, 1996: 139–157 and Young-Eisendrath, 1997c: 649–651 for a fuller discussion of this) for this patient and me. He has been stuck in rigidities for so long and has paid psycho-analysts so much money. Both of us seem stuck in preconceived positions. I have felt trapped in my double bind and he, too afraid to change. And yet, he says he feels closer to me than he has felt to anyone, having found that I can make sense of his darkest secrets. He also understands his motivations more objectively than ever before. When he says now that he does not think he will ever change because he is too afraid, I often say "maybe."

## Compassion and transformation

The successful outcome of a psychoanalysis relies on more than insight into emotional habit patterns, or even accurate empathy and emotional holding. Bald insight can increase a patient's self-condemnation, alienation, shame and despair. When any of us sees the range and blindness of our own emotional habits, we tend to feel hopeless. Bland empathy can seem weak and useless in the face of strong self-conscious emotions, especially shame. Only compassion for oneself, cultivated over time, seems to me to allow the effects of the analysis to ripen into a transcendent function or dialogical space that can be used fairly reliably in everyday life.

It has been my experience that many people finish (apparently complete) a psychoanalysis or psychodynamic treatment with a heavy dose of ongoing self-condemnation and/or an inability to use their analytic skills in the face of powerful emotional triggering. It may be fine to feel, as some well-known psychoanalysts do (see, e.g., Hunter, 1994) that one has been helped in an analysis without knowing exactly how or why. But if one has not increased one's skill in being able to use a method of self-examination and self-reflection in a way that enhances relationships and other engagements of everyday life, then I believe that the analysis has not been effective.

Compassion – meaning literally suffering-*with* – for oneself and others transcends interpretations and insights in a way that allows us to embrace and use the knowledge and skills we gain through insight. Moreover, it permits us to feel "only human," encouraging openness and transparency with others, especially those who are close to us, on whom we depend. By compassion, I mean a kind and loving response to the suffering and adversity of oneself or another. Compassion is more than pity, sympathy, or the urge to help. True compassion allows us to respond to difficulty and anguish in a way that is truly helpful and not simply reactive, trivializing, or premature. Compassion, we might say, is a response that keeps us open to the nature of the difficulty at hand – even when the difficulty stirs hatred, rage, impatience, or shame. True compassion allows us to respond to distress (our own or another's) in a way that is helpful because the compassion contains within it an awareness of the inevitability of human suffering, lessening our need to attack ourselves or others.

In psychoanalysis, there are two reliable means by which compassion is cultivated, although they are rarely described fully. The first is the patient's engagement in, and eventual awareness of, what I regard as a necessary unobjectionable idealizing transference crucial to the therapeutic action of the treatment. The term that I've been using for this form of transference, drawing on the work of Modell (1990: 46–52), is "containing-transcendent" transference. Modell names it the "dependent-containing" transference and shows how it underlies the transformative aspect of psychotherapy.

I prefer the term "transcendent" to "dependent" because this transference is filled with the hope of transcending symptoms, suffering, and other limitations. It also contains the belief that this particular analyst can help me transcend my suffering. This analyst is knowledgeable or caring or smart or something enough for me to trust her or him to be more powerful than my symptoms. Such feelings may initially or eventually be accompanied by the belief that the analyst is "wiser" or "more powerful" than other people in the patient's everyday life.

In my view, these feelings arise naturally in, and are enhanced by, the very conditions of the analytic ritual or therapeutic set-up (see Hoffman, 1998, for an expanded discussion of this). This kind of ritual invites and encourages the analyst to be seen as someone "special" or "powerful" by the patient. Hoffman (1998) calls this the "mystique" of the analyst and also believes it contributes to the therapeutic action of the treatment. If the patient cannot or does not feel that the analyst is powerful or special in these ways, several things may be happening. More common than failures, it seems to me, is a confusion: the analyst refuses (or feels too small for) such an unreasonable transference because he or she thinks it is about him or her *personally*, rather than about the transformative process or environment.

This kind of transference may be diminished or compromised over the course of treatment by the analyst's chronic failures of attunement, empathy or understanding of the patient. In a successful treatment, the containing-transcendent transference will strengthen as the iconic-projective transferences are analyzed and dissolved. In other words, as the patient becomes more skilled, appreciative, and grateful in the transformation of suffering, the patient feels even more impressed with the special qualities of the analyst (not knowing the analyst's personal failings in detail). This happens along with feeling that the analyst is limited, flawed and human – the outcome of understanding the defensive idealization of the analyst based on envy.

What the patient transfers, then, is her or his own potential for ongoing hope and transformation, a potential that can, if the treatment is successful, unfold into compassion for self and others. For some patients (especially those suffering from personality disorders and trauma), the experience of this kind of transference may be the first ever encounter with someone or something that seems to promise the hope for renewal. I believe that this kind of hope constitutes a big portion of the "placebo effect" commonly discussed in research on therapeutic effectiveness.

The second condition for the development of compassion is also related to the analytic ritual: the interdependence of the analyst and patient in the discovery of insight. Over time, the patient and analyst together deeply appreciate the discovery process in which they have engaged – a process enhanced by the constraints of the ritual. They both recognize how they have depended on each other and the treatment set-up, especially in times of tension and pressure. Repeatedly, in the most unlikely moments, when things have been particularly distressing, they have discovered new perspectives or ideas that have transcended their suffering. This has not been simply the imposition of the analyst's interpretations, expertise or authority. It has been a mutual engagement in a process of investigation of subjective life.

Experiencing this interdependence in the analytic process allows both patient and analyst to appreciate the multiple levels of human suffering and the human dilemma (accountability and responsibility with limited control). The analyst's interpretations of unconscious meanings are put into words and gestures that are meant to bring insight in such a way that the patient can see how he or she has unnecessarily created suffering. These interpretations are also expanded into narratives about the patient and analyst that reveal over the course of treatment how the patient creates this suffering with the analyst, and what the consequences are. Naturally the patient feels confused, despairing or enraged about being accountable for these actions. The effective analyst also sometimes feels confused, despairing, or enraged about being responsible for the task of transformation, as I discussed in my own case of the man with perversions.

The analyst's tolerance for her or his own uncertainty, openness to questioning, respect for the interdependent discovery of meaning, and acceptance of blindspots will convey to the patient a compassion for human limitation. This realistic acknowledgment of the limitations of expert authority seems to me to play an important role in counterbalancing the forces of the containing-transcendent transference, as well as clarifying that the analyst is unashamed of not-knowing. The limitation of expert authority must, however, be handled in a way that protects the patient's belief that the analyst does indeed "know" that it is possible for the patient to transform her or his suffering (for an example of this working well, see Renik, 2000). In other words, the analyst must retain a sense of confidence about analytic methods and the vitality of this specific therapeutic alliance.

In ordinary relationships of everyday life, we are constantly immersed in iconic-projective transferences, as well as less emotionally charged dynamics, with family, friends and strangers. The potentials for retaliation, the complications of interpersonal conflict, and various other impingements, make it difficult to study the consequences of our complexes, enactments, and fantasies. Within the framework of the analytic ritual, with its containing-transcendent transference, we have a unique opportunity to study the transformation of suffering because the context will "nourish some of the analyst's more 'ideal' qualities as a person" (Hoffman, 1998: 203) and promote hopefulness and desire for self-understanding in the patient.

The two kinds of transference present in the analytic situation guarantee a strong affective response – an emotional cooker – in which the transformation of suffering can be usefully studied as it is ameliorated. Conflicts of dependence–independence, trust–betrayal and engulfment–abandonment will be necessarily felt in every analytic treatment because they are built into the containing-transcendent transference: the analyst is the repository for the patient's hope for development and this is uncomfortable for both participants. Conflicts around this hope will be experienced and enacted according to the specific mix of an individual patient with an individual analyst, alongside the iconic-projective themes. In an effective treatment, patients discover that they can depend on and trust the analyst even in times of great despair and challenge. They discover that they will be neither engulfed nor abandoned, not because the analyst always knows what to do or how to think, but because the analyst knows how to work with her or his own emotional dynamics and shortcomings in a way that shows both limitations and a willingness to tolerate uncertainty – depending on the process of mutual discovery, again and again.

The potent alchemy of containing-transcending and interdependence is repeatedly demonstrated within sessions, along with other analytic and empathic methods for achieving insight into suffering and its creation. It is this alchemy that gradually provides the increase in compassion that allows the patient to leave treatment with an ongoing motivation to use the skills of self-understanding, and allows the analyst to embrace both the patient and oneself with feelings of love by the conclusion of the treatment.

## Keeping the faith

Analytic methods of interpretation, inquiry, and empathy were designed to transform individual suffering within the context of a vital, creative relationship – a relationship of discovery. In order to learn how to keep an open mind in the face of unconscious impulses, desires, intentions and the like, after treatment has ended, a former patient needs to believe that ongoing effort will continue to lead somewhere worthwhile. Otherwise, the conservative force of emotional habit patterns will overtake the personality in the absence of a therapeutic relationship.

When people enter into an intensive psychotherapy or psychoanalysis, they have typically already tried many other ways of ameliorating their suffering. With the possible exception of analytic candidates, psychotherapy or psychoanalysis is only moderately desired by the people who pay for it. Psychoanalysts also feel ambivalent about their commitment to a process that involves many troubling and chaotic emotional experiences and ongoing exposure to countless narratives of human cruelties and stupidities. Consequently, both patient and analyst are genuinely surprised when they come to feel deeply appreciative and loving toward each other. This "love affair," which in my professional experience has often come quite strongly just as the treatment was about to end, also undergirds the containing-transcendent transference to one's analyst over the remainder of a lifetime. It seems to allow the patient, as I hear in reports from people who come back for consultations after analysis (as well as from my own analyses), to continue to draw on a wise and compassionate "therapist within" in moments of challenge and powerlessness.

All of these lead to a fairly reliable faith in, and motivation to use, the transcendent function or dialogical space – to hold open experiential moments of emotional meaning when feeling emotional pressure to react. Ongoing examination of one's own omnipotent longings and desires, as well as one's tendency to project and identify with certain images and dynamics, should continue after treatment to lead to modesty about isolated uncorrected self-analyses. As I said earlier, appreciation of interdependence strengthens our compassion – our ability to suffer with ourselves and others – and our willingness to be more transparent about our failures and fears.

Of course, a patient has attained some self-knowledge of the personal habit patterns that shape the particular complexes and conflicts of her or his personality. In resolving the iconic-projective transferences with this particular analyst, the patient has experienced the possibility of trans-forming old habit patterns in the moment, or soon after, they occur. The patient has encountered shameful and difficult sexual, aggressive, cruel, hateful and envious feelings and images, and has found that even these were ultimately helpful and useful for understanding oneself.

In the last stage of a treatment, the patient has also worked collabora-tively to apply the skills gained in treatment sessions to the world outside, and felt the analyst to be a partner in that endeavor. All of these experi-ences have led to the transformation of suffering into insight, compassion, and renewal.

The transformative effects of a psychoanalytic treatment should live on forever. Even years after the death of one's analyst, news about him or her can have an effect on the treatment. This is a great responsibility for those who take on the role of analyst. It is a responsibility to remain an ethical and committed practitioner and person in order to allow for the containing-transcendent transference to flourish over time. And yet, as I mentioned earlier, it is a serious error for an analyst to believe that this transference is a personal matter. Although the analyst plays an important part in competently handling the constraints of the analytic ritual, this kind of transference arises spontaneously as the universal hope for the transformation of suffering when that hope can be sustained.

Mistakenly identifying oneself personally with the powers of this transference always leads to destructive errors and actions of which there are innumerable examples among charismatic therapeutic and psychoanalytic leaders. Such people have usually demanded that others adhere to their particular formulas and ideas – rather than to a process of inquiry and discovery – because they have believed that they have alone held some unique powers of transformation. Unfortunately, such a therapist or analyst will betray the effectiveness of the transcendent-containing transference, either through disastrous errors or by feeling beyond criticism. In my view, the stance of dogmatic certainty or isolated superiority is the reverse of what is demanded for effective transformation of human suffering. The adequate maintenance of the analytic ritual, with its ethical and generally non-retaliatory commitments, allows the analyst to engage openly in a process of discovery, without having to know in advance or even to know at all (in many ways) exactly how to interpret or understand particular enactments, images, and so on. Rather than demonstrating to the patient an attitude of being beyond criticism, the effective analyst will naturally show a willingness to be corrected and guided by the patient while also being confident about how the process or method of transformation works, and how insight and compassion are manifest in human actions.

In conclusion, then, I regard the aim of effective psychoanalytic treatment to be the amelioration of suffering that is revealed through the emotional habit patterns expressed in the iconic-projective transference, dreams, and reports of other relational patterns. This process leads also to an increase in compassion for self and others as the investigation of the patient's suffering takes place. The containing-transcending transference, as the transference of hope for renewal, will be strengthened over the course of effective treatment, rather than resolved. As a result, the patient leaves the treatment with not only new skills and perspective for increasing subjective freedom, but also with the motivation and humility to continue to do so. The latter come especially from ongoing compassion for oneself and others.

# Part 4

## Transcendence and subjectivity

# Chapter 16

# Psychotherapy as ordinary transcendence: the unspeakable and the unspoken

I have at times written and talked about psychotherapy as a spiritual practice that awakens us to how and why we create suffering and shows us a path toward compassion and interdependence. But I would rather not. I would rather talk about psychotherapy as its own practice: a practice of ordinary transcendence. This kind of transcendence provides evidence and insight that being human means being dependent, and that the life space we inhabit is one of interdependence, not independence. It also shows us that self-protectiveness, isolation and the ubiquitous human desire for omnipotence produce great suffering. This type of transcendence carries no special labels such as "mystical" or "spiritual." It frequently goes unnoticed outside of psychotherapy or other practices designed to reveal it, because it goes against the grain of our culture of individualism.

In effective psychotherapy, ordinary transcendence becomes focal and conscious through a process in which the participants sustain their respect and regard for each other in the midst of dangerous affective dynamics that are expressed and understood as part of a search for new insight and meaning. Specific individual knowledge about the patient increases while both parties learn what it means to be human. They repeatedly encounter limitations of their own power and knowledge while they discover their interdependence and mutual playfulness in expanding a shared purpose.

## Ordinary transcendence in context

In my clinical practice of psychotherapy, I see individuals in psychoanalytic psychotherapy in face-to-face encounters at the frequency of one or two (fifty-minute) sessions per week. I also work with individuals in more intensive psychoanalysis, sometimes using the analytic couch at the frequency of three or four sessions per week. Additionally, my husband Ed Epstein and I work together as a team seeing couples in a form of psychotherapy that we originated, called "Dialogue Therapy," which uses psychodynamic principles and psychodramatic methods to help couples improve their abilities for intimate communication and partnership. And finally, I supervise psychologists, social workers and psychiatric residents in the practice of psychodynamic psychotherapy.

In all of these settings, I witness the process of transcendence that I describe in this chapter. My professional preparation includes a background in developmental psychology, which I taught at the graduate level for a long time, and a wide variety of different trainings in psychoanalytic approaches (such as object relations and self psychology). Additionally, I have for many years been a practitioner of Zen Buddhism, Jung's analytical psychology and feminism.

As a Jungian analyst, I find myself uncomfortable with the habit among many Jungians of labeling certain experiences as "numinous" or "soulful" because of the dichotomy between spiritual and secular that is implied. Thinking and theorizing along the lines of a secular–spiritual dichotomy can, in my view, lead to overlooking spiritual yearnings that naturally arise through exploring ordinary problems. Urgent longings to understand why we are here and why we die may be revealed, for example, in discovering the meaning of being "workaholic" or seeing what is being communicated through the habit of being late for appointments. Without elevating or redeeming these troubles, they can unveil a profound search for life's meaning. So, I want to stand clear of calling certain states of mind or ways of seeing more extraordinary than others; I prefer not to predict what is, or where I or anyone might find, a moment of transcendence.

Can we speak of the spiritual value of our psychotherapeutic work and hold it lightly, without sounding like it is akin to meditation or religion? On one hand, we have the problem of not speaking too much about something that takes form and shape according to the needs and being of each individual. Although there are conditions within the therapeutic set-up that increase the possibilities for what I am calling ordinary transcendence, there are no guarantees that any particular therapist–patient dyad will reach this goal. The elusive spiritual quality of psychotherapy is – I believe – fundamentally "unspeakable" because it is hurt or even spoiled by too much theorizing or commercializing. Later I will say more about this unspeakable quality in terms of its unknowable character.

On the other hand, psychotherapy has certain transformative aspects that derive their strength precisely from putting into words that which has been "unspoken." These include not only the interpretation of transference and dreams, but especially the interpretation of projective identification. This latter experience is an unconscious communication of affective meaning for which language may never have been available. An unintentional attempt to communicate unconscious emotional memories through perceiving their frightening or stimulating implications in another's being, words or actions, this kind of projection tends to evoke an enactment of what is projected. The other person feels emotionally kidnapped by, and appears to identify with, the projection that the sender is unconsciously making. There are both "subject" and "object" poles in such a communication, and the person who receives and plays out the projected dynamic will be an actor in the other's inner theatre.

When the unspoken aspects of our hidden emotional intentions are revealed to us, they show us how we create a world through our projected meanings and fantasies. Witnessing this with a trusted therapist, in the moment it is happening, reveals the roots of our suffering. Perhaps the most widely read Buddhist text, *The Dhammapada*, begins with these lines: "We are what we think. All that we are arises with our thought. With our thoughts we make the world" (Bryom, 1993: 1). Effective psychotherapy shows us exactly this.

When I began my training to be a Jungian psychoanalyst in 1978, I was already a formal student of Zen Buddhism. Therefore, I have always practiced and understood depth psychology from a Buddhist perspective. Buddhism has assisted me in interpreting, revising and practicing analysis and psychotherapy from a "non-essentialist" perspective that typifies all Buddhist practices. Essentialism is a philosophical position that presumes that certain permanent unchanging essences underlie human experience and perception. These essences are believed to determine aspects of our world that exist outside our subjectivity, and are not matters of our own interpretation or perception. For example, a current popular form of essentialism is a belief that many of our moods, talents, and other characteristics are physical or biological traits. In earlier periods of time, essentialist beliefs were cast either as ideal forms (Plato) or mental categories (Kant) that determined human agency and experience. Non-essentialism rejects the notion of an unchanging essence or substance at the foundation of our experiences. Instead it assumes that nothing is permanent and unchanging. Even the very world that we perceive as solid and stable is constructed or created from our own perceptions and interpretations.

In Jung's later years, after 1944, he moved away from essentialist reasoning about archetype and complex, and the collective and personal unconscious. He unsystematically revised many of the principles of his theory to fit the prevailing new ideas about innate releasing mechanisms, predispositions to certain emotional enactments, and the role of interpersonal situations in emotional adaptation. Many later psychoanalysts (including most Jungians themselves) have overlooked this major change in his thinking. It is this "ethological" process-oriented approach that I have embraced in Jung, have further developed in my own writings and practice, and find consonant with Buddhism, and with contemporary constructivism. Psychological and biological constructivism – distinct from social constructivism – is a branch of postmodern theorizing that claims that our phenomenal world (the physical, emotional and psychological) arises from the constraints of our embodied consciousness imposed on an environment in flux that we can never know directly. What I write here exemplifies a dialogue between Buddhism and analytical psychology, but also outlines a constructivist psychology for understanding transcendence through effective psychoanalytic psychotherapy.

## Transcendence through multiple realities

I often think of the famous anecdote about the Zen patriarch Bodhidharma who is purported to have brought Zen or Chan (in Chinese) meditation from India to China. The eminent Chinese emperor Wu asked the great master Bodhidharma, "What is the highest meaning of the holy truths?" Bodhidharma said, "Empty, without holiness." The emperor said, "Who is facing me?" and Bodhidharma replied "I don't know." Here "empty" means without an essential nature. The answer cautions us not to elevate and separate out certain things as holy while assuming that other elements of our experience are inferior. The reply to the question of identity (Who is facing me?) is yet another reminder not to foreclose on meaning, and name just one identity when our identities are fluid and always changing.

Psychotherapy is a relationship founded on human suffering, attempting to alleviate it through an awakening – awakening to how we create worlds through our thoughts and intentions. When this drama is fully engaged, it always leads to the great spiritual questions – Why are we here? Who are we, as humans? Why do we die? – but it cannot provide answers to these questions because it is not designed to function at such a universal level. When spiritual questions arise in a therapy session, not defensively but earnestly, I respond with interest. I show by my manner that the questions merit futher inquiry. If an individual has an established spiritual context, a religion or practice, I direct the questions into that context. If the patient is confused and uninformed, I may suggest some extra-therapeutic reading or going to a center to pursue spiritual inquiry, but I clarify that I am a not a spiritual expert or teacher. Answering the great spiritual questions requires, in my view, a religious or spiritual practice or method that has been developed specifically to answer spiritual questions.

Psychotherapy was not designed to answer the great spiritual questions, but rather to deal with necessity, often in the face of pain and suffering. The ordinary transcendence that can emerge in psychotherapy arises from the necessity of dealing with overwhelming affective states (erotic, fearful, hateful, idealizing) in the context of respect and a search for personal understanding. Like taking out the garbage, mopping the floor, or feeding the dog, making use of overwhelming affective states is something we "have to do" in effective psychotherapy. Making use of these states takes us by surprise. Most people seek therapy not because they want to, but because they have to. Psychotherapy is only moderately desired at best by the people who have to pay for it. The negative affective states of patients are only ambivalently desired, at best, by the therapists who are responsible for containing and transforming them. Consequently, both therapist and client are really surprised when they suddenly feel deeply appreciative of their dependence on each other and the compassion that arises from it.

Effective therapy is transformative on a level beyond talk or interpretation. I have come to see its core process of transformation as an interaction between the patient's (and sometimes the therapist's) projections and the transcendent function: Jung's term for our ability to hold onto psychological and emotional openness in the face of pressure and impulses. The transcendent function, as a back-and-forth dialectic between different sides or images of a demanding conflict, permits the discovery of something new and unexpected, a creative solution that transcends the original conflict.

The transformation of troubling emotional patterns, through the transcendent function of psychotherapy, depends on the paradoxical and unknown, although it is guided by theory, knowledge and expertise. The therapeutic set-up is paradoxical itself. It renders the therapeutic relationship to be impersonally personal, empathically non-gratifying, erotically non-sexual, provocatively non-aggressive, and welcoming of spontaneous communications within a strongly bound time–fee–space limit.

A person coming for help, already in distress, is likely to want to create an order – an old emotional order – in such a paradoxical environment. The analyst or therapist, in response to what the patient imposes on the therapeutic relationship, is also likely to impose an old order in terms of theory, authority and/or her or his own unconscious emotional habits. But, the effective therapeutic process is like a Zen koan for both participants: it invites and defies old orders and known interpretations.

What permits psychotherapy to be transformative is the gradual ability on the part of the participants to penetrate the multiple layers of the therapeutic relationship and process. These multiple layers are explained by Arnold Modell (1990) who describes three "realities" in which patient and therapist are engaged.

We can envision Modell's three realities as concentric or nested frames that characterize different worlds existing simultaneously. Each new frame encompasses and reorganizes those within so that same experience can be felt to mean something different at each level. At the center is the projective transference. This is the transference of unconscious emotional memories in the form of psychological complexes. Within the projective transference, the patient and therapist experience highly charged emotional moments in which it seems to both parties that the underlying meanings and images are dangerous and overwhelming. This is a realm of sexual and aggressive longings, of demonic and intrusive fantasies, and of supernatural and idealistics images of all kinds.

Surrounding this projective swamp is the ordinary human connection of two people who are limited by their knowledge and embodiment, while they are attempting a task together: the amelioration of the patient's suffering through seeing how he or she creates it, to become free enough to stop.

The power of the patient to fire the therapist counterbalances the asymmetry of the projective transference. But the third therapeutic reality, the outer frame of the nested model, creates an effect that can hold sway over the other two layers. I call it the "containing-transcendent transference". This frame around the other realities of psychotherapy sets therapy apart from life by insuring that it is an interpersonal space in which the patient is safe to experience all affective dynamics without risk to life outside of therapy. This frame absolutely depends on the therapist's ethical conduct, emotional stability, professional training, and personal self-knowledge. For in order for the therapist to contain the multiple meanings of the paradoxical set-up I have been describing, she or he must be capable of tolerating and working with the full range of her or his own subjective experiences, as well as the patient's, without putting the patient at any risk of retaliation. Within the unobjectionable idealizing transference, the patient experiences the therapist as a very potent figure.

## Unspeakable transcendence

In my view, this idealizing transference provides the foundation for effective psychotherapy. In its absence, there is no psychotherapy. The other two realities present in therapy – projective transference and ordinary human connection – are the stuff of life outside of therapy. The idealizing transference provides a unique environment in which two people can discover the particular meanings of the patient's subjective life. The power of this transference, monitored by a genuinely ethical and interested therapist, allows psychological changes to occur because it is completely safe to express and examine what would otherwise endanger one emotionally or physically in the presence of others or in the isolation of oneself alone.

Moreover, the experience of the idealizing transference is an awakening of inchoate spiritual yearnings in the patient – yearnings for compassion and wisdom. Those yearnings are known to the patient at first through the hope and belief that *this* psychotherapist, can be (could be) helpful with things that no one else has ever seemed to help with. This hopeful belief is a direct by-product of a well-maintained therapeutic set-up, a good enough therapist *and* the patient's potential for individuation or development. It is experienced as a conviction that suffering will someday make sense and that life has a purpose that goes beyond one's own identity.

Jung describes this transference as a yearning for the *transcendent function*: the capacity to hold the tensions of conflict and struggle without collapsing prematurely into a judgment that "this is bad" or "this is good." Jung recognized that the idealizing transference has a purpose that cannot be reduced to childish longings or primitive impulses. It expresses the unconscious striving for spiritual development in the patient. Sometimes, maybe often, it is the patient's first authentic and sustained experience of the "unspeakable" unity of existence, the unnameable that is called God, the Tao, Buddha Nature, True Nature, and the like.

The effective treatment relationship is one in which the patient feels safely held and securely known so that she or he can encounter dangerous and troubling feelings in a safe environment in which both interdependence and compassion are discovered. Effectiveness can be disrupted and even permanently betrayed through a break in the idealizing transference. Of course, this can happen through an ethical violation by the therapist or through a gross mismanagement (for example, the therapist missing appointments or regularly showing up late) of the therapy. On a more subtle and more common level, effectiveness can be breached through the collapse of the idealizing transference into a chronic projective identification in which the therapist is experienced as yet another inadequate, uninformed or unempathic caregiver. Under these conditions, the therapist will seem to the patient to be still another caregiver who is not capable of helping, who has failed to treat the patient fairly and/or see the patient clearly. In my view, this kind of failure can also block the natural spiritual yearnings of the patient through a kind of hopelessness about ever being known or helped by an ideal figure.

Effectiveness can also be diminished through the therapist's (conscious or unconscious) unwillingness to admit to mistakes and/or to see his or her own failings. If a therapist cannot tolerate being seen in a negative light, she or he will avoid the patient's most dangerous affective dynamics in order not to make a mistake. Sometimes the patient actually improves, all the same, and feels entirely accepted and understood without encountering the frightening aspects of his or her emotional life, but the transcendent function will not be engaged because the conflict of opposites is not encountered. Under these circumstances, the patient will also feel a keen need to protect the therapist from dangerous affects. This too will be a repeat of childhood tendencies to protect one's parents, but will not be made known within the therapy.

More harmful than avoiding negative feelings is a therapist's longing for idealizing projections. If a therapist cannot tolerate being seen in a critical or negative light, she or he will have problems maintaining the constraints of the therapeutic set-up and will engage in granting special favors to the patient, or will give premature reassurances and support. Avoidance of negative emotions and images will rob psychotherapy of its heart through eliminating the possibility of transcending the patient's most troubling complexes.

While the projective transference is diminished or dissolved through mutative interpretation, the idealizing transference is enhanced and strengthened. The more the patient experiences the transformation of suffering, the more the patient will respect and even revere the analyst/therapist who seems to embody this means of understanding and developing. After an effective psychotherapy has come to an end, the idealizing transference continues to develop. Protecting this frame around the realities of psychotherapy is a lifelong ethical and compassionate task of any psychotherapist.

In a brief psychotherapy, the idealizing transference may never be spoken; it may only be felt as something very potent, very helpful. Near the conclusion of a more extended treatment, when the patient speaks of me in reverent tones, I name the agent as "the process of psychotherapy" reminding us how it allows us to witness our capacity to transform suffering and develop compassion. I express gratitude for having experienced psychotherapy with this particular patient, and point out that it was not me personally, but a process, that brought about the transformation.

## Speaking the unspoken

The goal of an effective psychotherapy or psychoanalysis is to have fairly reliable access to the transcendent function, especially in the midst of psychological complexes being triggered. This means an openness in one's attitude toward oneself and an interest in genuine dialogue between oneself and others. Experientially this is a willingness to be accountable for both conscious and unconscious intentions, moods and impulses – as they become known to oneself – and to recognize how one creates suffering through imposing old emotional habits, and wanting or wishing the world and others would conform to one's desires and ideals.

Patient and therapist move unevenly toward this goal through repeated encounters with the patient's psychological complexes, presented in dreams and the projective transference, and understood and transformed through effective interpretations. As I said earlier, such interpretations are transformative beyond words: they allow both patient and therapist to witness our interdependence in the discovery of emotional meaning and confront us with the multiple levels of reality in our affective lives. Effective interpretations emerge from the therapist's openness to uncertainty and new discoveries. In the midst of a patient's negative complex, this is a challenging task.

For example, when I attempt to interpret a self-hating attack that a depressed middle-aged man makes on himself, he immediately hears my interpretation as blame for his miseries. He says "you're saying that I sound like a victim, that I could do better and feel better if I just looked at myself differently, but I can't." Within the iconic-projective transference, he experiences me as a critical, disapproving father who has "told me many times how to behave" and he refuses. From his previous statements about me I know that he perceives me as a totally calm and centered person who could never be trapped in self-hatred. Within the containing-transcendent transference, he feels completely dependent on me to find "the way" out of his attacks on himself. He does not perceive me as an ordinary human being who is struggling to find words that will help him transform his attacks on himself into compassion for himself. I respond to the multiple realities by investigating with him each of his different perceptions of me – as critical father, as calm analyst, as super-human being. Together we discover a way that I can join him in making "baby steps" out of his self-hatred.

When a therapist is seen by the patient as unhelpful, inferior, inadequate, or uninformed and the therapist protects her professional authority too quickly with an implied "god's eye view" of the mess, then it's very likely that the therapist will get caught up in her own ego complex – feeling shame, pride, self-doubt or self-pity. And even more fundamental, a good therapist intuitively fears the destruction of the idealizing transference because then therapy suddenly becomes life. Then the patient and therapist are simply two people victimized by projective identification, both hurt and in a power struggle over what is going on. I have found it helpful to speak to the "big picture" of what's going on in these situations. In this case, I said "As your therapist I'm looking at what you've said with interest, and concern, and I'd like to look with you at a number of ways that we could understand it."

When patients believe that their views of me are *factually* based, not impressions based on their own subjective factors, I must become alert not simply to defend myself through stock interpretations or my own counter-transference – for example, the demand on myself that I should *always* be helpful. Keeping a modest tone of "this is how I'm seeing it," rather than "this is how it is," acknowledges the complexity of competing realities and the possibility of discovering what is truly new and previously unknown.

## Conclusion

Through the messy work of entering into and understanding projective transference, projective identification and the multiple realities of psychotherapy, patient and therapist learn to experience the freedom to choose among different meanings and discover that we are not condemned to repeat the emotional conditions into which we were born. We also learn that everything – from pain to excrement, from delusion to grandiosity, from pride to material wealth – can teach us spiritually because everything emanates compassion when it is perceived in the light of our interdependence, a light that shines through the idealizing transference and the transcendent function of effective psychotherapy.

# Compassion as resilience and transcendence

True compassion often emerges from attempting to help others with those conditions that we ourselves suffer. As before, the term "suffering" refers specifically to the discontent or anguish that almost always accompanies pain, adversity, loss, error, illness and other unhappy experiences. Suffering is different from life's necessary adversities because suffering is optional. It comes from the attitude or expectation that we bring to our experience and it adds to our misery.

Take, for example, a traffic jam or a bounced check. Neither of these is a serious adversity, but either one can occasion plenty of suffering if we are thrown off-balance and become opposed to the event. And, of course, it's only worse with major adversities such as illness or loss; then we add suffering to great pain or injury. Suffering itself – in the form of negative emotional habits and compulsions to repeat emotionally dangerous situations – is the very stuff of our neurotic conflicts and defenses. The experience of being off-center or discontent, is guaranteed to accompany our grandiose or overly idealistic expectations, as well as our feelings of self-deprecation. Suffering is something that we humans create through our own mental and emotional habits, and it can be alleviated or even dissolved with certain kinds of knowledge and attention, and the desire to change.

## Resilience

Resilience in response to loss, pain, failure or other adversity belongs to those who know the nature of suffering and how to overcome it. I define "resilience" as the capacity to thrive after adversity, to bounce back to life with hope and vitality, rather than linger in envy or resentment after life has dealt us a difficult blow. Clearly resilience is related to many factors, but a major one is the ability to reduce one's suffering.

In studies of the "protective factors" that contribute to resilience, we find that many people become resilient without the benefit of psychotherapy or any kind of intervention. They seem able to keep in mind something that gives them hope, beyond their own fears, losses or disappointments. They are able to encounter and understand very negative experiences in a framework that allows them to transcend their own individual feelings and to see some larger purpose connected to their adversities.

Like many others, I believe that there are steps or stages in the development of resilience. I have my own terms for naming those steps: self-awareness, compassion, self-knowledge and renewal. The first step of self-awareness is a "waking up." It is the recognition, often the ah-ha, that one is actually creating misery in oneself. When I was a child of about eight, I first woke up to the realization of how people create suffering. I began to see how my father created unnecessary suffering for himself and those around him. I saw clearly how he continuously hurt those that he loved without wanting or intending to. I tried desperately to stop him from his habits, but that only increased their intensity, and so I began to study him closely to try to figure out what was wrong.

Throughout my childhood, my father had an undiagnosed and untreated emotional disorder, the result of an extremely traumatic and impoverished childhood: we would now call it complex post-traumatic stress disorder or "borderline personality disorder." His unpredictable aggressive and paranoid states became known to me as his "craziness" – something that I learned to objectify and analyze by the time I was twelve or so. I could see, although I didn't have words to say so, that he was driven by some part of himself that he did not understand. I could see that his suffering was unnecessary, but that it also seemed unstoppable. As I look back on all of this now, I realize that my father's suffering helped me discern the self-created nature of repetition compulsions or psychological complexes: our tendency to recreate in adulthood the emotional dangers and difficulties that we could not master as children.

My father frequently attacked and derided me, but I began to develop resilience in the face of these attacks during my mid-teen years. I decided that I would use my difficult experiences to help others in the future. I decided to become a psychoanalyst. Even though I was the only child of a factory worker and a housewife who had never attended even high school, I managed to find out about psychiatry, psychology and psychoanalysis. I don't recall exactly how it happened, but my junior high school essay for Career Day was about becoming a psychoanalyst. Along the way, I realized that I would not be able to heal my father, that he could not accept the help I offered through my angry observations, but I pledged myself to help others in the future.

Compassion emerges from trying to help. In the case of my father, I tried to help him because I suffered from his outbursts, and in the future I wanted to help others who had suffered in similar circumstances, as well as those who wrestled with their own difficult feelings in trying to be effective parents. Compassion begins to develop through our first altruistic gestures and is expanded through our emotional attunements with others, and later our sympathy and our empathy if we can infer others' realities. Compassion is a special form of empathy if it develops to full maturity. In its most mature form, compassion is the ability to offer effective help to those who are in pain and suffering, having acknowledged and understood our own, at least to some extent.

Compassion literally means "to suffer with" – *com*-passion. Different from other forms of helping like charity and sympathy, in which the helper stands apart from the sufferer, in compassion the helper steps into the shoes of the sufferer. To develop compassion, we have to acknowledge our own suffering because we cannot suffer *with* unless we know that we too suffer. Joining with others in adversity and suffering, we gradually increase our self-knowledge, not necessarily in terms of who we are as individuals, but in terms of what it means to be human. We begin to see how compassion sustains us by opening new horizons of meaning and purpose. It does not leave us feeling exhausted, resentful or empty as other forms of helping sometimes do. I will say more about this soon, but first I want to relate a story about a parrot and a sailor that shows us something about the nature of compassion, something analogous to the story of my early attempts to help my father.

## The parrot of compassion

An old sailor owns a pet parrot. The sailor is a crusty, cantankerous sort who does not enjoy the company of other people; diagnostically, we would certainly label him "schizoid." Like many good schizoid people, he thoroughly enjoys his pet. In addition to the pet, the sailor enjoys his pipe which he has been smoking for years. Unfortunately, though, his parrot develops a chronic cough and the sailor begins to be afraid that the parrot has contracted a lung disease from passively inhaling pipe smoke over the years. Naturally this creates a conflict for the sailor: should he part with his pipe or his parrot? Because his parrot is his best friend, the sailor decides to give up his pipe. Some months later, the sailor is still worried about his pet and so he takes the parrot to the vet to be examined. After checking the parrot's lungs and listening to his heart, the vet pronounces the parrot entirely healthy. "But what about the cough that was going on for months?" the sailor asks. The vet approaches the parrot and coughs. Echoing him, the parrot coughs back.

The parrot had been *imitating* the sailor's chronic cough which the sailor had ignored in himself. The sailor would never have stopped smoking for himself, but he has done so for the love of his parrot. The parrot's "compassionate" cough, which mirrored the suffering of his master, is similar to my early impulse to help my father. The parrot's cough led to the sailor wanting to help that resulted in him being helped himself.

My initial mirroring of my father's suffering in my own impulse to help led to my complaint about how unfortunate *I* was to have a crazy father who wouldn't listen to me, but eventually led to my development as a competent helper. As a psychologist, a psychoanalyst and a Buddhist, I have benefited endlessly from my attempts to understand and help my father in his suffering.

## The great identity questions

My first role as a psychologist was as a developmental psychologist, and I still think in terms of developmental processes. In attempting to understand some of the ways that meaning evolves in our lives, I think in terms of three questions that I call the great questions of identity: Who are They? Who am I? and Who are We? These three questions characterize major trends in our desire to find meaning in our lives over time.

In our early years we all ask the first question: Who are They? They are the Big Ones who surround us: our parents, elders, older siblings who initially seem so incredibly powerful and command our curiosity and interest. Some people never answer this question to their satisfaction, and so they stay with it for the rest of their lives. These people are always gathering data about Them – the neighbors, the boss, the relatives, the President of the USA. But if we pay close attention to our answers about Them, we start to wonder about ourselves.

Who am I? Typically a question of late adolescence and early adulthood, "Who am I?" leads to the individual, personal search for a certain kind of self, career, family, relationships, and so on. Of course, many people remain with this second question throughout adulthood. Instead of feeling secure in themselves as individuals, they anxiously continue to be preoccupied with finding independence and uniqueness. Nothing satisfies the question of personal identity.

But those people who are truly resilient will eventually be moved to ask the third identity question: Who are We? This question addresses the issue of what it means to be human – to be so responsible and yet so weak, so knowledgeable and yet so ignorant. What is it about our species that we create so much suffering for ourselves and others? What's going on here, anyway? Compassionate actions and feelings gradually but inexorably reveal the answers to this third great identity question of what it means to be human. In the process, we learn how to renew ourselves and engage with life anew on a moment-to-moment basis. So these three questions – Who are They? Who am I? and Who are We? – exemplify different levels of development in relation to resilience in which the first is the level of helpless victims, the second of neurotic anxiety and conflict, and the third of compassionate resilience. Of course, we can reach the third level and still be bounced back to the earlier two in the face of adversity.

### The wise emperor

In the following story, a wise emperor who has reached the third level is attempting to search for meaning through asking three questions (different from above). This is a traditional Zen story that illustrates some of the ways in which compassion teaches the wise.

Once upon a time an emperor decided that if he knew the answers to three questions, he would always know what to do. The questions were these:

> When is the best time to do things?
> Who are the most important people?
> What is the most important thing?

The emperor offered a big reward for the right answers to these questions, and he received many answers, but none satisfied him.

Finally, he decided to travel to the top of the mountain to visit an old hermit who would perhaps know the right answers. When he reached the hermit, the emperor asked his three questions. The hermit, digging in his garden, listened attentively and said nothing. He returned to his digging. As the emperor watched him, he noticed how tired the old man seemed.

"Here," he said, "give me the spade and I'll dig while you rest." So the hermit rested and the emperor dug.

After several hours, the emperor was very tired. He put down the spade and said: "If you can't answer my questions, that's all right. Just tell me and I'll take my leave."

"Wait, do you hear someone running?" the hermit asked suddenly, pointing to the edge of the woods.

Sure enough, a man came tumbling out of the woods, clutching his stomach. He collapsed as the hermit and the emperor reached him. Opening the man's shirt, they saw that he had a deep wound. The emperor cleaned the wound, using his own shirt to bind it. Regaining consciousness, the man asked for water. The emperor hurried to a nearby stream and brought him some. The man drank gratefully, then slept.

The hermit and the emperor carried the man into the hut and lay him on the hermit's bed. By this time the emperor was exhausted, too, and he fell asleep.

The next morning when the emperor awoke, he saw the wounded man staring down at him.

"Forgive me," the man whispered.

"Forgive you?" said the emperor, sitting up, wide awake now. "What have you done that needs my forgiveness?"

"You do not know me, your majesty, but I have thought of you as my sworn enemy. During the last war you killed my brother and took away my lands."

The man went on to explain that he had been lying in ambush, waiting for the emperor to come back down the mountain when one of the emperor's own attendants recognized him as an enemy and stabbed him.

"I fled, but if you hadn't helped me when you did, I surely would have died. I had planned to kill you. Instead, you saved my life! I am so ashamed and so grateful."

The emperor was glad to hear the story and restored the man's land.

After the man left, the emperor looked at the hermit and said, "I must leave now. I shall travel everywhere looking for the answers to my questions."

The hermit laughed and replied, "Your questions have already been answered."

The hermit explained that if the emperor had not helped to dig the garden but had simply hurried off in search of answers to his questions, he would have been killed by his enemy on the way down the mountain. "The most important time for you was the time you were digging in my garden. The most important person was myself, the person you were with, and the most important thing was simply to help me," said the hermit.

"And later, when we met the wounded man, the most important time was that spent tending his wound, for otherwise he would have died – and you would not have become friends. And he was at that moment the most important person in the world, and the most important pursuit was tending his wound.

"The present moment is the only moment," the hermit continued. "The most important person is always the person you are with. And the most important pursuit is making the person at your side as happy as possible. What could be simpler or more important?"

## Transcendent compassion

To attain the real and immediate ability to pay attention to the present moment and to be truly effective in helping others, we must repeatedly engage our compassion by stepping into the shoes of those who suffer and staying with them to find the way out of their suffering. In doing so, we discover that we humans are not powerless victims of circumstances or dynamics beyond our control.

Compassion teaches about our uniquely human freedom: the freedom to make meaning that transcends pain and loss, and transforms it into connections with others. Through the knowledge of compassion we recognize that suffering is not only optional, but it is the bridge that connects us with others and the world. When we cross that bridge, our fears and self-protectiveness (as individuals, societies and nations) are repeatedly transformed into evermore deepened appreciation of our interdependence, as we find the world renewed through our compassionate perception of it.

# Chapter 18

# Locating the transcendent: inference, rupture, irony

As I have said, I believe that constructivism is consistent with Jung's later work, after 1944. In 1958 (Jung, 1916/1969: 67–68) he wrote a brief commentary for the publication of his 1916 essay "The transcendent function" that states succinctly that this function is "identical with the universal question: How does one come to terms in practice with the unconscious? . . . For the unconscious is not this thing or that; it is the Unknown as it immediately affects us". The "Unknown" indicates a kind of unconsciousness that is unknowable. This kind of unconsciousness is what psychoanalyst Jacques Lacan calls the Real and what objection relations theorist Thomas Ogden (1989) describes as lying beyond the "primitive edge of experience." These theorists specify that the Unknown, the Real, and what is beyond the primitive edge cannot be captured in language, images or even dreams. The Unknown is incoherent and unrevealed to human consciousness, although we infer it from our experiences. In the remainder of this essay I will use the term "the Unknown" to refer to this type of unconsciousness whose meaning is inferred in a variety of human contexts, but cannot be known directly even through our dreams and visions.

I shall discuss the Unknown and the transcendent function in two ways. First, I will discuss the role of inference and the interpretive context in our theorizing about the Unknown. Our claims for the unknowable archetype and the transcendental Self are significant Jungian inferences made within an interpretive context. They are not knowledge of the Unknown. If we forget that these concepts are based on hypotheses and inferences and speak as though they represent direct experiences, we lose the transcendent function in theoretical discourse among ourselves and with others.

My second discussion involves those occasions, especially in psychotherapy or analysis, when our sense of containment or coherence is disrupted. These are moments of horror, pain, fear or irritation that intrude into our apparent control. Such moments are ruptures in the analyst's and/or analysand's belief that analysis can come to terms with the Unknown. In such a moment the transcendent function may be lost or restored depending on how the analyst responds. It is an opportunity to come to terms with the Unknown.

Jung nowhere gave an exact definition of the transcendent function. In his 1916 essay, Jung (1916/1969: 69) said that "There is nothing mysterious or metaphysical about the term," which refers to a "union of conscious and unconscious contents". In a 1920 explanation he said it is "a complex function . . . that facilitates a transition from one attitude to another. The raw material shaped by thesis and antithesis . . . is the living symbol". I see this function as a capacity to move back and forth between layers of meaning, in a manner that psychoanalyst D.W. Winnicott (1971) described as inhabiting "potential space" or "play space." Author and Jungian analyst Carol Savitz (1990: 243) gives the following clinical description of the transcendent function: it is "a bridge to help cross the abyss between affects, between affect and memory, between self and ego, between analyst and patient". This bridge, in whatever form it may emerge, becomes the symbol of the psyche transcending dissolution and ultimately coming to terms with the Unknown.

## Inference and experience

My response to much contemporary Jungian theorizing and commentary on the Self is to remember Jung's repeated assertions that his concept of the Self as empty center is neither knowledge nor experience of the Unknown. In a 1955 (1955/1975: 259) letter, for example, he said of the Self: "Here the limit of possible experience is reached: the ego dissolves as the reference point of cognition". In the same letter he said, "If I call the 'ultimate' the self and you call it the 'absolute ultimate,' its ultimateness is not changed one whit . . . I see many God-images of various kinds . . . but I know that none of them expresses or captures the immeasurable Other" (p. 261). Implicitly Jung was stressing the transcendent function in recognizing the role of inference in our speculations about the Unknown. We cannot know this Otherness; we can only infer and attempt to understand it in context.

Jung wrote a great deal about the dialectic in a Hegelian sense of thesis and antithesis; we often describe the transcendent function as "holding the tension of opposites." I discovered the term "dialectical space" in Ogden's work (1989) and have come to see it as the basis for maintaining the transcendent function in both theory and practice. His dialectical process is one in which two opposing concepts inform, create and oppose each other in a dynamic relationship. So far, no different from Jung. Ogden empha-sizes, however, that the creative dialectic of human development takes place primarily in the "space" between symbol (image or word) and symbolized (experience) mediated by an interpreting self. In this dialectical space we are creative rather than simply reactive. We are "free" to invent or discover new meaning from old patterns. More emphatically than Jung, Ogden stresses the importance of our awareness of ourselves as thinking subjects – as interpreters within a context. If we lose this awareness, we invite a "pathology of dialectic" that Ogden (p. 216, emphases in original) describes as follows:

> The subject becomes tightly imprisoned in the realm of fantasy objects as things in themselves. This is a two-dimensional world which is experienced as a collection of facts. The hallucination does not sound like a voice, it *is* a voice. One's husband does not simply behave coldly, he *is* ice. One does not feel like one's father, one's father *is* in one's blood.

In Jungian discussions of the archetype or the Self, I find us frequently collapsing the space between the symbol (our concept) and the symbolized (the Unknown), and then forgetting that we do not directly experience these unknowables. For example, if we claim that some dreams are "archetypal" and others are "ordinary" without attending to the context of why this claim is made for a particular dream, but instead act as though this knowledge is immediately accessible either to the dreamer or the analyst, we have collapsed the dialectical space around the Unknown. In theorizing, we have a tendency to describe the Self as a human subject. In such a case, the Self is described as a subject with views, ideas, or guidelines that can be known to us. Here is a randomly chosen example from a contemporary Jungian text: "A man dreamt 'I am a lion.' This presented his Self's view of a potential lion force." If the Self is a concept inferred from a principle of unity, the Self cannot have a view. It is not a perceiving subject like a human being. If we want to infer that the Self is a perceiving subject, then we need to give an account in our theory to defend this assumption.

When we collapse the dialectical space around our theorizing about the Unknown, and seem to imply that we experience the Unknown directly, we forget to defend our assumptions. This tends to hamper us in dialogues with our colleagues in depth psychology or other fields. We sound as if we are making truth claims about experiences of the unknowable. Jung (1955/ 1975) was a critic of such truth claims made by theologians. In 1955, Jung (1955/1975: 261) wrote, "If theologians think that whenever they say 'God' then god is, they are deifying anthropomorphisms, psychic structures and myths. This is exactly what I don't do . . . Who talks of divine knowledge and divine revelation? Certainly not me".

If we lose the transcendent function in our theorizing about the Unknown, there is no space to explore how our interpretive context affects our views. (In Jung's words, the "name means far less . . . than the view associated with it" [p. 261]). What does an analyst's pronouncement about an analysand's Self mean within the therapeutic relationship at any moment? What is its purpose? Defensive? Loving? Aggressive? Why do some Jungians collapse the dialectical space around the concept of Self in Jungian discourse? What does this mean?

All inferences about the Unknown are made within a context. Holding the tension of the transcendent function can produce a new synthesis of meaning about the Unknown from differing contexts. As Jung said: When confronted with the Unknown "the ego can merely affirm that something vitally important is happening to it. It may conjecture that it has come up against something greater, that it feels powerless against this greater power . . . The ego has to acknowledge many gods before it attains the centre where no god helps it any longer against another god" (p. 259). Context and purpose in confronting the Unknown produce configurations of meaning that guide us in coming to terms with a moment or a larger theoretical issue.

Claims about the Unknown are made in many different languages: scientific, philosophical, mathematical, psychological, religious. These claims are not readily interchangeable because of the different viewpoints of the communities of speakers. Jungian speakers sometimes collapse the dialectical space between different languages and assume that concepts like the archetype or the Self encompass concepts from other disciplines (e.g., anthropology, physics or mathematics) in a way that is disagreeable to theorists in those disciplines. When this happens, we tend to subsume divergent assumptions about the Unknown under our concepts without adequate dialog with the other side. As scholar Wendy Doniger (1992: 8) said recently of Joseph Campbell's tendency to collapse the dialectical space: "He made the myths he retold his myths, instead of letting them tell their own story". Respecting the dialectical space means living within transcendent function, allowing for the emergence of new meaning from differing views of the Unknown.

I would like to see a new emphasis on the transcendent function in Jungian discourse about the Unknown. If we claim to hear the voice of the Unknown directly or know the view from the empty center, we have collapsed the transcendent function into a pathology of the dialectic. This leads to theoretical dogmatism with no potential space for moving back and forth between levels of meaning in coming to terms with ourselves and our reason for making this or that inference about the Unknown.

## Crisis and intersubjectivity in analysis

Although inferences about the Unknown are "experience-far," certain disruptive experiences are "close encounters" with the unspeakable. Ogden uses the metaphor of the "primitive edge" to allude to the "surface" or edge of our containment, particularly the containment we feel within a body. The primitive edge is the outermost surface of what seems under our control. Rupture of this edge leads to "unthinkable agonies" (falling forever, having no relation to the body, complete alienation, etc.), as Winnicott called them. The intrusion of the chaotic into the orderly may seem horrific or awesome depending on the context.

In therapy and in life, our close encounters with the Unknown are often shocking. A term for this encounter is "crisis" and Jungian analyst Verena Kast (1990: 11) gives a useful description of it when she says: "The term 'crisis' describes a very decisive moment . . . wherein . . . we can no longer solve a problem with known ways and means at a time when it matters a great deal to us that the problem be solved." Kast uses crisis to talk about a "creative process" in which we are faced with a gap, barrier or difficulty that we cannot overcome using ordinary solutions.

The particular crisis I want to discuss here is a rupture in the therapeutic relationship. This is a serious disruption in which the analysand doubts the analyst's ability to help and wants to quit therapy. At this point the analyst is faced with an intersubjective disorganization, a break in the trust on which analysis is based.

A woman in her late forties has seen me in analytically oriented therapy (with periods of crisis intervention) over almost five years, once a week. She had a chaotic, disruptive childhood: She was physically and sexually abused by her stepfather, lost her own father through desertion, was repeatedly misperceived by her mother who failed to protect her from the stepfather's cruelties, and was socially ostracized because of her mixed racial background. Had I heard her personal history out of context of her present life, I would have predicted that she would have a disabling borderline personality syndrome with overwhelming impulses to mutilate herself.

As it is, she is a very successful psychotherapist who works in a large metropolitan clinic as both a general practitioner and a drug and alcohol counselor. She has been married and divorced twice, has two grown daughters who live on their own and a preadolescent son who does well in school. She has great difficulty trusting the regard and love people feel for her. She also has a tendency to vomit when she feels out of control. Otherwise she has no serious symptoms. Her symptoms were more disruptive when she began treatment with me.

She came because she wanted "Jungian analysis" with hopes that she might train as an analyst some day. During the first year, she was a home-maker (having temporarily "retired" as a therapist) who made a comfortable home for her husband, son and one teenage daughter. (This was prior to her husband's leaving her "for another woman," someone she knew.) She had many dreams with frightening psychotic images: people being ripped apart, body parts fused with machines, deadly animals and weapons, her own violence and others' violence against her. She became afraid to tell me such dreams because she feared they were "true" in the way of prophecy. There had been events in her life that she felt had been prophesied by her dreams. Although I was deeply concerned about the psychotic images in her dreams, I was also convinced that she was a woman of complex development who could hold different meanings simultaneously and reflect on her inner states. I saw her literal interpretations of her dreams as a defense against her self-hatred. I placed my bets on this view.

Many months passed during which we were in a crisis mode after her husband left. I gave much advice – not my usual style. Her conduct with her divorcing husband benefited from my advice, her son benefited from her conduct, and so on. We were all quite contained. After most of the crisis had passed and her son was in treatment with a good psychiatrist and she was making a solid income and could see new possibilities, she lost faith in our treatment.

She complained that although she had followed my advice, was doing what she "needed to live," and had long since given up literal inter-pretations of her dreams (which had also become more humanized), she felt no better, especially in her body. Everything seemed "driven" from the outside with no personal satisfaction for her. She could see no future for herself and she was distractedly envious of her ex-husband. She worried that I had idealized her, believing she could transcend so many difficulties and develop herself into – something. We both felt a heavy depression and fear, and I was unsure about the paths I had taken with her.

This situation existed at the time of the Christmas holidays. For two years I had warmly accepted small gifts from her during the holidays and believed that she was symbolically putting parts of herself into me as a container. Because of the disintegration in her daily life I had decided to say nothing interpretive about the gifts. The third year she gave me a larger gift. It was a little stained glass window, a delightful design with colors that matched perfectly the stained glass I already had in my office. In the previous session she had expressed frustration that I "wouldn't just let her leave" therapy. The gift was presented with a sort of "here it is" gesture, and when I opened its wrapping and exclaimed how beautiful it was, she said that she felt very "lucky" to find it. Because of my uncertainty and the size of the gift, I made an interpretive remark about it. I said something like "There is a reason why you keep giving me gifts?" She was enraged. She said that she didn't want her gifts to be analyzed, and that I had not done that before. I felt a huge anxiety arise in me. I couldn't make out in my own thoughts anything except how much I cared about this woman and how stupid I felt. I remarked stupidly that sometimes people offer me gifts when they are angry with me; she was nonplussed. Then I said that perhaps she "wanted to leave parts of herself in me." She looked puzzled and angry. She announced that this was her last session. I responded emphatically that this was not a good time to quit. She agreed to come for another session and we finished this one in a daze.

In my reflection after the session, I knew my actions were contradictory and wrong. I had accepted the gift and destroyed the "magic" of it through an interpretation. Her faith in me had been wearing thin anyway and now I had destroyed something and hurt her badly. We spent the next session talking about her reactions to my statement. I opened by asking her why my words had hurt so much. She said she felt betrayed by my speaking about her gift. In that moment I had changed into someone who wanted to examine her motives for giving. I had become like her mother who could never simply accept her love, but always had to correct it. Movingly she told me how much she enjoyed choosing and giving me these gifts as a recognition of what I had given her during the crisis. She rejected the idea that she "was putting parts" of herself into me. With relief, I understood. I could see how I seemed like her mother who was never simply pleased by her. I said I believed in her capacity to continue developing, but recognized also that she did not believe in it. She felt relieved. She recommitted herself to therapy. The stained glass remains on my window sill and no further mention of it has been made.

The transcendent function is fostered by the unobjectionable idealizing transference, as I have said repeatedly. In the words of psychotherapy researcher Hans Strupp (1989: 723), this kind of transference can be understood as the "overriding significance of the interpersonal relationship between patient and therapist as the vehicle for therapeutic change". When I interpreted her gift, my analysand felt belittled. We lost the transcendent function and I became the Terrible Mother. She lost hope in me and was flooded with unspeakable agonies she had experienced with enraged and unpredictable childhood caregivers. In reflecting on the session afterward, I remembered a statement from a self psychologist: In a therapeutic rupture, attune yourself to the analysand's subjective experience.

Attuning to the analysand's subjectivity restores the containing-transcendent transference that I have described in other essays here. After this is re-established, together the analysand and I can examine the conscious and unconscious meanings of what happened. I take this as a new Basic Rule for analysis: When an analysand threatens to quit and accuses me of being at fault, always emphasize and explore the analysand's subjective state. Then examine the meaning that has emerged to see how it fits the narrative of our analytic work. A therapist who feels accused may unconsciously react to guilt and shame through projective identification. Reductive or genetic interpretations of the rupture imply "you caused this impasse" to the other person and tend to evoke guilt and shame in the other.

In 1916 Jung (1916/1969: 74) described the transcendent function of the idealizing transference. At this early date he observed that the process of transformation is rooted in the idealization of the analyst. The

idealizing transference allows an analysand to encounter powerful unconscious material with the belief that the analyst embodies the transcendent
function, the capacity to come to terms with the Unknown. Jung said:

> For the patient . . . the analyst has the character of an indispensable
> figure absolutely necessary for life. However infantile this dependence
> may appear to be, it expresses an extremely important demand which,
> if disappointed, often turns to bitter hatred of the analyst.

When the containing-transcendent transference is lost the analysand is at
the primitive edge. On the other side is the Unknown, the unspeakable, the
incoherent. The analysand experiences the analyst as having evoked this
chaos and wants to escape the relationship in which the chaos is occurring.
When the therapist empathizes and accepts the analysand's experience as
valid, for example, "I seem to be causing you overwhelming pain and you
feel as though I cannot be trusted," the analysand can begin to re-establish
trust in the therapeutic relationship.

In general, this idealizing transference should not be interpreted, unless
the analysand requests it, but should be understood by the analyst as
necessary for transformation to occur. If the containing-transcendent transference never takes place, there is no possibility of transformation through
the therapy. If this transference is lost, the possibility for transformation
dies. The analysand will never again risk much with the analyst because they
went to the edge and the analyst failed. If this transference is restored after a
rupture, together the two witness the living symbol of their relationship as a
means for coming to terms with the Unknown, bridging the most chaotic
unconsciousness with conscious meaning.

## Irritation and irony

A therapeutic rupture is a crisis that brings us face to face with the
unspeakable Unknown. Smaller moments of irritation, for example, when
an analysand "forgets" a session, face us with similar but less critical
disruptions. Irritating remarks and assaults, aggression, rage and humiliation are opportunities enacted by the analysand for creative transformation,
occasionally for feeling the transcendent function. Sometimes a negative
transference is interpreted genetically in terms of conscious projections and
images, parts of a psychological complex. Sometimes a negative transference
is interpreted interpersonally in terms of a difficulty arising in the therapeutic
relationship. With the hope of understanding conscious and unconscious
meanings, analysand and analyst come to know how to speak about the
various levels of meaning of negative emotions in a context of trust. I am a

great believer in the value of negative emotions in analysis, provided that neither analyst nor analysand destroys the containing transference. There are few intimate relationships in life in which envy, rage, or hatred can be spoken, acknowledged and understood without serious threat or danger. Allowing myself to be seen and experienced as hated, demanding, aloof and unloving have been moments of grace when they can be transformed through empathic understanding, followed by a collaborative interpretation of what happened.

Understanding the transcendent function has led me gradually to an ironic view of therapy, development, and even human life. Psychoanalyst Roy Schafer (1976: 50) defined ironic as a readiness "to seek out internal contradictions, ambiguities, and paradoxes" without the momentous implications of the tragic. I tend to see the classical Jungian view as romantic and the classical Freudian view as tragic. My own approach to Jungian analysis has been colored by irony through my years of struggling to sustain the transcendent function in my life and work. Here is Schafer's (p. 51) full description of the ironic vision that describes what I have learned about holding the tension of opposites:

> The ironic vision . . . aims at detachment, keeping things in perspective, taking nothing for granted, and readily spotting the antithesis to any thesis so as to reduce the claim of that thesis upon us. In this respect the ironic vision tends to limit (not minimize) the scale of involvement in human difficulty while continuing to insist on the inherent difficulties of human existence.

I read the term "detachment" here in line with Buddhist teachings about it. It is an attitude in which we let go of our own egocentrism and get a bigger perspective.

The perspective of irony, taking nothing for granted, enlivens our work. If we remain alert to the dialectical space of our own theorizing, I believe we are better able to attend to the subjectivity of the analysand on the primitive edge of experience. It is not our theory about the Unknown that will awaken us to the meaning of disruption, chaos, or unity. It is rather our capacity to remain attuned to the meanings that emerge. I conclude with a few verses from poet Howard Nemerov's (1977: 379–398) poem about the paradox of imposing meaning on emergent experience:

> Across the millstream below the bridge
> Seven blue swallows divide the air
> In shapes invisible and evanescent,
> Kaleidoscopic beyond the mind's
> Or memory's power to keep them there.

Fully awakened, I shall show you
A new thing: even the water
Flowing away beneath those birds
Will fail to reflect their flying forms,
And the eyes that see become as stones
Whence never tears shall fall again.

O swallows, swallows, poems are not
The point. Finding again the world,
That is the point, where loveliness
Adorns intelligible things
Because the mind's eye lit the sun.

# Chapter 19

# Self and transcendence: a postmodern approach to analytical psychology in practice

In the foreground of Jung's contributions to psychodynamic theory is the idea that the unity of personality is a struggle, both in the moment and over time. Although everyone strives for a coherent and continuous sense of self, this state of being is not easily sustained or ever finally secured. According to Jung, personality is structured as multiple centers of subjectivity, loosely organized around the ego complex with its core of the archetype of self. These "psychological complexes" are experienced as motivating forces with core affective and image components that are highly arousing.

In the following account, I show how Jung's theory of psychological complexes fits with contemporary research on emotions and emotional memory, and how his dissociative model of personality is balanced by a theory of integration and unity through the archetype of self. Additionally, I argue that analytical psychology is consonant with postmodernism when its models and methods are understood from a non-essentialist viewpoint which is, in my view, not a revision but an extension of Jung's own thinking.

## Archetype and complex

Core states of human life, such as bonding, attachment, separation anxiety, and grief, are expressed among human beings everywhere in similar gestural, facial and proto-communicative forms, and are infused with emotions. Human emotions – first the primary emotions that are recognizable at birth (see Izard, 1992; Tompkins, 1962, 1963) and then the "self-conscious" emotions (such as shame, pride, envy, guilt, embarrassment; see Lewis, 1991b) that emerge in the second year – create universal motivational and relational tendencies. From those who study emotional memory (e.g., Edelman, 1989; LeDoux, 1996), we know that memories play a large part in the human construction of the so-called "present moment." Gerard Edelman (1989) has referred to our emotionally charged memories as the "remembered present" to stress the categorical or metaphorical (rather than veridical) nature of representational memory. Joseph LeDoux (1996: 224) further expands our understanding of memory by showing that emotional memories can be representational or non-representational. For example, he explains that the hippocampus formation of the brain is "well-suited for establishing complex memories in which lots of events are bound together in space and time . . . No particular response is associated with these kinds of memories – they can be used in many different ways in many different situations". Representational memories are complex affective images that I would call "metaphors" (in the sense of Lakoff, 1987: 224), because they map cues from earlier domains of experience to later ones. By contrast, memories that are triggered in the amygdala are "rigidly coupled to specific kinds of responses . . . wired so as to preempt the need for thinking about what to do". In non-representational memories, we react to immediate stimuli because they have elicited a primitive emotion – usually fear – sometimes without conscious perception of them.

In Jung's later theory (after 1944), he claimed that innate potentials – called *archetypes* (meaning primary imprint) – predispose us to form *coherent affectively charged images* (archetypal images) that are expressed unconsciously in dreams, mythologies, folklore, art, religion, rituals and literature in similar forms the world over. In Jung's view, archetypal images were "living symbols" intimately connected to emotional life, not "signs" that could be translated through cultural or linguistic systems. This definition of archetype as an action-potential was the product of Jung's acquaintance with evolutionary biology and ethology, and comparable to Tinbergen's idea of innate releasing mechanisms. The archetype as core arousal state, connected to affective images, is now supported by Edelman's and Ledoux's work on emotional memory, and Goleman's (1995) model of emotional intelligence.

Psychological complexes form around archetypes and their images, as personality develops. Experiences of an individual's psychic reality – needs, perceptions, fantasy, action patterns, motivations, cognitions – cohere into associated dynamics because of the emotional energy of particular affective images that may be completely unconscious. All complexes are composed of core arousal states and emotional memories (in representational and non-representational forms) that may be either re-enacted or remembered. Psychological complexes are both universal and personal, both collective and individual, in that they form around archetypes and express the psychic reality of an individual life.

Complexes are similar to "subjective objects" because they are a mix of "subjective" and "objective" experiences patterned from emotional adaptation, and expressed in dreams, projective identifications, unconscious roles and other enactments in ordinary daily life. They play out individual adaptations to archetypal themes with survival purpose for our emotional lives, although they may block development as the emotional environment changes over time. Complexes may be enacted between oneself and others (e.g., playing the "victim child" to someone's "terrible father"), or within oneself (e.g., the ego complex being constantly threatened by intrusions from a negative mother complex).

In humans everywhere, we find such common complexes as "mother," "father," "child" and "ego." All of these have positive (e.g., "great mother") and negative ("terrible mother") expressions because of the dichotomizing tendencies that develop from the earliest distinctions between pain and pleasure, and because our early care was a mix of good and bad. Also each complex includes a subject pole (originally the experience of the subject) and an object pole (originally experienced as the object), but after adolescence, we can usually identify with either pole and project the other in an enactment or projective identification.

When unconscious complexes overtake ordinary consciousness, they invite or offer or demand that another participate. Enactments of complexes often become projective identifications that may be acute or chronic, in which one person communicates unconsciously through inviting another to play out some aspect of the first's complex. The receiving person will have fertile ground in her or his psyche to be familiar with the projected material, because of the universal nature of archetype and emotion. Identifying with another's projection, we play a role in another's inner theater that fits closely enough with something of our own. Jung called this *participation mystique*, borrowing the term from anthropology and describing clearly the mix of the unconscious dynamics between people.

### Self as archetype and ego as complex

What keeps us from forever drifting off into unconscious complexes in our everyday interactions? Why and how do we differentiate from constant enactments of our emotional memories, from re-experiencing ourselves as helpless children and others as powerful parents? Jung theorized a predisposition towards ever-evolving consciousness and knowledge of ourselves through the "archetype of self." This archetype endows each of us with a developmental potential to become a "psychological individual" who can be accountable for multiple centers of subjectivity and competing motivations. This potential is, obviously, no guarantee that the process will be realized because, as Jung notes in many places, becoming aware of and responsible for, our unconscious motives and complexes is an *opus contra naturam*, a work against nature.

The archetype of self is, first and foremost, a predisposition for integration and unity of the personality. It is experienced everywhere as the tendency to develop an ego complex with a coherent image of an individual embodied subject. In Jung's later theory of self (see Young-Eisendrath and Hall, 1991, and Young-Eisendrath, 1997a and 1997b for a full discussion of this), he describes this central archetype as the capacity or ability for increasing integration of the personality over time.

If development proceeds smoothly, the first expression of the archetype of self is the beginning of a rudimentary ego complex at around eighteen months to two years of age (marked by the expression of self-conscious emotions) evolving toward an embodied, subjective, gendered identity by the age of thirty-six months or so. The age of six or seven years heralds the experience of a unique identity: "I am somebody." This identity grows through relationships and rational self-awareness in childhood and adolescence until it culminates in what Piaget dubbed "formal thought operations" – the ability to think about our own thoughts and feelings, and to deduce our own motives from our behaviors. If all has gone well in the development of the ego complex, by the end of adolescence an individual will have some version of responsibility and intentionality for her or his own actions, according to the norms of the surrounding culture.

The self-conscious affects – pride, shame, envy, guilt, embarrassment and self-pity – arouse the ego complex interpersonally and intrapsychically. They call attention to self-other distinctions and again and again compel us, through the archetype of self, to create an image of an individual subject: a unified, separate being who must be defended and protected. As we bump up against unknown parts of ourselves and unfamiliar parts of the world, we are triggered through our emotional memories to impose the same affective images and action patterns of a particular embodied identity, defended through identifications and projections.

From a Jungian perspective, in order for development to proceed beyond adolescent defenses of the ego – identifying with its *persona* (social look or mask) and projecting its *shadow* (alien or unwanted aspects of the personality) – an individual must experience some breakdown of normal ego functioning.

Recall that the archetype of self forms the core of the ego complex. The four invariant characteristics of this archetype display the universal features of individual subjectivity: coherence, continuity, agency and affective relational patterns. *Coherence* is the integration of diverse and competing subjective experiences into the unity of body-being. Coherence means that we feel contained and held into this sack of skin. *Continuity* refers to what Donald Winnicott calls "going on being" and develops into a personal narrative, a life story, for each individual. Depending on the cultural and relational surroundings, a person may have a story of self that emphasizes individuality – like the bounded, masterful self of Western societies – or one that emphasizes honor and collectivity – like the Japanese do. To be in possession of one's narrative history, of one's continuity over time, is valued in all cultures and societies. *Agency* is the experience of being the author of one's own actions, of being an agent in the world. Jean Piaget recognized that this invariant of the self develops from the sensorimotor schemes of infancy into the capacity for abstract reasoning about means and ends, and finally into the experience of being a personal cause, a mover and shaper. *Affective relational patterns* arise from the interdependence of persons in the formation of selves. The work of John Bowlby (e.g., 1988) and his followers in the investigations of human attachments, and the work of the affect researchers (e.g., Izard, 1977) and theorists has demonstrated that human emotions, and emotional dependence are communicated in recognizable patterns the world over. This work substantiates the claims made by self psychologists, attachment theorists, relational psychoanalysts, and feminist psychologists that the human self is fundamentally relational throughout life.

The four invariants of self – coherence, continuity, agency, and affective relational patterns – shape a particular ego complex to function more or less well in maintaining the unity of the subject over time. Disruptions or disturbances in the functioning of these invariants bring people into psychotherapy; disturbances in these self-functions form some part of everyone's presenting problems. Below, I will detail how I work with the ego complex, and its archetype of self, in analysis, but for the moment, I want to conclude my brief history of the development of a healthy ego complex.

In the healthiest development, Jung regards a neurosis as necessary to becoming a psychological individual who can gain self-knowledge of the multiple centers of subjectivity. Without a break-up of adolescent defenses of the ego, or breakdown of ego functioning, an individual will remain childish or adolescent throughout life, rationalizing her or his unconscious complexes and defending the ego through identification and projection. Neurosis brings the awareness of inner conflict, generally through the disruption of agency and the experience of being unable to meet the goals, or carry out the desires, that one has for oneself. When a neurosis is the focus of analytical treatment, the patient eventually becomes a psychological individual, decentering the ego and recognizing that other complexes are motivated differently, and must be accounted for in desires and actions.

Gradually a perspective develops in the patient's personality that is "midway" or "between" the ego and the other complexes: this new viewpoint encompasses both the ego and the others within the personality. I have named this perspective a "transcendent coherence" (Young-Eisendrath, 1997c) of the self, in light of Jung's (1916/1969) idea of a transcendent function of the psyche – the ability to hold conflict and tension without enactment, foreclosure on meaning, or projection, in order to discover something new. I call it "transcendent" because it transcends ordinary ego consciousness, forging new understandings of hidden motives, altered states, intuitions, and synthetic processes (such as dream image production) that are not-ego. Transcendent coherence is experienced as a multi-leveled, nuanced understanding of what it means to be human, with a greater compassion for ourselves and others as we recognize how we are limited and fallible. And yet we find we are capable of an understanding that exceeds the ordinary boundaries of our self-protectiveness and self-consciousness.

The transcendent coherence of the self is expressed in yet another way in our everyday lives, one that psychoanalysts rarely mention. From our beginnings we can explore and predict, operate on and change the phenomenal world around us, in a manner that we do not invent and that proves our intimate connection to it. The connection between "knower" and "known" is seen as an aspect of the archetype of the self in analytical psychology, as part of our predisposition to an experience of psychic unity with the world around us. And so, Jung's psychology is a precursor to those theories of psychological and biological constructivism, like Piaget's, that claim that we construct and create our physical world through our embodied interactions with an environment in flux.

## The self in analysis

The four invariants of the self – coherence, continuity, agency and affective relational patterns – are the core issues that I rework and relive with patients in psychotherapy and analysis. In the abstract, these issues transcend the particulars of a person's complexes, ego or otherwise, but in the immediacy of a transferential field between a patient and me, between life partners, between a child and parent, these universal themes take on meanings and metaphors that give a personal signature to the sweeping brush stroke of self.

The following is a rudimentary map of analysis of the self. In all cases, in any form of psychotherapeutic treatment – individual or couples – I draw on transferential material (including countertransference), defenses, dreams and the history of complexes to make interpretations and other interventions. The first step in personality development, as I explained above, is to come fully into possession of the experience of being an individual subject – the ego complex. And so my first consideration in treating someone is whether or not she or he has achieved a relatively stable identity and object constancy. A healthy ego is experienced as a set of beliefs, images, experiences, and so on that permit an individual to be fairly coherent and continuous in the face of pressure from the inside and the outside. The adequacy of early relationships, temperament, and body image will have all contributed significantly to the ego complex of an adult.

If early relationships were not adequate, if there was a great deal of confusion, and/or trauma in the development of self-determination, then my analytic work will begin at the primary level of the formation of a healthy ego. This is usually called "pre-Oedipal" analysis in Freudian circles. In such a case, I will pay great attention to establishing a secure holding environment, providing certain "emotionally corrective" aspects in the therapeutic relationship, and presenting my thoughts and interpretations in ways that are intended to be empathic and supportive, rather than challenging. My goal will be to strengthen such ego functioning in intiative-taking, self-determination, memory and momentary self-awareness while we name and differentiate major unconscious complexes – usually negative parental complexes, and complexes that have formed due to trauma.

If development has progressed, through therapy or life, into a functional ego complex, the patient will usually report some version of inner conflict as part of the presenting problem; defenses of the ego will be somewhat dystonic. For example, the patient may report beginning more than one intimate relationship with the intention of making it last, but feeling unable to become committed. Although there may be some rationalization, usually the patient will be aware of her or his own difficulties in some ways. In such a case, analysis will challenge the defenses of the ego – such as reaction formation, rationalization, humor – that keep the persona intact. Through transference and dreams, patient and therapist begin to name and understand non-ego complexes and their inner lives. These complexes, sometimes in complicity with each other and sometimes with the ego, always involve forms of dominance and submission, sex and aggression, wish-fulfilling and despairing attitudes and enactments that the person has repeatedly disowned, even while they are being used.

In a successful long-term psychotherapy or analysis, both the patient and I come to read her or his history – the complexes of the personality – as an aspect of the archetype of self, as fundamentally human. Then we learn to accept and tolerate a range of emotion and image without necessarily acting upon them. This capacity to reflect metaphorically on the whole personality within an analytic frame is what Ogden (1986) calls sustaining "dialogical space" and what Jung (1916/1969) dubs the transcendent function, and what I've been calling the transcendent coherence.

Ogden emphasizes not only the tension of opposites, but also the awareness of a human subject as interpreter. Our subjective freedom lies in the space between an experience (the symbolized) and a symbol (the expressed). In this space, we can begin to see multiple meanings and to make new discoveries. Calm self-reflection and a capacity for the transcendent function will open the door to greater self-knowledge and transcendent coherence. Through a successful analysis, we encounter our interdependence – both in the therapeutic relationship and intrapsychically between complexes – as we witness multiple meanings and motives in ourselves and discover new insights through dialogue.

What I have just described is a non-essentialist, postmodern approach to analytical psychology. In my view, it is clinically and theoretically sound to stand clear of positing a Self (often capitalized in Jungian literature) that superintends the whole personality with views of its own. Such an idea seems to me to be a conflation of a psychological function (the archetype of self) and a human subject (a person) who wills and and intends. Additionally, I hold us accountable for our actions and intentions, rather than determined by some suprapersonal function. And yet this accountability is paradoxical. Only psychological individuals can be reasonably accountable for what they say and do; yet, through their self-knowledge, they become aware of the fallibility of their own accounts and knowledge of their motives.

Ultimately, though, we are responsible for the multi-subjectivities of the personality and our sometimes contradictory intentions. I agree with Carlo Strenger (1991: 62–63) who says the following about psychoanalysis:

> The assumption is that every aspect of human behavior is intelligible; i.e. behavior is seen as intentional action all the way down. Furthermore, it is assumed that by correctly understanding the meaning of actions, we help the patient to take full responsibility for who he is, and give him the freedom to change if he truly wants to.

With this freedom we can be more flexible because we trust that mistakes can be corrected and damages can be repaired.

In the later developments of individuation, we are able to dissolve some of the defenses of the ego complex and become less mired in self-conscious emotions. We feel the reality of our interdependence more fully and become more mature in our dependence, as Fairbairn has noted. The complexity of an evolved self makes clear that the human personality is a gathering of subjectivities, with plenty of contradictions, existing on the foundation of a particular embodiment.

## The transcendent function and projective identification

To move from painful enactments of complexes into the transcendent function or dialogical space is, as I see it, the major work of a long-term psychotherapy or analysis. When this is achieved, the patient can see motivations and desires from more than one perspective, moving back and forth in levels of meaning. It is my belief that a successful analytic treatment is aimed at helping people hold onto the transcendent function in the face of powerful emotional tendencies to enact, project and identifiy with images from primitive emotional states. Stephen Mitchell (1993: 83) seems to agree when he writes: "the capacity to bear, hold and play with an interpretation, neither surrendering to it as powerful magic nor rejecting it as dangerous poison – [is] . . . a criterion of readiness to terminate."

Over time, the gains of analysis lead to an appreciation of uncertainty, openness to discovery, and readiness to reflect on one's motives. These gains can lead to an ongoing development of the transcendent coherence of the self as a process of discovery through dialogue with objective and subjective factors of experience.

Projective identification – for example, from patient to therapist — can overtake the transcendent function or the dialogical space during treatment. When this happens, there is a significant standstill, and a tendency for both therapeutic partners to feel victimized by the dynamics. New discoveries are blocked by power struggles, devaluation or idealization. By projective identification, I mean a person's attempt to communicate unconscious material by projecting it into another and evoking from (and with) the other a playing out of what is projected. As Modell (1990: 56) aptly describes it:

> When the analysand projects his inner life into the analyst, it is as if the analyst is an actor who receives stage directions from the patient, but the entire process remains outside the consciousness of both participants. For some patients it seems that their affective experiences need to be placed within the other because language itself is inadequate, and some other means must be found to communicate.

All long-term treatments will contain, in my view, signficant projections of the patient's inner life into the therapist. Difficult and disturbing emotional memories are triggered in the therapeutic relationship, and will be played out through projective identification. (Of course, projective identification can also move from the therapist to the patient, and then it has to be detected in the therapist's countertransference responses.) Especially in the process of working through a chronic projective identification, both patient and analyst experience the transformation from enactment to transcendence, from repetition to dialogue.

If a therapist were so consistently neutral in the face of a patient's projections that the therapist never identified, then it seems to me, the therapist would be too remote to be helpful. On the other hand, if a therapist simply were to play out the identifications and never be able to stand back and interpret what is being communicated, then the treatment comes to a standstill, even a dead end. Jung believed that both analyst and patient are "in therapy" and that both must be transformed by it. Many times it is the working through of projective identifications that transforms me, allowing me to know myself and the patient better through the transcendent function.

## Conclusion

Mapping the psyche by following the images and affects (the emotional memories) that have cohered into complexes, analyst and analysand trace the personal evolution of a particular self. Interpreting transference, projective identifications, and dreams, they gradually encounter the transcendent function that encourages a perspective midway between ego and other complexes.

Over time, in a successful analysis, this perspective opens to the recognition that truth is a way of living, not something we discover outside ourselves. This kind of truth is related to our own knowledge of the complexity, fallibility and limitations of being human, and to gratitude for those on whom we depend to help us find ourselves. Challenged by this perspective – a transcendent coherence between subjective and objective experiences – individuals can never wholly return to a belief in a masterful, bounded ego that knows itself and needs no one else.

# Chapter 20

# From myth to metaphor: transcending realism

To borrow a metaphor, this chapter is a tiny drop in the ocean of possible commentaries on metaphor and myth. I originally allowed this drop to fall from two of my pools of personal mental absorption: (1) how myth and metaphor differ and how psychotherapy transforms the former into the latter; and (2) how our contemporary myth of scientific realism does injury to the meaning of psychodynamic psychotherapy.

It is my habit to load even little drops with a lot of meaning, and so I begin by scanning a wide range of topics in order to raise some questions about how we understand science and myth at the beginning of the twenty-first century.

## Metaphor and myth

Within the human sciences, especially linguistics and anthropology, there has recently been a lot of theorizing and investigation of metaphor. For example, the linguists George Lakoff and Mark Johnson have outlined the ways in which our human embodiment is used in the symbolic development of categories that are the basis of our conceptual systems. From their research and studies, they argue that reason has a bodily basis and that imaginative aspects of reason, such as metaphor, are central to our conceptual and intellectual development. Metaphor is defined as the mapping of one domain of experience with images from another domain: for example, "I'm exploding with anger" or "I can't contain my desire" are statements that use the metaphor of body-as-container to describe feeling states. What is implied, of course, is that the speaker feels as if the body will explode, not that the body is actually exploding.

Back in the 1960s, psychiatrist Harold Searles investigated the inability of actively psychotic patients to use metaphor symbolically. Instead of speaking as if one domain of experience mapped onto another, these patients experienced concretely one domain (the emotional) *as* the other (physical sensation and reaction). A patient's depression did not feel like a brick, but was experienced as a force falling on her head. A memorable example, described by Dr Searles (1965: 565), illustrates this condition. The quote begins with the patient,

> "Always angry – my therapist is always angry at me," and then said in the same tone of discouragement and exasperation, that his sister had written that she had purchased some chairs for her apartment . . . made of heavy iron, so heavy that one could move them only with great difficulty. I [Searles] replied, "And you feel, perhaps, that your therapist is like the heavy chairs – very hard to move?" He laughed as though my comment were ridiculous, saying, "No, I know you're not a chair, Dr. Searles . . . There's a chair," he said, pointing to my chair over at my desk, "and there's Dr. Searles."

Two years earlier this patient had experienced himself as part of the bed he was lying on, and Searles as part of the chair he was sitting in. Searles says about the patient at the time of the above incident, ". . . as yet he could just *barely* distinguish between the chair and his therapist, even at a *concrete* level; and that if he had to struggle to discriminate such perceptions at a concrete level, he was in no condition as yet to attempt the facile symbolizing of one by the other which metaphorical thinking entails" (p. 565, emphases in original).

From Searles' work with deeply disturbed patients, he witnessed what developmental psychologists see in the formation of categories in children's thinking: holding the distinction among the three great categories of being – object, animal, and human – is an achievement of emotional and conceptual development. When emotional experiences flood and overwhelm the conceptual apparatus, we are not able to hold these distinctions reliably. When the distinctions are not reliable, then metaphorical mapping from one domain to another does not work well.

Most of the contemporary investigations of metaphor fail to include any serious consideration of mythology. From my work in Jungian psychotherapy and psychoanalysis, I regard mythology as a whole context of meaning: the Big Story that tells us why and how things are the way they are. Over millenia, collective human mythology has developed narratives about the universal conditions and constraints of being human. Mythology, in my view, is not a thing of the past, but rather a necessity for people to go on being.

We are born into a family in which a great drama is already underway and the emotional image traces of our earliest relationships and meanings compel us, throughout life, to experience our attachment bonds and some aspects of our needs as mythic, as larger-than-life. These affective imaginal categories do not function as metaphor, but more as concrete reality, like bricks falling on our heads. We perceive and experience ourselves and our parents and siblings as the monsters, gods or goddesses, heroes, hags and demons under the sway of our early myths. Carl Jung called this tendency to experience our emotionally charged relationships in this way "archetypal." *Archetype* means "primary imprint" and points to the fact that human beings are universally predisposed to form emotionally compelling images of positive and negative figures that are idealized and feared.

Our early patterns of attachment, and the images or representations that accompany them, extend into lifelong habits of thought and action. Carl Jung called these habits "psychological complexes" and believed that personality was composed of a loose association of these affectively charged dynamics, each cohering around an archetype. As adults we experience our complexes as subpersonalities, as almost trancelike states in which we are engaged by a hidden reality that demands expression.

Psychological complexes are transferred and repeated (especially through projective identification) with our partners, our children, our therapists and others on whom we depend as adults. Whenever we feel locked into a relationship, unable to escape the influence of another, then we tend to draw on our emotional mythology about how to deal with danger when escape is impossible. And so the child who perceived his mother as depressed, weak, and empty will try to protect himself from his wife if she cries, complains, or criticizes in a way that sounds or looks like "mother." The old story will be imposed on the new situation.

### From myth to metaphor

Psychotherapy is a retelling of a life. When patient and therapist reach what is called the "end" of therapy – although it is not by any means the end of the treatment which should continue to have an ameloriative effect over a lifetime – they have reformulated and recast the patient's life into new meanings. Much that was myth has now become metaphor. Much that had been taken as reality is now seen as a subjective account of reality as if it had been true.

When people come to psychotherapy, they do not come to change their myths. They come because they are suffering, often because something in their psychological complexes is causing pain to themselves or others. Whatever the sustaining myth, the individual will regard that story as "only natural." For example, when I have asked young women, who are starving and abusing their bodies with laxatives and exercise, "Why do you want to be so thin?", the answer I most often hear is "Doesn't everyone want to be thin?" After all, even the Duchess of Windsor once said it was impossible to be too thin or too rich. On some level, we all justify our symptoms with a myth that seems to be reality.

One of my tasks in psychotherapy or analysis is to help people appreciate the human origin of all accounts of reality. The images and stories, as experienced in the transference and dreams, will come to be understood as a way of surviving or adapting to an emotional reality that somehow makes sense. As author Daniel Goleman says it, we all develop "emotional intelligence" that differs from practical and cognitive reasoning.

A person in therapy cannot surrender an old myth until she or he can trust a new account of reality. This new account has to encompass and reorganize the reality of the painful myth. In order to change something at the basis of reality, patients have to trust that they are being accepted, seen and protected in exactly those ways that they had been failed in the past. Because of the levels and types of transference in an effective therapeutic relationship, creating this fundamental trust requires time, skill, and a secure ethical foundation. Current social and economic reactions against long-term psychotherapy are provocative misunderstandings of the subjective basis of psychological complexes as living myths.

The idea that a medication or a cognitive restructuring will ameliorate suffering ignores the basis of emotional intelligence. Serotonin levels and negative self-talk certainly affect our capacity to pay attention and con-centrate, but they did not create the myths, nor can they change them. Psychoanalysis or long-term psychotherapy offers a replacement myth, the story of the intentional life: responsibility for one's own subjective states and actions. Self-awareness and insight into one's subjective life gradually transform the original myth of the monsters, dragons, witches or heroes into the myth of an intentional human life.

## Scientific realism

Not long ago, the story of the intentional life was considered to be a part of science. Studies of motivation, ego development and perspective-taking were being conducted to support findings of personality change in long-term psychotherapy. In fact, many well-designed studies of long-term psy-chotherapy have supported claims that patients' fundamental functioning changed for the better and remained effectively changed.

Today we are living within a myth of science. By this I mean that science has replaced religion and philosophy in advancing a full-scale worldview of reality and truth. Jung once called science the "great spiritual adventure" of our age. Renowned geneticist Richard Lewontin (1991: 8–9) says the following about how science forms the basis of our reality:

> Not only the methods and institutions of science are said to be above ordinary human relations but, of course, the product of science is claimed to be a kind of universal truth. The secrets of nature are unlocked. Once the truth about nature is revealed, one must accept the facts of life. When science speaks, let no dog bark.

This particular moment of science is so dangerous to psychotherapy because we have suddenly become concrete realists about genetics and evolutionary biology.

The theory of natural selection is assumed to be an objective paradigm, beyond the reaches of human opinion. Although there have been widespread social and spiritual consequences from the notion that living beings are determined by their genes, we rarely hear these discussed. Our genes and the DNA molecules that make them up are now described almost as a form of grace: we will understand who we are when we know what our genes are made of. The world outside poses certain problems which we do not create, but rather experience as a result of our genes. All of our struggles, such as finding a mate or becoming an altruistic person, are recast according to the outcome of leaving the greatest numbers of offspring. It appears that it is our genes that are propagating themselves through us.

Genetic explanations play a major part in my work as a supervisor and educator of psychiatric residents. Contemporary biological psychiatrists, neuroscientists and sociobiologists tell us that we are the way we are because of our genes and brain chemistry. When we hear that depression is "really a biochemical imbalance," and that alcoholism, criminality and even happiness are genetic conditions, we are persuaded to surrender our beliefs in the power of human intention.

The notion that our own intentions can be used to change our thoughts, feelings and actions – even our brain chemistry – has rather suddenly become outmoded in many training programs for psychiatrists and psychologists. Most of the psychiatric residents I supervise would have no idea of how to talk to a patient about motivations and intentions, whether conscious or unconscious. These residents have learned only how to diagnose symptoms and determine appropriate medications, and to conduct brief symptom-oriented counseling. Moreover, the suffering people who come to our offices are asked to believe that they will be cured by some form of biological treatment, not through a change in awareness or intention.

It seems to me that a great deal of harm has already occurred from our losing track of intention and meaning in our explanations of psychological suffering. This is not to say that we should disregard the important advances that genetics and biochemistry have provided to psychotherapy and medicine, both in understanding ourselves and in medicating serious psychiatric conditions. Indeed we have a much better understanding of the brain and our emotional processes than we had even ten years ago. And yet we need to become alert to the consequences of relating to our collective myth as the last word on meaning.

I am supportive both of science and scientific research; indeed, I have done a fair amount of psychological research myself. But I *am* opposed to being a concrete realist about genes and brain chemistry, believing that we have now discovered the "truth" about human actions and motivations.

There is no doubt that human beings wish that science could defeat death and illness and could tell us who we are. As a psychoanalyst, I believe that is magical thinking or, to put it another way, a dangerous aspect of our contemporary living myth.

## Subjects of our own desires

When we recognize ourselves as subjects of our own desires, we feel the freedom of taking a point of view. As I've noted throughout this collection of essays, psychoanalyst Thomas Ogden calls this securing a "dialogical space" within oneself and Jung calls it the "transcendent function." They both describe it as a capacity to hold tensions and pressures with an attitude of openness, without moving too quickly to a dogmatic answer about what is right or true. Being able to hold open the space around one's most primitive and demanding needs and fears, a space in which one can raise a question like "What's going on here?", means being able to examine one's experience in terms of both the inner demands and the possibility of discovering something new in the moment.

Believing, as I do, that humans cannot get beyond mythology – our best account of reality at any moment – I want to open questions about the mythology we use to explain human psychology to those who are suffering. Perhaps we can open some dialogical space around the assumption that we should call "genetic" everything from evil to happiness. Perhaps we can wonder if we should put down the mirror of self-recognition and blame Nature for our miseries. Perhaps we could even find a way to transform the images of genes and DNA into metaphors that enhance the story of an intentional life.

# Bibliography

Appleyard, B. (1998) *Brave New Worlds: staying human in the genetic future*, New York: Viking.

Bateson, M.C. (1989) *Composing a Life*, New York: Atlantic Monthly Press.

Bateson, M.C. (1994) *Peripheral Visions: learning along the way*, New York: HarperCollins.

Baruch, G., Barnett, R. and Rivers, C. (1983) *Life Prints: new patterns of love and work for today's women*, New York: McGraw-Hill.

Belenky, M.F., Clinchy, B.M., Goldberger, N.R. and Tarule, J.M. (1986) *Women's Ways of Knowing: the development of self, voice and mind*, New York: Basic Books.

Bellah, R., Madsen, R., Sullivan, W.M., Swidler, A. and Tipton, S.M. (1985) *Habits of the Heart: individuation and commitment in American life*, New York: Harper & Row.

Bem, S.L. (1974) "The measurement of psychological androgyny", *Journal of Consulting and Clinical Psychology*, 42: 153–162.

Bem, S.L., Martyna, W. and Watson, C. (1976) "Sex typing and androgyny: further explorations of the expressive domain", *Journal of Personality and Social Psychology*, 34: 1016–1023.

Beneke, T. (1982) *Men on Rape*, New York: St. Martin's Press.

Bordo, S. (1986) "The Cartesian masculinization of thought", *Signs*, 11: 439–456.

Bowlby, J. (1988) *A Secure Base: parent–child attachment and healthy development*, New York: Basic Books.

Breger, L. (1974) *From Instinct to Identity*, Clifton Heights, NJ: Prentice-Hall.

Broverman, I.K., Broverman, D.M., Clarkson, F.E., Rosenkrantz, P.S. and Vogel, S.R. (1970) "Sex-role stereotypes and clinical judgments of mental health", *Journal of Consulting and Clinical Psychology*, 34: 1–7.

Broverman, I.K., Broverman, D.M., Clarkson, F.E. and Rosenkrantz, P.S. (1972) "Sex-role stereotypes: a current appraisal", *Journal of Social Issues*, 28: 59–78.

Brownmiller, S. (1984) *Femininity*, New York: Ballantine.

Broyard, A. (1992) *Intoxicated by My Illness and Other Writings on Life after Death*, New York: C. Potter.

Bruner, J.S. (1986) *Actual Minds, Possible Worlds*, Cambridge, MA: Harvard University Press.

Bruner, J.S. (1990) *Acts of Meaning*, Cambridge, MA: Harvard University Press.

Byrom, T. (trans.) (1993) *Dhammapada: the sayings of the Buddha*, Boston, MA: Shambhala.

Chodorow, N. (1978) *The Reproduction of Mothering: psychoanalysis and the sociology of gender*, Berkeley, CA: University of California Press.

Cleavely, E. (1993) "Relationships: interaction, defense and transformation", in *Psychotherapy with Couples: theory and practice at the Tavistock Institute of Marital Studies*, London: Karnac.

Csikszentmihalyi, M. (1993) *The Evolving Self: a psychology for the third millenium*, New York: HarperCollins.

Daly, M. (1978) *Gynecology: the metaethics of radical feminism*, Boston, MA: Beacon Press.

Deaux, K. and Lewis, L.L. (1984) "Structure of gender stereotypes: interrelationships among components and gender label", *Journal of Personality and Social Psychology*, 46: 991–1004.

Dharmasiri, G. (1989) *Buddhist Ethics*, Antioch, CA: Golden Leaves Publishing.

Douglas, C. (1990) *The Woman in the Mirror: analytical psychology and the feminine*, Boston: Sigo.

Douvan, E. (1970) "New sources of conflict in females at adolescence and early adulthood", in J.M. Bardwick, E. Douvan, M.S. Horner and D. Gutmann (eds) *Feminine Personality and Conflict*, Westport, CT: Greenwood Press.

Eagly, A. (1983) "Gender and social influences: a social psychological analysis", *American Psychologist*, 38: 971–981.

Eagly, A. (1987) *Sex Differences in Social Behavior: a social-role interpretation*, Hillsdale, NJ: Lawrence Erlbaum Associates Inc.

Edelman, G. (1989) *The Remembered Present: a biological theory of consciousness*, New York: Basic Books.

Elkind, D. and Bowen, R. (1979) "Imaginary audience behavior in children and adolescents", *Developmental Psychology*, 15: 38–44.

Engler, J. (2003) "Being somebody and being nobody: a reexamination of the understanding of self in psychoanalysis and Buddhism" in J. Saffran (ed.) *Psychoanalysis and Buddhism: an unfolding dialogue*, New York: Wisdom Publications.

Erikson, E.H. (1950) *Childhood and Society*, New York: W.W. Norton.

Erikson, E.H. (1965) "Inner and outer space: reflections on womanhood", in R.J. Lifton (ed.) *The Women in America*, Boston, MA: Houghton Mifflin.

Erikson, E.H. (1968) *Identity: youth and crisis*, New York: W.W. Norton.

Frankl, V. (1984) *Man's Search for Meaning: an introduction to logotherapy*, New York: Simon & Schuster.

Freud, S. (1914/1963) "On narcissism: an introduction", in P. Rieff (ed.) *General Psychological Theory 3*, New York: Macmillan.

Gilligan, C. (1982) *In a Different Voice: psychological theory and women's development*, Cambridge, MA: Harvard University Press.

Goldenberg, N. (1979) *Changing the Gods: feminism and the end of traditional religions*, Boston, MA: Beacon Press.

Goleman, D. (1995) *Emotional Intelligence*, New York: Bantam Press.

Grosholz, E. (1988) "Women, history, and practical deliberation", in M. Gergen (ed.) *Feminist Thought and the Structure of Knowledge*, New York: New York University Press.

Grünbaum, A. (1984) *The Foundations of Psychoanalysis: a philosophical critique*, Berkeley, CA: University of California Press.

Guttentag, M. and Longfellow, C. (1977) "Children's social attributions: development and change", in C.B. Keasey (ed.) *Nebraska Symposium on Motivation*, Lincoln, NE: University of Nebraska Press.

Haley, A. (1976) *Roots*, Garden City, NY: Doubleday.

Hare-Mustin, R. and Marecek, J. (1988) "The meaning of difference: gender theory, post-modernism, and psychology", *American Psychologist*, 43: 455–464.

Harré, R. (1984) *Personal Being: a theory for individual psychology*, Cambridge, MA: Harvard University Press.

Harré, R. (1989) "The 'Self' as a theoretical concept", in M. Krausz (ed.) *Relativism: interpretation and confrontation*, Notre Dame, IN: University of Notre Dame Press.

Haseltine, E. (2003) "The joy of jitters: a whole lot of shaking helps bring your eyes into sharp focus", *Discover Magazine*, 24: 88.

Heilbrun, C. (1988) *Writing a Woman's Life*, New York: W.W. Norton.

Hesiod (1959) *The Works and the Days; Theogony; the Shield of Herakles*; trans. R. Lattimore, Ann Arbor, MI: University of Michigan.

Hiley, D., Bohman, J. and Shusterman, R. (eds) (1991) *The Interpretive Turn: philosophy, science, culture*, Ithaca, NY: Cornell University Press.

Hill, J.P. and Lynch, M.E. (1983) "The intensification of gender-related expectations during early adolescence", in J. Brooks-Gunn and A.C. Peterson (eds) *Girls at Puberty*, New York: Plenum Press.

Hoffman, I. (1998) *Ritual and Spontaneity in the Psychoanalytic Process: a dialectical-constructivist view*, Hillsdale, NJ: The Analytic Press.

Horne, M. (1998) "How does the transcendent function?" *The San Francisco Jung Institute Library Journal*, 17: 21–41.

Hunter, V. (1994) *Psychoanalysts Talk*, New York: Guilford Press.

Irigaray, L. (1985a) *Speculum of the Other Woman*, Ithaca, NY: Cornell University Press.

Irigaray, L. (1985b) *This Sex Which Is Not One*, Ithaca, NY: Cornell University Press.

Izard, C.E. (1977) *Human Emotions*, New York: Plenum Press.

Izard, C.E. (1992) "Basic emotions, relations among emotions, and emotion–cognition relations", *Psychological Review*, 99: 561–565.

Izard, C.E. (1994) "Innate and universal facial expressions: evidence from developmental and cross cultural research", *Psychological Bulletin*, 115: 288–299.

Jung, C.G. (1916/1969) "The transcendent function", in *The Collected Works of C.G. Jung: the structure and dynamics of the psyche 8* (pp. 67–91), trans. R.F.C. Hull, Princeton, NJ: Princeton University Press.

Jung, C.G. (1917/1966a) "The persona as a segment of the collective psyche", in *The Collected Works of C.G. Jung 7* (pp. 156–62), trans. R.F.C. Hull, Princeton, NJ: Princeton University Press.

Jung, C.G. (1917/1966b) "The eros theory", in *The Collected Works of C.G. Jung 7* (pp. 19–29), trans. R.F.C. Hull, Princeton, NJ: Princeton University Press.

Jung, C.G. (1917/1966c) "The mana-personality", in *The Collected Works of C.G. Jung 7* (pp. 227–44), trans. R.F.C. Hull, Princeton, NJ: Princeton University Press.

Jung, C.G. (1917/1966d) "Phenomena resulting from the assimilation of the unconscious", in *The Collected Works of C.G. Jung 7* (pp. 273–79), trans. R.F.C. Hull, Princeton, NJ: Princeton University Press.

Jung, C.G. (1920/1971) "Definitions", in *The Collected Works of C.G. Jung: psychological types 6* (pp. 408–87), trans. R.F.C. Hull and H.G. Baynes, Princeton, NJ: Princeton University Press.

Jung, C.G. (1925/1954) "Marriage as a psychological relationship", in *The Collected Works of C.G. Jung 17* (pp. 187–204), trans. R.F.C. Hull, Princeton, NJ: Princeton University Press.

Jung, C.G. (1939/1992) "Commentary on the 'Tibetan Book of Great Liberation'", in D.H. Meckel and R.L. Moore (eds) *Self and Liberation: the Jung-Buddhism dialogue*, New York: Paulist Press.

Jung, C.G. (1946/1966) "The practice of psychotherapy", in *The Collected Works of C.G. Jung: the practice of psychotherapy 16*, trans. R.F.C. Hull, Princeton, NJ: Princeton University Press.

Jung, C.G. (1955/1975) *Letters, 1906–1950*, trans. R.F.C. Hull, Princeton, NJ: Princeton University Press.

Jung, C.G. (1961) *Memories, Dreams, Reflections*, New York: Random House.

Jung, C.G. (1973) *Letters, 1906–1950*, trans. R.F.C. Hull, Princeton, NJ: Princeton University Press.

Kast, V. (1990) *The Creative Leap: psychological transformation through crisis*, trans. D. Whitcher, Wilmette, IL: Chiron Publications.

Kazin, A. (ed.) (1946/1968) *The Portable Blake*, New York: Viking Press.

Kernberg, O. (1995) *Love Relations: normality and pathology*, New Haven, CT: Yale University Press.

Klein, A. (1995) *Meeting the Great Bliss Queen: Buddhists, feminists and the art of the self*, Boston, MA: Beacon Press.

Kohut, H. (1977) *The Restoration of the Self*, New York: International Universities Press.

Kopf, G. (1998) "In the face of the other: psychic interwovenness in Dogen and Jung", in A. Molino (ed.) *The Couch and the Tree: dialogues in psychoanalysis and Buddhism*, New York: North Point Press.

Kuhn, T. (1970) *The Structure of Scientific Revolutions*, Chicago, IL: University of Chicago Press.

Kuhn, T. (1991) "The natural and the human sciences", in D. Hiley, J. Bohman and R. Shusterman (eds) *The Interpretive Turn: philosophy, science and culture*, Ithaca, NY: Cornell University Press.

Kukil, K.V. (ed.) (2000) *The Unabridged Journals of Sylvia Plath, 1950–1962*, New York: Anchor Books.

Labouvie-Vief, G. (1994) *Psyche and Eros: mind and gender in the life course*, Cambridge, UK: Cambridge University Press.

Lacan, J. (1982) "Feminine sexuality", in J. Mitchell and J. Rose (eds) *Feminine Sexuality: Jacques Lacan and the école Freudienne*, trans. J. Rose, New York: W.W. Norton.

Lakoff, G. (1987) *Women, Fire and Dangerous Things: what categories reveal about the mind*, Chicago, IL: University of Chicago Press.

LeDoux, J. (1996) *The Emotional Brain: the mysterious underpinnings of emotional life*, New York: Simon & Schuster.

Levinson, D.J. (1978) *The Seasons of a Man's Life*, New York: Alfred A. Knopf.

Lewis, M. (1991a) *Shame: the exposed self*, New York: Free Press.

Lewis, M. (1991b) "Self-conscious emotions and the development of self", *Journal of the American Psychoanalytic Association*, 39: 45–73.

Lewontin, R. (1991) *Biology as Ideology: the doctrine of DNA*, New York: Harper-Collins.

Lipman-Blumen, J. (1983) *Gender Roles and Power*, Atlantic Highlands, NJ: Humanities Press.

Loevinger, J. (1976) *Ego Development: conceptions and theories*, San Francisco, CA: Jossey-Bass.

Loevinger, J. (1979) "Construct validity of the sentence completion test of ego development", *Applied Psychological Measurement*, 3: 281–311.

MacCoby, E.E. (1990) "Gender and relationships: a developmental account", *American Psychologist*, 45: 513–520.

MacIntyre, A. (1977) "Epistemological crises, dramatic narrative, and the philosophy of science", *The Monist*, 60: 453–472.

MacMurray, J. (1957, reprinted 1978) *The Form of the Personal, Vol. 1: the self as agent*, Atlantic Highlands, NJ: Humanities Press.

MacMurray, J. (1961, reprinted 1979) *The Form of the Personal, Vol. 2: persons in relation*, Atlantic Highlands, NJ: Humanities Press.

Magid, B. (2003) "Your ordinary mind", in J. Saffran (ed.) *Psychoanalysis and Buddhism: an unfolding dialogue*, New York: Wisdom Publications.

Mattoon, M. and Jones, J. (1987) "Is the animus obsolete?", *Quadrant*, 20: 5–22.

McNeely, D. (1992) *Animus Aeternus: exploring the inner masculine*, Toronto: Inner City Books.

Miles, J. (1999) "Foreword" in J.F. Revel and M. Ricard, *The Monk and the Philosopher: a father and son discuss the meaning of life*, New York: Schocken Books.

Miller, A. (1981) *The Drama of the Gifted Child*, New York: Basic Books.

Miller, J.B. (1976) *Toward a New Psychology of Women*, Boston, MA: Beacon Press.

Minuchin, S. (1974) *Families and Family Therapy*, Cambridge, MA: Harvard University Press.

Mitchell, S. (1993) *Hope and Dread in Psychoanalysis*, New York: Basic Books.

Mitchell, S. (2003) "Commentary: somebodies and nobodies", in J. Saffran (ed.) *Psychoanalysis and Buddhism: an unfolding dialogue*, New York: Wisdom Publications.

Modell, A. (1990) *Other Times, Other Realities: toward a theory of psychoanalytic treatment*, Cambridge, MA: Harvard University Press.

Modell, A. (1993) *The Private Self*, Cambridge, MA: Harvard University Press.

Nemerov, H. (1977) *The Collected Poems of Howard Nemerov*, Chicago, IL: University of Chicago Press.

Neumann, E. (1954) *The Origins and History of Consciousness*, Princeton, NJ: Princeton University Press.

Ogden, T. (1986) *The Matrix of the Mind: object relations and the psychoanalytic dialogue*, Northvale, NJ: Jason Aronson.

Ogden, T. (1989) *The Primitive Edge of Experience*, Northvale, NJ: Jason Aronson.

Ogden, T. (1994) "The concept of internal object relations", in J.S. Grotstein and D.

Rinsks (eds) *Fairbairn and the Origins of Object Relations*, New York: Guilford Press.

Putnam, H. (1988) *Representation and Reality*, Cambridge, MA: MIT Press.

Renik, O. (2000) "Subjectivity and unconsciousness", *Journal of Analytical Psychology*, 45: 2–20.

Rich, A. (1976) *Of Woman Born: motherhood as experience and institution*, New York: W.W. Norton.

Rorty, R. (1992) "Inquiry as recontextualization: an anti-dualist account of interpretation', in D. Hiley, J. Bohman and R. Shusterman (eds) *The Interpretive Turn: philosophy, science, culture*, Ithaca, NY: Cornell University Press.

Rose, J. (trans.) (1982) "Introduction", in J. Mitchell and J. Rose (eds) *Feminine Sexuality: Jacques Lacan and the école Freudienne*, New York: W.W. Norton.

Rosenau, P. (1992) *Postmodernism and the Social Sciences: insights, inroads and intrusions*, Princeton, NJ: Princeton University Press.

Ruble, T.L. (1983) "Sex stereotypes: issues of change in the 1970s", *Sex Roles*, 9: 397–402.

Samuels, A. (1989) *The Plural Psyche: personality, morality and the father*, New York: Routledge.

Samuels, A. (1993) *The Political Psyche*, London: Routledge.

Samuels, H. (1994) *Jung and the Post Jungians*, London: Routledge.

Sanday, P. (1981) *Female Power and Male Dominance: on the origins of sexual inequality*, Cambridge, MA: Cambridge University Press.

Savitz, C. (1990) "The double death", *Journal of Analytical Psychology*, 35: 241–260.

Schafer, R. (1976) *A New Language for Psychoanalysis*, New Haven, CT: Yale University Press.

Schafer, R. (1978) *Language and Insight*, New Haven, CT: Yale University Press.

Schafer, R. (1992) *Retelling a Life: narration and dialogue in psychoanalysis*, New York: Basic Books.

Searles, H.F. (1965) "The differentiation between concrete and metaphorical thinking in the recovering schizophrenic patient", *Collected Papers on Schizophrenia and Related Subjects*, New York: International Universities Press.

Shotter, J. (1975) *Images of Man in Psychological Research*, London: Methuen.

Shotter, J. and Logan, J. (1988) "The pervasiveness of patriarchy: on finding a different voice", in M. Gergen (ed.) *Feminist Thought and the Structure of Knowledge*, New York: New York University Press.

Singer, J. (1973) *Boundaries of the Soul: the practice of Jung's psychology*, Garden City, NY: Anchor Press, 1973.

Singer, J. (1976) *Androgyny: towards a new theory of sexuality*, New York: Doubleday.

Smith, J.H. and Kerrigan, W. (eds) (1983) *Interpreting Lacan*, New Haven, CT: Yale University Press.

Spence, J.T. and Sawin, L.L. (1985) "Images of masculinity and femininity: a reconceptualization", in V.E. O'Leary, R.K. Unger and B.S. Wallston (eds) *Women, Gender and Social Psychology*, Hillsdale, NJ: Lawrence Erlbaum Associates Inc.

Spruiell, V. (1984) "The analyst at work", *International Journal of Psychoanalysis*, 65: 13–30.

Strawson, P.F. (1959) *Individuals: an essay in descriptive metaphysics*, London: Methuen.

Strenger, C. (1991) "Between hermeneutics and science: an essay on the epistemology of psychoanalysis", *Psychological Issues*, monograph 59, Madison, WI: International Universities Press.

Strupp, H. (1989) "Psychotherapy: can the practitioner learn from the researcher?", *American Psychologist*, 44: 714–717.

Sullivan, H.S. (1953) *The Interpersonal Theory of Psychiatry*, New York: W.W. Norton.

Swan, J. (1985) "Difference and silence: John Milton and the question of gender", in S.N. Garner, C. Kahane and M. Sprengnether (eds) *The (M)other Tongue: essays in feminist psychoanalytic interpretation*, Ithaca, NY: Cornell University Press.

Taylor, C. (1985) *Human Agency and Language*, Cambridge, UK: Cambridge University Press.

Taylor, C. (1989) *Sources of the Self: the making of modern identity*, Cambridge, MA: Harvard University Press.

Thurman, R. (trans.) (1994) *The Tibetan Book of the Dead*, New York: Bantam Books.

Tompkins, S. (1962) *Affect, Imagery and Consciousness: the positive affects*, New York: Springer.

Tompkins, S. (1963) *Affect, Imagery and Consciousness: the negative affects*, New York: Springer.

Unger, R. (1989) "Sex, gender and epistemology", in M. Crawford and M. Gentry (eds) *Gender and Thought*, New York: Springer-Verlag.

Urberg, K.A. (1979) "Sex role conceptualization in adolescents and adults", *Developmental Psychology*, 15: 90–92.

Victoria, B. (1997) *Zen at War*, New York: Weatherhill.

*Webster's Ninth New Collegiate Dictionary* (1985) Springfield, MA: Merriam-Webster, Inc.

Wehr, D. (1987) *Jung and Feminism: liberating archetypes*, Boston, MA: Beacon Press.

Winnicott, D.W. (1971) *Playing and Reality*, London: Routledge.

Wolf, N. (1991) *The Beauty Myth: how images of beauty are used against women*, New York: William Morrow.

Young-Eisendrath, P. (1984) *Hags and Heroes: a feminist approach to Jungian psychotherapy with couples*, Toronto: Inner City Books.

Young-Eisendrath, P. (1987) "The female person and how we talk about her", in M. Gergen (ed.) *Feminist Thought and the Structure of Knowledge*, New York: New York University Press.

Young-Eisendrath, P. (1990) "Rethinking feminism, the animus and the feminine", in C. Zweig (ed.) *To Be a Woman*, Los Angeles, CA: Tarcher.

Young-Eisendrath, P. (1993) *You're Not What I Expected: learning to love the opposite sex*, New York: William Morrow.

Young-Eisendrath, P. (1996) *The Resilient Spirit: transforming suffering into insight, compassion and renewal*, Reading, MA: Addison-Wesley.

Young-Eisendrath, P. (1997a) "The problem of realism in analytical psychology",

*Gender and Desire: uncursing Pandora*, College Station, TX: Texas A & M University Press.

Young-Eisendrath, P. (1997b) "The self in analysis", *Journal of Analytical Psychology*, 42: 157–166.

Young-Eisendrath, P. (1997c) "Jungian constructivism and the value of uncertainty", *Journal of Analytical Psychology*, 42: 637–652.

Young-Eisendrath, P. (2000) "Self and transcendence: a postmodern approach to analytical psychology in practice", *Psychoanalytic Dialogues*, 10: 427–441.

Young-Eisendrath, P. (2001) "When the fruit ripens: alleviating suffering and increasing compassion as goals of clinical psychoanalysis", *Psychoanalytic Quarterly*, 70: 265–285.

Young-Eisendrath, P. and Hall, J. (1991) *Jung's Self Psychology: a constructivist perspective*, New York: Guilford Press.

Young-Eisendrath, P. and Wehr, D. (1988) "The fallacy of individualism and 'reasonable violence' against women", in C. Bohn (ed.) *Christianity, Patriarchy and Abuse*, Philadelphia, PA: Pioneer Press.

Young-Eisendrath, P. and Wiedemann, F. (1987) *Female Authority: empowering women through psychotherapy*, New York: Guilford Press.

# Index

abandonment trauma 170

accountability 107, 109, 167–8, 170, 186, 207, 211

action 47, 211; distinction from happenings 167; rendered meaningful 168–9

adolescents: and the beauty myth 132–3; egocentrism 119–20; gender issues 120–1, 132, 133; identity 118–21, 132; persona 131, 132; self 118, 119–21

affect theory 78

affective relational patterns 57, 207, 208, 209

agency: female 109–10, 111; of the self 56–7, 207–8, 209

agentic natures 94, 95

Aitken, Roshi, Robert 7

ambivalence: to love 139–40, 141, 146, 149; maternal 89–90, 141; to stressful transferential situations in therapy 159

analyst: containment 68; ego complex of 187; idealization of 31, 32, 34, 148, 172–3, 184–6, 187, 200–1, 202; identification with the containing-transcendent transference 148–9, 176, 185; interpretations of 145, 146, 159–60, 173, 199–200; and the kinship relationship 145; limitations of 31–2, 145–6, 160, 173–4, 187, 199–201; love for the patient 147; making mistakes 31–2, 185, 199–201; moments of irony 202–3; moments of irritation 201–2; mystique of 67, 143–4, 147, 172; patient's belief in their capacity to help 68; patient's hatred of 31, 32, 34, 148; patient's

love for 146–7; patient's transference of their potential for transformation onto 143; and projective identification 144–5; uncertainty of 145–6, 160, 186; *see also* psychoanalysts

analyst–analysand relationship: and the alleviation of suffering 165; case study 65–73; deadlock/standstill 65, 67–8, 71–2, 73; *folie-à-deux* 72; going crazy together 65; interdependence 162–3, 173, 174, 175, 183; as interpretive community of self 48, 50; as "love affair" 175; order in 183; projection in 158, 160–1; projective identification in 65, 66–7, 71–2; ruptures of 67, 198–201; uncertainty in 64–5, 73–4; *see also* kinship relationship; transference

analytic psychotherapy 64, 151

analytical psychology 42, 124; and Buddhism 182; postmodern approach to 204–13; potential of 44; and sexism 43

androcentrism 94–6, 101, 105, 108–11, 113

anima 36, 123, 124, 127–9

animus 36, 123, 124, 127–9

anti-Semitism 43

anxiety 192

Aphrodite 81

appearance-as-worth complex 134

Appleyard, Brian 22, 27

archetypal images 77, 78, 87, 205

archetypes 3, 33, 53–5, 194, 196–7, 204–11; of contrasexuality 123; defining 54, 63, 77–8, 157, 205, 216; emotional meanings as 79; of family

from biological sex 92–4, 96–7,
124–6; equality 90; female person
100–15; as fixed entity 50–1;
identification with 93, 122; in neurosis
and individuation 132–6; new ways of
understanding 13, 116–21; other
50–1, 93, 122, 123, 126–7, 128, 136; as
social construction 124–5; stereotypes
43, 91–6, 106–7, 120–1, 136; and
subjectivity 50–1
gender difference 93–7, 98; and cultural/
familial relativism 97, 98
gender-splitting 126–9
genetic determinism 19, 21–3, 26–7, 29,
218–19
Gilligan, Carol 95, 112
God 185, 196
gods 197
Goldenberg, Naomi 110
Goleman, Daniel 205, 217
gossip 89
grand narratives 61
grief 79
Grosholz, Emily 101

Hall, James 36
happenings 167
Hare-Mustin, Rachel 90, 95, 96
Harré, Rom 6, 32, 46, 47, 56–7, 104,
105, 107, 119
Haseltine, E. 9
Hegel, Georg Wilhelm Friedrich 40,
52
Heidegger, Martin 40, 41
Heilbrun, Carolyn 92
helplessness 83, 192; male 134;
transcending 193
Hephaestus 80–1
hermeneutics 24–5, 40–1, 52
Hermes 81
heroines 92
Hesiod 80, 81
Hoffman, Irwin 143–4, 146, 172
hope 144, 146–50, 169, 173–6, 184–5
human beings, what it means to be
191
human genome 27
human sciences 23–9, 40–1, 42, 52–3

idealization 35; of the analyst 31, 32, 34,
148, 172–3, 184–6, 187, 200–1, 202;
of the beloved 142

idealizing transference 30–1, 35, 37,
184–7, 200–2; breakdown 201
identification: with the female beauty
myth 82; gender 93, 122; idealized 31,
35; see also disidentification
identity: adolescent 118–21; as cultural
invention 117–18; defensive function
117; defining 116–18; development
207; as narrative dependent on self-
reflection 121; new ways of
understanding 116–21; questions of
191–3
images: archetypal 77, 78, 87, 205;
universal 78, 86, 87
imaginary audience 119–20
*imago* 55
impulsiveness 48
individualism 77, 80; fallacy of 101–2,
104–5, 109–12; and identity 118, 119,
120, 121; and the imaginary audience
119; and the personal fable 120;
Western privileging of 125
Individualistic stage of ego development
49–50
individuality, pretend 131
individuation 53, 55, 56, 129–36;
defining 129–30; through
psychotherapy 57–9; see also
separation–individuation
inference 195, 195–7
inferiority, female 91, 94, 102–3,
105–10, 113, 121, 123, 133–4
inflation, male 121, 133–4
innate releasing mechanisms 54, 77–8
insight: and the alleviation of suffering
165, 166–71; emotional challenges of
having achieved 167–8
integration 49–50, 134, 136, 206, 207
intention 19, 20, 23–4, 26, 109, 217–19;
power of transformation 154; science
of 20–1, 28–9
interdependence 142, 158, 183, 187, 208,
210, 211; in the therapeutic setting
145, 159–63, 173–5, 183
internal objects 128
interpretations: incorrect 200–1;
therapeutic 145, 146, 159–60, 173,
199–200
interpretive context 194, 195–7
intersubjectivity 197–201
intuition 112–13
Irigaray, Luce 103–4